VISUAL DESIGN for the
MODERN WEB

PENNY McINTIRE

New Riders

Visual Design for the Modern Web

Penny McIntire

New Riders
1249 Eighth Street
Berkeley, CA 94710
510/524-2178
510/524-2221 (fax)

Find us on the Web at: www.newriders.com
To report errors, please send a note to errata@peachpit.com

New Riders is an imprint of Peachpit, a division of Pearson Education

Copyright © 2008 by Penny McIntire

Project Editor: Wendy Sharp
Development Editor: Wendy Katz
Production Editor: Becky Winter
Compositor: Danielle Foster
Indexer: Emily Glossbrenner
Cover & interior designer: Charlene Charles-Will

ISBN 13: 978-0-321-51538-4
ISBN 10: 0-321-51538-2
9 8 7 6 5 4 3 2 1
Printed and bound in the United States of America

CONTENTS

One stunning autumn day a number of years ago, I was chatting with my boss, Rod Angotti, Chair of the Department of Computer Science at Northern Illinois University. I complained that some faculty member in our department, any faculty member, needed to create a web design course, because I really wanted to take it. I said, in a fit of pique, "Well, if someone doesn't develop a web design course soon, I'm going to be forced to do it myself!" Of course, I wasn't at all serious. I didn't know anything about web design. I had been teaching computer science for almost two decades, yes. I had been an artist in other media all my life, yes. But web design? I was clueless.

Two weeks later, the spring teaching schedule came out, with me listed as the professor on record for our new web design course. What could I do? I got up to speed, fast. Luckily, that first semester I was able to hand-pick both my teaching assistant, Jeff Cernauske (who had an undergraduate degree in art, including web design) and my students (only top students who were eager to share the adventure and who understood that we were in this together). As the semester progressed, I often had to say, "I'm sorry, I don't know the answer. Let's figure this out together." Nonetheless, we had a blast; it was one of my most exhilarating semesters. There's something to be said for challenging the professor as well as the students.

It's been a while since that first semester, but web design is still fascinating. I don't say "I don't know" so often anymore, but even so, my students teach me new tricks every year. I'm not ashamed to admit that I'm a much better teacher of web design than I am a designer. In fact, my students' design abilities, with training, often surpass my own. That delights me immensely.

How did that saga lead to this book? Through the years, I have never been able to find a good, comprehensive web design book. HTML, CSS, and JavaScript books abound, both in textbook and reference form. There are books that are mainly eye candy, showing gorgeous web sites, and even books that teach design by what *not* to do. But I never ran across a concise book that systematically presented design concepts and how to apply them to a web site. I hope this is that book.

So what topics, exactly, does this book cover?

First, let's talk about what this book is *not*. It's not about the following, all of which deserve dedicated books:

- Introductory HTML or CSS. I assume that you already know the basics of both, and perhaps a little JavaScript as well (although that knowledge is certainly not required). I do give lots of practical HTML and CSS examples, however, to show how to implement the principles under discussion.

- Adobe Creative Suite. Although I don't teach these tools themselves, I do use screenshots from them to illustrate many techniques that could be accomplished in other development environments as well.

- Server-side technologies such as ASP, JSP, ColdFusion, Perl, and PHP.

- Multimedia, including sound and video.

What this book *does* teach are design concepts and how to implement them for a web site using HTML, CSS, and baby JavaScript. As a clever reader might guess from the title, the book concentrates on visual design and the characteristics that make a web site usable, engaging, and memorable. Web design is tough, frankly, because of considerations ranging from the technical to the organizational to the aesthetic. As a matter of fact, it's so tough that the preliminary title for this book was Web Design Alchemy, because medieval alchemy blurred the lines between science, art, and magic, and while a wonderfully designed web site may not be medieval gold, it is indeed magical.

Target Audience

My only assumption is that you know at least the fundamentals of web technology, including basic HTML and CSS. Beyond that, my target audience is anyone who wants to take this technology further by developing his or her aesthetic abilities in web design:

- **Techies**, who know computer programming but often desperately need to learn the aesthetic side of web design. This book can be used and understood by folks with no formal art training. Although technical web developers in the corporate world often have graphic designers to do their visual design work, they still need to know enough about aesthetics to communicate with the designers and evaluate their work. Also, there are many techies in smaller companies that are required to do web design without benefit of any training in design theory. Despite the fact that technical web developers are only rarely able to approach the design levels of trained artists, they can be taught to understand enough design to create professional and appealing web sites. After all, the best programmers are highly creative.

- **Artists and designers**, who understand aesthetics but are often baffled by how to translate those aesthetics to the technical medium of the web. Color mixing is a good example. Given pots of red, yellow, blue, black, and white paints, an artist can mix any imaginable color. But how does that same artist mix a hue when the medium is pixels represented with hexadecimal numbers, and the primary colors are red, green, and blue? The fact that yellow is a mix of red and green pixels is completely foreign to most artists. This book can teach traditional artists how to transfer their skills to the web.

Features of This Book

The book consists of eight chapters: Introduction, Site Analysis, Navigation, Page Layout, Color, Graphics, Typography, and Forms. Throughout the chapters, I present numerous "code reviews" to show exactly how to implement the design concept under discussion. Keep in mind that code examples are often abbreviated to show only the code relevant to the issue at hand. I use local CSS styles—rather than the more preferred external style sheets—for clarity and brevity.

Feel free to contact me if you have questions or suggestions for future editions. If you're a teacher or professor using this book for a course, please contact me for PowerPoint slides and other materials that might support your teaching efforts.

The book's web site, **www.VisualDesignModernWeb. com**, contains all sorts of bonus topics and interesting tidbits. I hope to have the site up and running by the time the book is published, but I will also be adding content in the future as I create or run across things I think might interest you.

Acknowledgments

My deepest appreciation goes to all of the following:

My reviewers. Their suggestions and criticisms have improved this book beyond measure. Their input makes me look much smarter than I really am. I thank all of you profusely: Anita Philipp, Oklahoma City Community College; Anne Marie Shanley, County College of Morris; Antony Gauvin, University of Maine at Fort Kent; Arta Szathmary, Bucks County Community College; Blaine Robertson, Brigham Young University, Idaho; Bruce Long, University of North Carolina, Charlotte; Carol Buser, Owens Community College; Catherine Pace-Pequeno, Crafton Hills College; Chang Miao, DeVry University, DuPage Campus; Charles Goodman, College of DuPage; Christine L. Moore, College of Charleston; Craig Baehr, Texas Tech University; Dale Craig, Fullerton

College; David Alger, Tidewater Community College; David Tarnoff, East Tennessee State University; Diana Hill, Chesapeake College; Diane M. Coyle, Montgomery County Community College; Don Bonidie, University of Pittsburgh; Donna Hendricks, South Arkansas Community College; Dorothy Harman, Tarrant County College, NE; Dr. Connie D. Lightfoot, Indiana Wesleyan University; Dr. Jerry Isaacs, Carroll College; Dr. Rich Rice, Texas Tech University; Dr. Richard L. Thornton, New England College; Dr. Sue Casey, Weatherford College; Edward A. Hoisington, Bedford School District K-12; Elizabeth B Kilroy, Temple University, Philadelphia and NYU, NYC; Elizabeth Drake, Santa Fe Community College; Fred Wells, Florida State University; Gary Kidney, University of Houston, Clear Lake; Gerald J. Ross, Lane Community College; Jack Brzezinski, DePaul University; James Gifford, University of Wisconsin, Stevens Point; Janet Pickard, Chattanooga State Technical Community College; Jayne Klenner-Moore, King's College; Jeanine Meyer, Purchase College/ SUNY; Jodi Neely-Ritz, University of Florida; John Avitabile, College of Saint Rose; John H. Humphrey, Asheville Buncombe Technical Community College; Joyce M. Dick, Northeast Iowa Community College, Peosta Campus; Judith Scheeren, Westmoreland County Community College; Judy Scholl, Austin Community College; Kathryn M. Baalman, Webster University; Ken Wanderman, California State University, Monterey Bay; Kenneth Wade, Champlain College; Kevin Floyd, Macon State College; Kevin R. Parker, Idaho State University ; Kristin Benner, Saddleback College; Liz Boese, Colorado State University; Lynn Komarek, Spokane Community College; Maria Martinez, University of Miami; Mark Van Beek, Tacoma Community College; Martin Granier, Western Washington University; Martin Kollman, Fort Hays State University; Melissa Swanson, Bay de Noc Community College; Michael Gildersleeve, University of New Hampshire; Michael Sturgeon, Lee University; Rebecca Hayes, American River College; Ric Heishman, Northern Virginia Community College, Manassas Campus; Robert J. Clougherty, Tennessee Tech University; Robert Kelly, Stony Brook University; Robert Kueper, Queensborough Community College; Sam Blanchard, Anderson University; Sheryl R. Schoenacher, Farmingdale State University; Shyamal Mitra, University of Texas at Austin; Srikanth Siva, Northwest Missouri State University; Steve Perry, Palomar College; Ted Shaneyfelt, University of Hawaii, Hilo; Teresa Pelkie, Palomar College; Thomas G Luce, Ohio University, Athens; Thomas Michael Smith, Austin Community College; Veronica Noone, Community College of Baltimore County; Will Devenport, Southern Illinois University, Carbondale; Yilin Fang, Diablo Valley College

The folks at the three publishers this book was with before it even went to press: Richard Jones and Jean Coston, from Scott-Jones (which was acquired by Addison-Wesley while the book was in progress). They had faith that this book would create a market out of thin air. Without that faith, this book wouldn't exist. They did much of the handholding through its early stages, finding a slew of wonderfully insightful reviewers and building a market before the book was even written. Michael Hirsch at Addison-Wesley, who passed the book on to Peachpit Press/New Riders, my dream publisher. All the friendly, helpful, and talented folks at Peachpit Press/New Riders, who took my concept for what I hoped would be a beautiful design book and put it into production. Wendy Sharp saw the book's potential and was my evangelist at Peachpit, pushing for the book's publication. Charlene Charles-Will created a wonderful book design, Becky Winter put it into production, and Danielle Foster was the excellent compositor. Wendy Katz, editor extraordinaire, deserves my most heartfelt thanks for making me appear to be a much more graceful and articulate writer than I really am. The fact that she could make me snort with laughter with 2 a.m. emails was an unexpected and delightful bonus.

My students, who have made my teaching experience at NIU so very rewarding. Students who truly want to learn are just the very best at teaching me how to be a better teacher. Because of them, what I intended as a temporary teaching job while my daughters were babies turned into my life-long career.

Rod Angotti, my boss and Chair of the Department of Computer Science at Northern Illinois University 1983–2006. Rod has been unfailing in his support, friendship, and leadership throughout those and subsequent years, and I would have absolutely forbidden his retirement had it been in my power. His advice and commiseration pulled me and many others in our Department through one particularly rough year in academia. As my opening story attests, I have Rod to thank for my entry into the web design field. Thank you, Boss, for always having the faith that I could pull "it" off, regardless of what "it" was—I would not be where I am today without you. And always remember, "The demise of COBOL is imminent." Not.

My new Chair, Nick Karonis, who in the short time he's been Chair has already proven himself to be a skilled tactician and caring leader. His good judgment is a much-needed steadying influence on the Department. Now, what can we do to convince you to stay on when your two-year stint is up, Nick?

The faculty and staff of the Department of Computer Science at Northern Illinois University, as well as university administration. Recently, circumstances dictated that we band together to fight the good fight. We did, and the Department is all the better for it. Although I simply must mention Mary Letheby and Kai Rush, the rest of the list is far too long. You know who you are, and I thank you all.

My dear friend, Jeff Denton. He went bravely into the world of web design before me, and then held out his hand to pull me in. His assistance in structuring my first web design class as well as this book was invaluable. And to think our friendship started simply because we both loved Mary Stewart's *The Crystal Cave*! Jeff, your knowledge, technical help, and encouragement made this book possible. Your friendship is gift.

Dear friends (or partners in crime, depending upon your viewpoint) Mindy Cleary, Kathi Davis, Marge Dixon, and Kay Tallyn (in alphabetical order, Ladies!), for an aggregate total of 120 years and counting. They have helped me grieve, cope with crises, remodel my house, and fight the good fight. "A good friend will bail you out of jail. A better friend is sitting in jail next to you, saying, 'Hot damn, that was fun!' A best friend will help you bury the body." Girlfriends, I know that all four of you would show up bearing shovels, chocolate, and Cabernet.

My daughters, Shelley and Abby Kendall, the lights of my life, who have enriched it beyond measure. They have both grown up to be "good people," with compassion and unquestionable integrity. They usually manage to conceal the fact that they think their mother is a bit, well, quirky, not to mention the "ditziest smart person we know." I do have to admit, their teenage years drove home the statement that growing older doesn't cause gray hairs—growing *kids* causes gray hairs. Despite that, I'm so very proud of your accomplishments and of the women you have grown up to be, Girls.

My parents, Carroll "Jiggs" and Ethel (Ferrill) McIntire, and my cousin, Pat (Hiller) Strum, a surrogate older sister/second mother. I was unbelievably lucky to be raised by a kind and supportive family. They were always there when I needed them, and they never doubted that I could do absolutely anything I truly wanted to do. The confidence they instilled in me has stood me in good stead, although arguably, "fearless" and "foolish" have more in common than just alliteration. I miss you.

My readers. With any luck, you will like this book well enough that there will someday be a second edition (OK, maybe a *lot* of luck). Enjoy!

Penny (Kendall) McIntire
Department of Computer Science
Northern Illinois University
penny@pennymcintire.com
pmcintire@niu.edu
penny@VisualDesignModernWeb.com

CHAPTER ONE

Introduction to Visual Design for the Modern Web

A. MICHAEL GILDERSLEEVE, UNIVERSITY OF NEW HAMPSHIRE:

"So much of web design sounds like plain old common sense after you read it or hear it. But if it really were plain old common sense, there would be far more attractive and usable web sites on the Web."

The web is, first and foremost, a form of communication. A web designer's goal should be not just to make things visually appealing, but to communicate with the audience.

In face-to-face conversation, words convey only a portion of the message. In fact, a great deal of the message is carried by tone of voice, facial expression, and hand gestures. Web content, like the words of a conversation, is influenced by presentation. Visual elements such as color, layout, typography, and images shape a site's personality, or voice. The voice gives a site a unique tone, ambiance, and attitude; generates emotional impact; and makes the site engaging. Every element on the site should contribute to its unique voice.

● ● ●

QUIPS AND QUOTES

"We must discover what information the audience needs, then deliver it to them in a way they can absorb." –*Creativeprose Weekly*, July 12, 2005, *http://www.creativepro.com/ storyarchive/newsletter/458.html*

The voice of a site should depend upon its purpose and its target audience, both topics we'll explore within this book. For now, though, suffice to say that a site promoting the latest rap star will have a very different voice than one peddling expensive baby bassinets. If we were to reverse the look and feel of these two sites, both audiences would be confused and unlikely to frequent their respective sites in the future.

Web design is, therefore, not just about technology. In fact, it's the melding of web-based technologies with content (the message), site architecture (the way the content is organized), visual design (the visual presentation), and interaction (your site's behavior as it responds to a visitor), as shown in **FIGURE 1.1**. This collision of forces can explode as stunning fireworks—or it can fizzle out as a confusing and unappealing visual muddle.

FIGURE 1.1 The Five Interdependent Components of Web Design

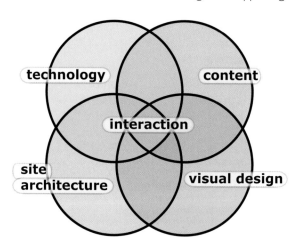

* * *

COMPANION WEB SITE

The web site accompanying this book, *www.VisualDesignModernWeb.com*, provides myriad bonus materials, including chapter-by-chapter review questions and exercises, nuts and bolts information about creating a site, pre-written JavaScripts, and a tutorial for using Fireworks and Dreamweaver to create rollover buttons.

The need to define content, organization, and visual design is nothing new in communication design; designers have been struggling with these three components in the print medium since papyrus was de rigueur. Always, technology has been a factor, from the aforementioned papyrus to quill pens to today's digital presses. Still, never before has the presentation medium been so closely bound to the technology as it is on the web. Additionally, the web has advanced communication a step further, into interaction…well, that's a whole new wrinkle in the communication arena. Until computers, the most interaction an audience could experience was turning the pages of a book or fast-forwarding through a video. With the advent of the web, though, interaction in the form of navigation and visitor input has become not only pervasive, but essential.

Before we delve into the specific yet interconnected areas of web design—technology, content, site architecture, visual design, and interaction—let's agree on the fact that these components are integral characteristics of a first-rate web site. We need to address them all in order to create a site that is:

- **Easy to maintain:** It must be flexible and scalable so that ongoing updates throughout the life of the site can be accomplished with a minimum of time and effort.

- **Aesthetically appealing:** It must be an attractive and engaging sensory experience for its target audience.

- **Easy to use:** That is, user-friendly, effective, and downloads rapidly. Visitors should encounter a high degree of success in finding what they are looking for or in accomplishing their missions, without wasting time.

- **Technically solid:** It behaves predictably, without any broken links.

We will start with a quick review of web technologies, as highlighted in **FIGURE 1.2**, before progressing into the other aspects of web design shown in Figure 1.1.

FIGURE 1.2 Web Technology

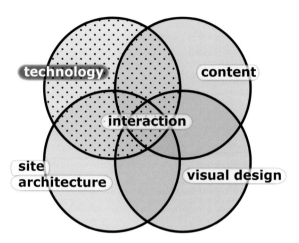

Review of Web Technology

Before we can delve into any artistic endeavor, whether it's sculpting in clay, painting in watercolor, or bending red-hot iron into decorative curlicues, we must understand the medium. Web design is so closely linked to the technology that every artistic decision has technological consequences, and vice versa. As a result, we should start off by ensuring that we have a general understanding of the technology as well as its strengths and weaknesses. Additional technological concerns will be addressed throughout the book, as appropriate.

TWELVE MODEL SITES

Throughout the book, when controversial issues arise, we will look at how twelve popular but randomly selected sites handled each issue as of June 2007. Those twelve sites are:

- adobe.com
- amazon.com
- cnn.com
- ebay.com
- imdb.com
- mapquest.com

- microsoft.com
- msn.com
- msnbc.com
- randmcnally.com
- ticketmaster.com
- yahoo.com

Screen prints of these sites are included on the book's web site. Of course, as we all know, in web time, even a year is a very long time. By the time this book is actually in print, these web sites may well have evolved such that they no longer exhibit the same characteristics.

The millions of web surfers who could potentially view our site have a wide variety of computer systems, which means that we do not have complete control over how our web site appears on a visitor's system, so bear in mind the following axioms:

- Colors and fonts display differently in different browsers, on different monitors, and on different systems. For example, a hue that looks barn red on one system might look magenta or old rose on another. We will look at these differences in more depth in the Color and Typography chapters.

- Elements on the page can't be guaranteed to display at a particular size, because different systems have different resolutions. A font size that looks perfect on one system may appear too large on another system and too small to read on yet a third. We will delve into these problems in the Page Layout chapter.

- Most brand new computers are not displaying at their best or highest settings. Manufacturers often configure new boxes a notch or two down from their maximum capabilities. Worse, many computer owners are unaware that they can change their display properties to enhance the view.

This is just a sampling of why designing a good web page is much trickier than designing a good printed page, because you simply cannot predict with any accuracy the system setup your visitors will have. In effect, WYSIWYG (the computer programmer's acronym for "What You See Is What You Get") should really be WYSI^{NN}WYG ("What You See is Not Necessarily What You Get").

On the other hand, one of the rewards of web technology is that we possess powerful tools like animation, user interaction, and "free" color that we wouldn't have when designing a printed page. Additionally, search engines can aid visitors in finding our site out of the millions of web sites competing for attention.

As you know, the web connects clients (the visitor's computer) and servers (the system on which the web site resides). Let's do a quick review of both client-side and server-side technologies, as well as identify which elements will be covered in this book.

Client-side Technologies

In a web environment, a *client* consists of the visitor's computer (hardware) and the browser application (software) that displays a web page.

Browsers

The browser's mission is to request, retrieve, and display documents (another term for web pages) for the visitor. There are currently dozens of browsers and browser versions in use. Alas, each one may have its own quirky (the polite way of saying "maddeningly buggy") way of rendering a document.

If you are fortunate enough to be coding for a corporate intranet environment, everyone in the organization probably uses the same version of the same browser. In such a case, you can simply code to and test on that specific browser. But if you are building a public-access internet web site, you need to keep in mind that many features are interpreted idiosyncratically by different browsers, or even different versions of the same browser.

Microsoft Internet Explorer (IE) has dominated the browser marketplace for years, but other browsers (notably Firefox) have steadily gained market share. **FIGURE 1.3** shows browser market share as of July 2007. It seems safe to say that we should test all public web sites on at least the latest versions of Internet Explorer and Firefox.

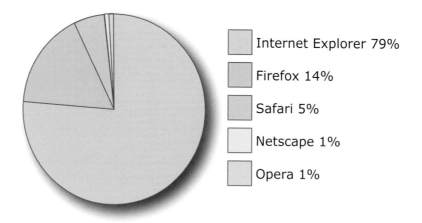

FIGURE 1.3 Browser Prevalence (statistics compiled by http://marketshare.hitslink.com/report.aspx?qprid=0, July 2007)

Internet Explorer 79%

Firefox 14%

Safari 5%

Netscape 1%

Opera 1%

It's also a good idea to test a site against the W3C validator, which can identify HTML that is not following standards (meaning "it has a higher potential to break in the different browsers"). Fortunately, one promising trend is that newer versions of browsers are more compatible with each other than earlier versions have been, as any designer charged with building a web site that functioned flawlessly in older versions of IE as well as Navigator 4.7 will attest.

If the code turns out to be incompatible with at least one browser that it *has* to work with, we can deliver a separate page tailored to a specific browser by "sniffing the browser," that is, identifying the browser in use and then routing a visitor to a page specifically optimized for that browser. Regrettably, creating and maintaining multiple versions of each and every page is a difficult and tedious chore; we need to assess the number of visitors we might have who use a particular browser, and then determine whether the cost is worth the effort for our particular circumstances. Still, it could be an option for perhaps just a few critical pages within the site.

In addition to testing a site within multiple browsers, we should also test on different platforms—Windows, Mac OS, and Unix. For instance, Internet Explorer renders some code differently on a Mac than it does on a Windows PC.

For all of our target browsers and platforms, the site should be error-free, although it could be acceptable if some "bells and whistles" degrade gracefully; that is, the features don't appear at all, but in such a way that nothing is obviously broken. The end result should be that the viewer is not aware that anything is missing.

A browser employs HTML, Cascading Style Sheets (CSS), JavaScript, Flash, and multimedia (audio and video) to render documents. Let's briefly review each of these components.

HTML/XHTML

HTML (Hypertext Markup Language) is a tag-based language used by web browsers to render text and images on the visitor's monitor. When a visitor requests a page from a web site, the HTML document is downloaded to the visitor's hard drive and displayed from there. Relevant HTML will be presented in sidebars throughout this book.

One of the best ways to expand your knowledge of HTML is to view the source code of other web pages. To do so, simply right-click (or Control-click on the Mac if you don't have a two-button mouse) anywhere on the page other than over an image or a form element, and then choose View Source or View Page Source. The HTML for the page will be loaded and displayed in your default HTML editor.

• • •
HTML VALIDATION

When using the W3C validator, you choose between two standards: HTML strict (the most modern but least flexible) or HTML transitional (which is more forgiving). Most designers choose transitional because it's less likely to break in these days of rapidly evolving browsers. See www.w3c.org.

Although HTML includes commands for visual presentation (color, fonts, and so on), it's really best used for structural indicators such as header levels and bulleted lists. As a result, HTML formatting is now deprecated (discouraged) in favor of CSS formatting (see the upcoming section).

BONUS TOPIC:
Setting up a Web Site on a Service Provider

See the book's web site for an overview of purchasing a domain name, choosing a web hosting provider, and uploading to the server.

This book follows the latest HTML standard, referred to as XHTML, but we'll use the more generic and common term, just plain HTML, in all our discussion. The World Wide Web Consortium (W3C—www.w3.org) provides the current specification for HTML, along with proposals for future additions to the standard. Additionally, it offers an online HTML validator that can check that the HTML on a site is following modern standards.

· · ·

REFORMATTING OLDER HTML TO XHTML STANDARDS

Some HTML development environments, including Adobe Dreamweaver, can reformat HTML to the XHTML standard as you type, as well as upgrade legacy (existing) HTML files to XHTML (choose File > Convert).

Cascading Style Sheets

Cascading Style Sheets (CSS) define the visual presentation of a web page, including color, sizes, fonts, background images, borders, margins, underlines, and even positioning. CSS can stipulate formatting options that are not available with HTML alone, such as absolute positioning (placing an object at a precise location on a page) and text rollovers (when the visual characteristics of a text link change as the mouse rolls over it). Relevant CSS will be presented in sidebars throughout the book.

Although the greatest benefit to using CSS is accrued by linking to external CSS files, we will normally use in-line CSS (that is, embedded in the HTML) in the examples in this book, because external files make for unwieldy examples. Keep in mind, however, that any in-line CSS can be easily pulled out into an external CSS file for production use.

• • •

CROSS-BROWSER COMPATIBILITY

Don't leave anything to the browser default. That is, don't assume that all browsers display a white page background, use identical margins and padding, or treat visited links just like normal links unless you specify otherwise. These assumptions can result in pages that don't render the same from browser to browser. To be safe, pull control out of the hands of the browsers and explicitly lock in every critical formatting characteristic (particularly margins, cellpadding, cellspacing, and borders) with CSS.

Scripting Languages

HTML alone is static—its only responsibility is to display text and images. That is, it can't do anything that requires changes to the page after it's loaded, nor can it perform tasks such as adding two numbers together. As a result, we need scripting languages, which are nothing more than "lite" programming languages, to accomplish tasks such as performing calculations, editing input data, or changing visual presentation on the fly. The two browser-based scripting languages are JavaScript and Microsoft's VBScript. The latter has proprietary features that are recognized only in a Microsoft environment, so from here on out, we will deal only with JavaScript.

Even so, you need not have any knowledge of JavaScript to use this book. Luckily for non-programmers, simple JavaScript effects, such as image rollovers (replacing one image with a different image on mouse rollover), can be implemented within a development environment such as Dreamweaver (discussion follows in a few pages) without any real knowledge of actual programming.

Adobe Flash

Flash began its life as graphic-animation technology, but is now being used for entire web sites. Everything from navigation to server-side database access can be accomplished in Flash, using Flash's programming environment, Flex/ActionScript. Although it's likely that Flash-based sites will continue to increase in popularity, it's unlikely that Flash will completely replace HTML in the near future. Instead, it's a question of using the right technology for the intended purpose. We'll briefly look at Flash as a page-delivery tool in the Page Layout chapter.

**BONUS TOPIC:
JavaScript**

See the book's web site for a quick tutorial on creating a navigational image in Fireworks and then embedding it in a web page with a rollover effect using Dreamweaver.

Multimedia: Audio and Video

Sound and video effects can, in the right circumstances, add a great deal to a web site. For instance, fans of a musical group might appreciate being able to download a sample from the band's latest track, or a news site might offer videos of the latest world events. The downsides are:

- CD-quality, uncompressed files can be huge and impractical to download from the web. Fortunately, file formats for the web use advanced compression algorithms that can alleviate the performance issue at least somewhat. To boot, many such formats can begin playback as soon as a portion of the file is down-loaded, while the remainder of the file downloads in the background, thereby delivering content to the visitor faster.

- If a visitor is surfing the web from work, audio can alert everyone within earshot that someone who should be working is instead goofing off.

- Unrequested sound interferes with any music the visitor might already be play-ing on his or her computer.

Because of these problems, sound and video files should rarely execute automati-cally when a visitor drops in on a site. Instead, visitors should always be given a choice; they should be required to click on a link in order to see or hear the effects. Put more generally, multimedia should be an option that is under control of the user, rather than being solely under the control of the site designer.

Common audio formats include MIDI (Musical Instrument Digital Interface), WAV (Windows Waveform), and MP3 (MPEG Layer 3). MP3 is probably the superior format for general-purpose usage. Common video formats include AVI (Audio Video Interleaved), MPEG (Motion Picture Experts Group), MOV (QuickTime movie), and RealOne Player.

Server-side Technologies

The term *web server* can refer to both the server software (like the Apache web server) and the computer hardware upon which the server software runs. The web server receives the web page request and processes it, eventually ship-ping the assembled web page off to the requesting client (the visitor's computer and browser). The process is somewhat different, depending upon whether the requested web page is static (all of the displayed information is embedded in the HTML itself) or data-driven (much of the displayed information was actually pulled in from a separate database). Let's look at each.

Static Web Pages

The top image in **FIGURE 1.4** illustrates an interaction for a simple static page, which functions somewhat like this:

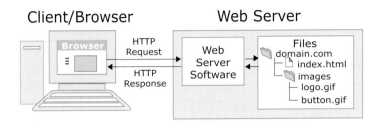

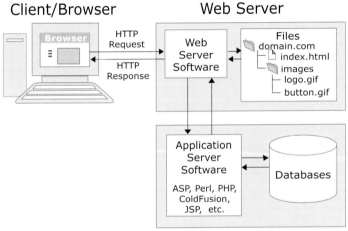

FIGURE 1.4 Client-Server Interaction: Static Web Page (top) and Data-driven Web Page (bottom)

1. The client sends a request for a page to a web server using HTTP (Hypertext Transfer Protocol), which in English means "the client types in a URL."

2. The web server software requests and returns the requested HTML document as well as all associated CSS, JavaScript, and multimedia files.

3. The client displays the received files as a completed page.

4. The web server disconnects the client. Any future requests from the client are treated independently of any prior requests.

Data-driven Web Pages

It's a bit more complicated if the page is data-driven, requiring access to a database on the server. For example, Amazon provides information on hundreds of thousands of books. It would be virtually impossible, not to mention expensive, for Amazon to hand-code a web page for every book. Instead, a skeleton book page is set up, with data about individual books pulled in from the books database at the time each page is requested.

When a site is data-driven, we must use application programs written in PHP, ASP, CGI/Perl, ColdFusion, JSP (JavaServerPages), or some other programming language. The bottom image in Figure 1.4 illustrates this process:

1. The client sends a request for a page to a web server. The request usually includes embedded variables that give the server additional information about the request. For instance, if a visitor attempts to purchase a book from a web site, the request would include data that identifies the book as well as the quantity desired.

2. The web server passes control off to an application server (software and the computer it runs on), notifying it to run the appropriate application program. In many cases, the application program retrieves and/or updates records from a database.

3. The application server passes control back to the web server, along with any information the web server needs (such as database records) to assemble the response page.

4. The web server merges the application program's data with the appropriate HTML file. It ships the newly composed HTML file as well as any image, CSS, and JavaScript files off to the client.

5. The client's web browser merges the received files and displays the completed page.

6. The web server disconnects the client. Any future requests from the client are treated independently of any prior requests.

If a page requires security of some sort, such as if credit card numbers or other confidential data needs to be passed, HTTPS (Secure Hypertext Transfer Protocol) is used instead of HTTP.

Although you do need to have a basic understanding of how this process works, we will not cover server-side technologies (such as how to pull in data from a database) in any depth here. Once again, that is a topic that deserves an entire book (or, for that matter, several books) of its own. We will, however, look briefly at two fairly new additions to our server-side technologies: XML and Ajax.

XML

XML (Extensible Markup Language) is a methodology for transporting data. With XML, the data is self-describing; that is, each of the fields is wrapped in a container that specifies the field name. See the sidebar for an example of XML as it might be used on a page that includes news feed articles from a news service. Note how the "wrappers" use an HTML-like syntax.

XML EXAMPLE

```
<newsArticle>
    <title>Webby Award Winners Announced</title>
    <shortDescription>This year's Webby Awards were announced at last
    night's annual banquet in Seattle, Washington.</shortDescription>
    <articleText>This year's Webby Awards were announced at last night's
    annual banquet in Seattle, Washington. Among the attendees were...
    </articleText>
</newsArticle>
<newsArticle>
    <title>Cat Rescued from Treetop</title>
    <shortDescription>An impromptu liberation effort brought out the best
    in a suburban community.</shortDescription>
    <articleText> An impromptu liberation effort brought out the best in
    a suburban community, at least for long enough to save the cat,
    share cookies and iced tea, and discover neighborliness in a large
    apartment building. Thanks to "Fluffy", the residents of...</articleText>
</newsArticle>
```

Any web page can make use of XML data as long as the page knows the data's structure and naming conventions. The primary advantage to XML is that it allows independent programs (including web pages) to talk to one another after agreeing on a common format for the data.

Ajax

One fairly recent development, Ajax, has the potential to change the way we manipulate web page display. Ajax uses a powerful amalgamation of JavaScript, XHTML, CSS, XML, and server-side data requests to refresh data on the current page without reloading the entire page. Only the new data is sent from the server and merged

• • •

XML TUTORIAL

See John Shirrell's www.xmlbook.info for a concise introduction to XML.

• • •

MORE ON AJAX

"Ajax" is commonly thought to stand for Asynchronous JavaScript and XML, although there's debate on whether that was really the intention of the folks who coined the term. For further information on AJAX, see the seminal article by Jesse James Garrett, http://www.adaptivepath.com/publications/essays/archives/000385.php.

with the document already on display in the browser, so the response time is faster. Several popular sites are already using Ajax, including Google Suggest, Google Maps, Flikr, and Amazon's A9.com search engine.

Integrated Development Environments

Integrated Development Environments (IDEs) such as Adobe Creative Suite (including Adobe Dreamweaver) and Microsoft Expression Web have been among the best advancements to come along in web development. Although web pages can be coded manually within any simple text editor, an IDE can certainly streamline the writing of HTML, CSS, and JavaScript.

Exactly how can an IDE simplify the web page creation process?

- A split-screen environment (as shown in the Adobe Dreamweaver interface in **FIGURE 1.5**) lets us choose between writing the HTML manually in the top half of the window or using the more visual, drag-and-drop features in the bottom half, leaving the actual code composition to the IDE. In either case, we see the results of our efforts in the bottom half of the window. Either method is legitimate; we can be flexible, depending upon which seems easier and faster at the time.

FIGURE 1.5 Split Screen in Dreamweaver

• • •

FREE TRIAL VERSIONS

Free trial versions of Adobe Creative Suite and Microsoft Expression Web are available at www.adobe.com and www.microsoft.com, respectively.

- Site management features allow us to move or rename files almost effortlessly. The environment checks site-wide for all other files that reference the renamed one, and offers to update those references automatically (**FIGURE 1.6**).

FIGURE 1.6 Updating File References in Dreamweaver

- Powerful search and replace features allow us to replace a bit of code or content on just the current page, on all pages that are currently open, or on the entire site at once (**FIGURE 1.7**).

FIGURE 1.7 Search and Replace in Dreamweaver

- Coding is more efficient because of commands that can quickly reformat code, comment out or hide from view irrelevant areas of code, or offer suggestions for how to complete a line of code. **FIGURE 1.8** shows a drop-down code-completion tag list.

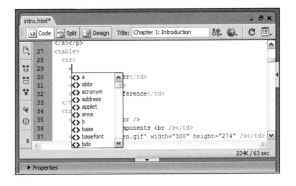

FIGURE 1.8 Code Completion in Dreamweaver

- Error-checking features can validate links site-wide, check for invalid code, or update the code to the latest coding standards with a single mouse-click.

- Reusable library assets like images or menus can be updated from within a library, which means that any changes to the asset, such as a new alt attribute, are automatically reflected wherever the asset is used.

- Templates (empty page layouts that store repetitive design elements like logos, navigation, and color schemes) can be linked to each new page. We then need to add only the variable content on each new page.

- Many development environments ship with built-in behaviors for common elements such as image swaps for rollover effects and pop-up menu scripts, as shown in **FIGURE 1.9**. Often extensions (downloadable plug-ins) for other behaviors are available, for free or for a fee, from third-party providers.

FIGURE 1.9 Behaviors Menu in Dreamweaver

All in all, development environments can remove much of the tedium of creating a web site. As of this writing, the web versions of Adobe Creative Suite seem to be the leader for professional web designers. The suite's development environment includes:

- Dreamweaver for creating HTML, CSS, and JavaScript.

- Fireworks and/or Photoshop for creating images.

- Flash for animation as well as creating entire web sites, including data-driven web sites.

- Contribute for content editing.

- FlashPaper for converting printable files into Adobe PDF or Flash documents.

Web Site Development Life Cycle

In the traditional "waterfall" model of system development, as illustrated in **FIGURE 1.10**, each phase must be completed before a subsequent phase can commence. Although web development is not generally as straightforward as this diagram makes it look, we still need to understand each phase individually before we can understand how they fit together for a web design project. To that end, a summary of the individual phases is presented in **TABLE 1.1**.

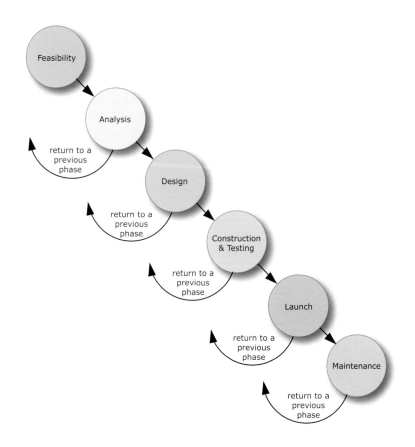

FIGURE 1.10 Development Life Cycle

TABLE 1.1 WATERFALL MODEL OF THE SYSTEM DEVELOPMENT LIFE CYCLE

Phase	Purpose	Principal Tools
Feasibility	Deciding whether a web site is needed, or whether an existing web site needs modification. If "yes," determining rough costs and benefits.	• Fact-gathering techniques such as interviewing the organization's management and proposed visitors • Cost-benefit analysis that ascertains whether the benefits are worth the associated costs
Analysis	Determining the purpose, target audience, and proposed content and functionality for the entire site. In short, deciding *what* is needed.	• Fact-gathering techniques • Cost-benefit analysis • Preliminary site architecture models
Design	Designing a site (both organizationally and visually) that fulfills the requirements determined in the analysis phase. In short, creating a "*how*" that provides the "*what*" from the analysis phase.	• Site architecture models • HTML, CSS, JavaScript, and integrated web development environments (such as Adobe Dreamweaver) for site prototyping • Image editors such as Adobe Photoshop or Fireworks for creating site graphics
Construction and Testing	Building and testing the web site. (Note that construction and testing can't be separated into independent phases, since testing should begin as soon as the first few lines of code are written. That way, problems are identified early in the process, rather than at the end when the entire site might end up needing major modifications to correct those problems.)	• HTML, CSS, JavaScript, and integrated web development environments (such as Adobe Dreamweaver and Flash) for site prototyping • Image editors such as Adobe Photoshop or Fireworks for creating site graphics • Accessibility validators • Live testing with prospective visitors
Launch	Uploading the site to the server, performing final site-wide tests, and bringing the site live. (See Bonus Topics on the web site for more on FTP and uploading to the server.)	• FTP or its equivalent
Maintenance	Repairing, upgrading, and overhauling the system as necessary.	All of the tools mentioned in the prior phases

Although the tasks represented in Figure 1.10 need to be completed for a web development project just as for a classic programming project, web design is much less cut-and-dried and linear than the diagram and table imply. Yes, we do still follow the waterfall model for the high-level process of web design; most of the overall site analysis and design is indeed done before much construction begins. But the construction and testing phase also includes tasks normally included in the independent analysis and design phases. This is because much of the analysis and design for individual pages is deferred until the construction and testing phase for those pages, since every page has unique requirements that often can't be ascertained until it's under construction. The result is that each page requires its own miniature life cycle, as shown by the connecting, spiraling circles of **FIGURE 1.11**. Each page is represented by a concentric circle, and each page progresses through its own analysis, design, and construction and testing phases. Now, all of the phases are tightly coupled with all of the other phases. Thus, to put a fine technical sheen on it, building a web site is iterative and recursive instead of rigidly sequential.

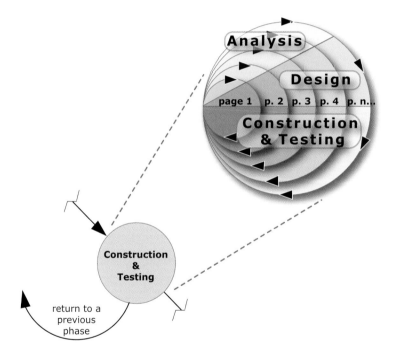

FIGURE 1.11 Web Site Construction Is a Spiral.

The iterative nature of web site construction also means that sometimes we need to revisit a page that we thought we had already completed. As a result, we often move backward, not just forward. For instance, several pages might be so closely related that none of them can be finalized until all of them are finalized, as would be the case with the multiple pages of a shopping-cart application. A good suggestion made by a user or manager for the 25th page might cause revisions on all earlier pages. We might discover that an error or missed requirement on a later page has implications for prior pages. All in all, creating a web site is indeed a spiraling, reiterative process.

Prototyping/Rapid Application Development

Another reason the lines between analysis, design, and construction and testing are blurred is that we use prototyping, also called rapid application development (RAD), in web development. That is, rather than designing a site on paper first, perhaps with dozens or even hundreds of pages of formal specifications, we rapidly "sketch" the pages in the development environment itself. The "sketch" is thereby in HTML already, so we can continue to refine the page until managers and testers are happy with it. At that point, our demo page is close to being a finished product anyway. Thus, we complete analysis, design, and construction and testing without ever noticing that we progressed through all of the steps along the way.

In effect, the system development phases are no longer distinct entities in web site development; the boundary lines have blurred, perhaps even disappeared, and the phases have become more integrated. You might even say that the phases have become tasks instead.

Now we'll look at overviews of content analysis, site architecture analysis, usability factors, visual design, interaction design, and accessibility, all as introductions to the chapters that follow.

Introduction to Content Analysis

If you build it, they will come. If you build good content, that is. Content, highlighted in **FIGURE 1.12**, is why visitors seek out a web site in the first place, why they stay once they get there, and why they return. Content is king; if a site does not have good content, it will not have visitors. Chapter 2 will delve into creating content.

FIGURE 1.12 Content

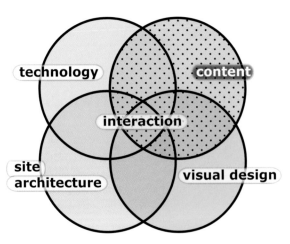

Introduction to Site Architecture Analysis

Information architecture—the organization and structure of any type of information—has been around since mankind began assembling libraries. For example, the Library of Congress Classification system is an information architecture system for categorizing, labeling, and organizing books in libraries. Similarly, site architecture, as highlighted in **FIGURE 1.13**, is nothing more than information architecture applied to a web site. It entails many of the same tasks as information architecture for libraries: categorizing, labeling, and organizing the bits and pieces of information that the site will present. Just as library patrons would be unable to find a specific book in a library if the books were jammed on shelves randomly, our visitors would be unable to find what they need if our web sites were not arranged on top of some underlying organizational principles.

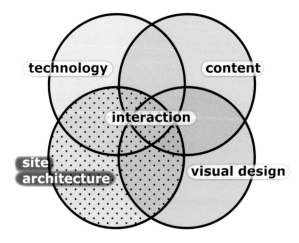

FIGURE 1.13 Site Architecture

Introduction to Usability Factors

Usability, also called user-centric design or human factors, is a hot topic these days. Whatever term you call it by, it refers to the underlying principle that we should be nice to our visitors; we should make it easy for them to do what they want to do and to find what they want to find. Web sites should be polite and considerate, much like your favorite restaurant waiter—helpful when a visitor needs help and out of the visitor's way when help isn't needed. The site should be likeable and should not intrude upon the visitor's experience.

Usability Principles

Usability principles are based on increasing visitor satisfaction, which determines whether or not the visitor stays on our site and returns to it later. Usability factors promoting visitor satisfaction include the following:

- **Self-evidence.** The site must be easy to use. Viewers will quickly leave a web site that is too complicated or that requires extensive onscreen explanations. In either case, the designers have not put enough thought into the design. We need to do the thinking so that users don't have to. A consistent and predictable organization, presentation, and interaction style promotes a faster learning curve and a resulting increase in visitor efficiency, and therefore, of course, user presence and loyalty.

- **Speed.** Visitors have no patience for slow. Unfortunately, some visitors are still on dial-up lines with slow modems. Consequently, we should limit the sizes of our files, a topic discussed more fully in Chapter 4. We also shouldn't require excessive clicks from visitors, because every new page requires a page load. We must establish clear and concise navigation so that visitors don't take wrong turns, again slowing them down. Ideally, we would like to deliver a visitor to his or her target within three clicks.

- **Feedback.** If the visitor must wait for something, we should warn her of that fact. For instance, a small animation that visually illustrates progress can indicate that the system is indeed doing something and hasn't just locked up. It's much like background music on a telephone call when you have been put on hold—you might not like the music, but at least it confirms that the connection isn't broken.

- **Accuracy.** Professional web pages shouldn't have broken links, missing images, JavaScript errors, or anything else that obviously doesn't work. You must make absolutely certain that none of these flubs turn up on your pages. Moreover, you should test the site in multiple browsers and browser versions.

Although the word "usability" may not be mentioned on every page of this book, it's certainly an underlying theme. Keep in mind that all of the aesthetic and interaction factors we are going to examine determine the usability of a site. For instance, a poor layout or irritating color scheme will, of course, degrade usability. After all, what is usability if not the result of effective design choices?

It's all well and good to talk about what makes a web site usable. Nevertheless, the only way to really know if we have satisfied those guidelines is to test against real users, which is the subject of our next section.

● ● ●

DON'T MAKE THEM THINK!

Alfred North Whitehead said, "Civilization advances by extending the number of important operations which we can perform without thinking about them."

Usability Testing

Long before unleashing your site on the world at large, you must test the site extensively with real users. Usability testing should be incremental, beginning as soon as there are several pages that are complete enough that testers can get some idea of at least the navigation. Even if the navigation is not yet wired up to go anywhere, you can show it to testers and ask, "Where do you think this will go? What would you expect to find if you click this link?" If the testers' view of how the navigation works differs from the way it was actually intended to work, you have a problem. Better to discover that problem now, when only a few pages are constructed, rather than later, after hundreds of pages are just a few days shy of deployment.

Of course, early testing does not in any way eliminate the need for later testing. In fact, you should test early, fix the problems, test again, and continue testing throughout the entire development cycle, as shown in **FIGURE 1.14** (an expansion of just the "testing" phase from Figure 1.10). Retest at least once each month throughout the project. If you are really, really good at listening to what your testers tell you, you won't have any major problems left to fix on your final test.

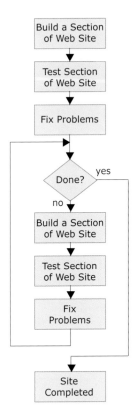

FIGURE 1.14 Testing Process

Just how involved, expensive, and time-consuming does usability testing have to be? Until just recently, many experts believed that *bigger* testing was *better* testing. They thought there needed to be bloated scenarios involving hundreds of testers, expensive usability labs with video taping of all tests, and convoluted and extensive reports complete with statistical analysis. The end result of such an overblown testing mentality is that testing was rarely done at all. Today, though, the belief is that more informal, less involved testing (termed "discount testing") can produce huge benefits—certainly more benefits than grandiose testing scenarios that aren't done at all. Major usability issues tend to become quickly obvious even with informal testing.

How do you do discount testing? Choose three or four testers with widely different technical abilities for each round of testing. Avoid using team members as testers; only people who are "off the street" and have not actually helped to create your site can give you unbiased, laypersons' opinions of what will and will not work with real visitors. Feel free to enlist friends and family in the test, as long as you are sure they will give you that unbiased opinion. For instance, your mother's "Yes, dear, this is just a wonderful site. I am soooooo proud of you!" might be a wonderful ego stroke, but it's of little practical value as a critique. What you truly need here is blunt honesty. Only frank critiques can improve the site (as well as protect your reputation as a professional web designer). And what should be your reaction to a brutally honest review? A sincere, heartfelt, "Thank you so much for identifying these flaws, so that now we can fix them!"

When you are testing, you are actually looking at two key issues: do the testers "get it," and can they accomplish the necessary tasks? The first refers to whether or not they understand the purpose of a site, its value, how it's organized, and how the navigation works. For this question, it's best to ask the users to think aloud, and then turn them loose, observe what happens, and listen very carefully to their comments. A few well-considered questions can always spur more in-depth evaluation as well. Did areas of the site irritate or baffle them? Why? And what would they change? What drew the testers' attention first on a page? Second? Third? Probe for specifics in all of these areas.

To evaluate the second of the two key issues—whether or not the testers can accomplish tasks—you might want to use tasks of their own choosing as well as assign specific tasks that you feel will be critical to future visitors. Again, what confused them or lost them?

On the other hand, were there areas of the site that engaged them, or amused them, or intrigued them? Why? What would they suggest that would allow you to propagate those positive aspects to other areas of the site?

Although you definitely need to take notes and perhaps even record each test session, a 30-page report detailing the results is overkill and very much a waste of your

• • •

HEAR FOR YOURSELF

What if management insists that certain elements of the site be done in a certain way, despite being informed those elements violate usability standards? Simple—invite the management to sit in on the testing. Let them hear for themselves the complaints and responses of their potential customers.

time. That time would be better spent in fixing the problems, not documenting them. A two-hour session with team members should allow you to focus on the major issues that simply must be fixed, as well as prioritize those issues that would be nice to repair but aren't so critical.

Be particularly wary of requests for additional features, so-called "scope creep." These features can end up cluttering the site to the point of *un*-usability, can have other unanticipated negative consequences to the site, and might be of value to only a very small subset of visitors—not to mention the extra time, effort, and costs to construct the additional features. Often, you must find a way to halt such scope creep in its tracks, because it can derail both the project's budget and its timetable.

Once you have incorporated what you learn from each set of testers, test the site again. And again. And yet again, until you and the latest set of testers are happy with the results, and the site can be launched.

Introduction to Visual Design

The visual design, or aesthetics, of a web site is the primary focus of this book. Webster's New Collegiate Dictionary defines aesthetics as "artistic" or "a pleasing appearance or effect." Aesthetics for a web site encompass anything with visual communication characteristics: color, layout, graphics, fonts, input forms, and navigation. We use visual elements to clarify the site's underlying structure and to provide an appropriate look and feel, or context. The design should provide a visual identity and visual consistency that carries throughout the entire site. Just like a design for a building or an automobile, the visual design for a web site must be appropriate. **FIGURE 1.15** highlights how visual design interacts with the other elements of web design.

FIGURE 1.15 Visual Design

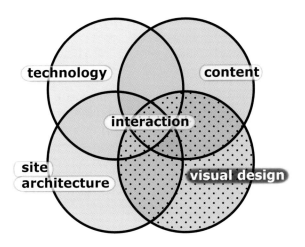

Why are aesthetics so important? Well, we *do* judge a book by its cover (envision the cover of a romance novel versus a book of photography of Ireland), a restaurant by its exterior (think McDonalds versus Olive Garden), and, ultimately, a web site by its design. If visitors are looking for children's toys, they are probably going to spend very little time on a site with a dull visual design, all in shades of grey.

Visual Design versus Usability

There have been two starkly opposing viewpoints when it comes to the visual design of a site. Usability gurus like Jakob Nielsen (www.useit.com) have traditionally expounded that web sites should be usable, not pretty. Almost anything done just for visual effect, he believes, gets in the way of usability. Starkly functional minimalism is the goal; images, colored backgrounds, and fancy layouts should all be avoided. Black text on a white background with few or no graphics would be the ideal web page. To be fair, the usability folks have softened their position a bit in the last few years, but nonetheless, the stricter advocates still favor "plain vanilla" web sites.

The opposing viewpoint promotes the web as an "experience." Consequently, web sites should take advantage of the uniqueness of the medium…stretch the limits of the medium…challenge/engage/mystify/amuse/enthrall the visitor. A terrific visual design creates meaning, provides context, and evokes emotion. It can engage a visitor and reassure him about the professionalism and reliability of the site. It can also establish focus, create emphasis, establish relationships between site elements, and guide the user to accomplish his mission. All of this is important for the visitor's experience as well as his understanding of the site. The flip side is that the "web as an experience" folks, left unchecked, might well deliver gorgeous web sites that are mystifying to navigate, difficult to decipher, and nightmares to download.

Fortunately for all of us using the web, neither side of the argument is totally right, nor totally wrong. In fact, usability and aesthetics don't have to be at odds on the web any more than they are in architecture. After all, a talented architect can craft a building that is both eminently functional and beautiful to behold. In the architecture of a building, form (the visual design) can indeed follow function (the building's usability).

Why can't the same balance apply to the web? Why can't we have beauty and functionality? After all, the web is, as we said right off at the beginning of this book, first and foremost a communication medium, much like print media. If we encountered a magazine with no pictures, in most cases we would dismiss it as an amateur production, cheaply made. So too it is on the web. And over time, this idea of balance is starting to inch toward the mainstream. In fact, some usability gurus (notably Jared Spool, www.uie.com) have grasped the fact that that web site form and function are not necessarily at odds with each other.

So let's do our best to balance form and function. If usability factors make a site functional, visual design makes it memorable. We aim for both.

- - -

ENGAGING THE VISITOR

"If the presentation is not clear, your audience might not be able to make it to your content. If the presentation is not engaging, your audience might not be motivated to try."
–From *Site-Seeing: A Visual Approach to Web Usability*, by Luke Wroblewski.

Branding: Creating an Identity

As mentioned earlier, one of the tasks of visual design is to make sure that a site has visual consistency. That is, all of the pages must look like they're cut from the same cloth. They'll have the same logo, and same color scheme, and (for the most part) the same layout. A visitor who has viewed one page in the site should be able to recognize immediately all of the other pages within the site. Additionally, that consistent look and feel should support the "branding" of the site.

What, then, is branding? It's the overall impression made by a product or the entire organization. It encompasses logos, packaging, advertising, presentation, reputation, and, of course, the web site itself. An effective brand has an identity, a personality, and an individuality of its own, with a distinct look and feel that appeals to its target audience. It evokes emotion and separates a product, service, or organization from its competitors. Most importantly, it's memorable.

Let's look at some examples of effective branding:

- **Oreo® cookies.** We can recognize an Oreo from just a small piece, and most of us immediately think of an associated glass of milk, and twisting the cookie apart (or not).

- **Jaguar.** The name instantly conjures up an image of a cool, high-performance, luxury vehicle with the evocative jungle cat hood ornament. We see sleek lines and a leather interior and imagine being the envy of all of our friends if we owned one.

- **Ben and Jerry's Ice Cream.** The overall image is funky and humorous. We can practically taste Ben and Jerry's rich ice cream in unusual but wonderful flavor combinations.

- **UPS™.** Very boring, very brown—but a UPS truck can be recognized blocks away. That boring brown has come to epitomize reliability, and UPS has capitalized on that image, to the point where the company uses the tag line "What can Brown do for you?"

- **Cheerios®.** Again, they are recognizable from just a tiny piece.

Other examples of effective branding include Disney, Godiva Chocolates, Victoria's Secret, Olive Garden, Harry Potter books and movies, and Nike's "swoosh" mark.

Now let's look at an example of ineffective branding. Think of the difference between Office Depot and Office Max…OK, time's up. Can't come up with anything? That's just it. Ineffective branding is in evidence here because there is little differentiation in the consumer's mind, little that is memorable. Their names, logos, and products are similar; the stores even have a similar look. Most consumers would just as happily go to one as the other and might not even remember which one of the two is located just a few blocks away in their own city.

A web site, then, must reflect the branding of its organization or product if it is to be memorable. Ideally, a coherent visual identity consistent with branding would allow visitors to guess the name of the organization even if we removed the name and logo from all of the pages. A coherent visual identity imparts a "sense of place" and, again, makes a site memorable.

Not only does the visual design furnish an instant impression of a site's branding, it also affects the site's perceived credibility, as verified by a Stanford University study:

> "The number one factor by which people actually judge Web site credibility was by their first impression of the visual design…If it doesn't look credible or it doesn't look like what they expect it to be, they go elsewhere. It doesn't get a second test. And it's not so different from other things in life. It's the way we judge automobiles and politicians." –*B.J. Fogg, Director of the Stanford University Pervasive Technology Lab*

Notice that what is being judged here is not just the ambiance or mood of a site, but its credibility. Today's web is a dangerous place; identity theft and web sites that install malware (adware, spyware, viruses, and so on) have trained web surfers to be cautious about the sites they trust. Yet now we are told that it's not a site's privacy policy, not its warranty statements, or not how long the site's been around that builds trust, but its *visual design*. With the visual design carrying such a heavy load, we certainly cannot give it short shrift.

Creating a Web Site with Appeal

Appeal means that visitors enjoy and become engaged in the site. We have already established that a web site must be easy to use or visitors won't find it appealing. But what are the characteristics of the visual design that can *make* a site appealing? It should be aesthetically pleasing, a unique experience, and evocative. Let's look at each characteristic in turn.

- **Aesthetically pleasing.** The site should "look right" for its purpose, its branding, and its audience. It could be fun, or professional, or cutting edge, or elegant, or futuristic, or grungy, or hip, or friendly, or formal, or down-home, or no-nonsense, or cozy, or flashy, or silly, or childlike…you get the idea. It all depends on purpose and audience. Once a style is nailed down, then every single element on every single page should sustain that style. It's worth repeating that visual design isn't just decoration; it colors the visitor's view of the product, the organization, and the site's credibility. Much of the rest of the book will be devoted to determining how to make a site aesthetically appealing.

- **A unique experience.** The experience should be unique to the medium. Avoid trying merely to duplicate the print medium, because you're missing an opportunity to leverage web technologies like color and interactivity. The buzz-word these days is "experience design:" Use the experience to draw the visitors into the site. Think of a restaurant like Olive Garden, where the food, the décor, the printed menus, and the service are all a part of the experience. The experience becomes immersive, captivating, and intriguing.

- **Evocative.** The site should, if possible, bring up positive emotions, whether satisfaction in a job accomplished, pleasure from viewing an artistic design, or eagerness to read a fascinating article.

Most of the remainder of the book concentrates on how to use the tools of site layout, color, graphics, typography, and input forms to create appeal. Before we get to specifics, however, we need to introduce a few broad design concepts that may help to create that appeal. We will discuss the use of metaphor and then examine several overall design hints.

Metaphor as a Design Tool

The use of visual metaphor is pervasive in web design, particularly for navigation. For instance, a computer desktop, complete with icons of files, folders, and a recycle bin is a familiar metaphor. Navigation buttons often look like real buttons that we could press to accomplish some task in the real world. Adding a rollover effect to "depress" the button heightens the effect. A few other common web metaphors are navigation controls that look like file folder tabs and icons that look like printers, computer disks, and shopping carts.

We can employ metaphor in a more global way as well, for the site as a whole. If you can identify an organizing metaphor that lends itself well to a visual interpretation, the entire design task becomes easier. For instance, a hotel's home page might look like the lobby of a hotel, complete with a check-in desk, the entrance to a restaurant, and a concierge desk. Each of these elements could be clickable, leading to reservations, a restaurant menu, and local attractions, respectively.

The benefit to visitors is that common metaphors can convey immediate understanding. To be effective, though, a metaphor needs to be appropriate both conceptually and visually. For instance, it's appropriate for United Airlines to use a globe as a logo, because their airplanes do indeed circle the globe. It's not appropriate for a pet supply retailer to use a globe, just because it has a presence on the "world wide" web.

Although engaging to visitors, metaphors can also be dangerous, particularly if the metaphor can't extend to cover all the necessary categories. If some of our categories must exist outside of the metaphor, we've introduced inconsistencies in our visitor's mental model, something we generally try to avoid.

● ● ●

BOLDNESS

"When you've chosen a style, make that style as clear and distinctive as you can. Be bold about it. Make it stand out." –From *User-Centered Web Design*, by John Cato.

Overall Design Hints

Upcoming chapters will deal with design hints and guidelines, organized by chapter topic. Here, though, we need to discuss a few more global hints that aren't limited to specific topics:

- **Less is (often) more.** Although some designers have difficulty embellishing a page enough to make it interesting, most have the opposite problem: They try to cram too much on a page. If you fall into this second category, review your designs for elements that can be eliminated or streamlined. For instance, rarely does a page look good with 15 different typefaces on it; it instead begins to look like a ransom note. Keep in mind that simple isn't always boring—often it's modern and elegant instead.

- **Maintain a "tickler file" of ideas.** Make note of images, color schemes, layout plans, interesting typefaces, and snippets of code that do interesting things. Other web sites can generate ideas, of course, but so too can magazines, books, opening credits of movies, or displays of color-coordinated bedding and towels in a department store or mail-order catalog. Keep your eyes open for inspiration at all times.

- **Use restraint.** For instance, gratuitous animation can be annoying and increases download time, perhaps so much so that visitors become impatient and abandon the site. You may also have to use restraint by ditching a clever idea that you absolutely love. Sadly, sometimes those clever ideas end up not really sustaining the purpose of the site you are currently working on. In that case, table the idea for now, but stash it in your tickler file, and consider it for your next project. (Admittedly, deciding to abandon a beloved "pet" idea can be one of the most gut-wrenching decisions that a web designer has to face.)

- **Check out competing sites.** Don't pass up the opportunity to leverage the experience of others. View competing sites as free prototypes. Analyze those things that the competitors do well, and the things they do poorly. Contemplate how you could avoid merely equaling the competing sites, but instead surpass them. Then consider whether you want to use a design style very similar to the competing sites (on the theory you shouldn't fix what isn't broken), or radically different (so that your site is memorable). Either choice can be a legitimate one, depending on the circumstances.

- **Cross-browse.** When browsing in bookstores, frequent the art and design section as well as the web development shelves. Some web-related books seem to appear only in the design section—Krause's Index series (*Layout Index*, *Color Index*, and so on) and Rockport Publishers' *Color Harmony for the Web* come to mind. Of course, non-web related design books can be inspirational, too.

- **Be judgmental.** At last, a situation in which you are encouraged to do this! Take note of and learn from the characteristics you personally like and dislike on the web sites you visit yourself. What annoys you? What delights you? Those same characteristics have the potential to annoy or delight your visitors as well.

- **Focus on solving design problems.** Keep in mind that although design is an art, it's not just art for art's sake. An artist creates something that is purely appealing, that doesn't need to have a purpose or satisfy an audience (well, unless the artist likes to eat). She can paint or sculpt whatever she chooses. The only constraints are those of the medium, whether paint or clay or fiber. A designer, on the other hand, must solve communication problems that have inherent restrictions: budgetary guidelines, business goals, existing branding, target audiences, and the organization's management. In the design field, pure art often gets in the way of communication. Designers who were artists first and entered web design later seem to have a particularly hard time dealing with these issues.

More specific elements of visual design will be covered in all the chapters in the book, except for Chapter 2.

Introduction to Interaction Design

Interaction, as highlighted in **FIGURE 1.16**, refers to anything that requires some action from the visitor, such as clicking on a link or filling out a form, as a way to, or the next step toward, reaching some goal. Interaction design goes beyond visual design, because we now expect visitors to be active participants, not just passive observers.

FIGURE 1.16 Interaction

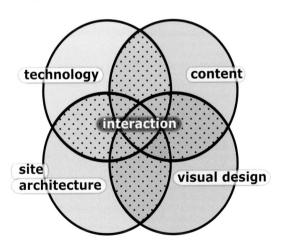

• • •

INVISIBILITY

"Perhaps the most easy-to-use products are the ones you don't notice." –From *User-Centered Web Design*, by John Cato.

Poor interaction design is distracting to a visitor, like a small splinter. It annoys even though it might not be truly painful. In contrast, visitors won't even notice how successful an interface is if we do our jobs properly; the design will be transparent, invisible to the visitor (just like we don't notice when we *don't* have a splinter). An interface that seems so natural and intuitive that the user doesn't notice it at all is the very definition of a successful interface.

How many hoops your visitors are willing to jump through to get to that goal depends, again, on its importance to the visitor. Visitors will typically tolerate long and drawn-out processes only if the end result is of high personal salience.

• • •

COMPLEXITY

"If you add features to your program that are necessarily complex to manage, users will be willing to tolerate that complexity only if the rewards are worth it. This is why a program's user interface cannot be complex to achieve simple results, but it can be complex to achieve complex results (as long as such results aren't needed very often)." –From *About Face 2.0: The Essentials of Interaction Design*, by Alan Cooper and Robert Reimann.

Interaction design will be covered in more depth in both Chapters 3 and 8.

Introduction to Web Accessibility

One of the ongoing themes of this book is accessibility, also called universal design, which refers to providing access for all users regardless of physical abilities. As we go through each chapter, we will look at accessibility guidelines that relate to the topic at hand. For instance, in Chapter 5, we'll examine how to make a colorful site look great while at the same time making sure that the site is legible to individuals who are color-blind. Nonetheless, before looking at specifics in the following chapters, we need to understand the overarching principles that underlie those specifics.

We can, with thoughtful universal design, provide access for everyone. Why should we bother, when the vast majority of our visitors don't have physical limitations? The foremost reason is for humanitarian purposes—it's the right thing to do. Furthermore, many accessibility initiatives support usability for all visitors. For instance, choosing high-contrast colors to ensure they are legible to those with color vision problems can also render the site easier to read for other visitors with no such impairments.

Yet another reason is that Section 508 of U.S. government regulations requires that technology used within the U.S. federal government be accessible to people with various disabilities. Many local and state governments follow suit and may refuse to do business with non-governmental business organizations that don't comply voluntarily.

The general rule for web sites is that they should provide identical content in accessible formats whenever possible, or equivalent content in a different format when not. We can do so by providing compatibility with a variety of techniques and devices used by people with disabilities. For instance, screen-reader technology can read the words of a web page to people with visual disabilities, as long as we make sure our page is compatible with those screen readers.

Types of Disabilities

What general types of disabilities should we consider?

- **Visual impairment.** This can range from the extreme of total blindness to a less severe color-blindness or the loss of visual acuity encountered by people as they age. For the former, we accommodate screen readers by including such design elements as column headers on tabular data and alt attributes on all images. For folks with a milder disability, we make sure that our pages don't override any browser setting that they have specified for larger type or custom colors. (Fortunately, modern browsers won't allow our specifications to override the visitor's preferences.)

- **Hearing impairment.** If we provide content sound (sound that is more than just for entertainment—it carries information as well) such as an instructional video or an audio file of a lecture, we should provide an alternative for the hearing impaired. For instance, we could offer captioning or a link to a text transcription.

- **Physical impairment.** Visitors who can't manipulate a mouse should be able to use the tab key or control keys to access all interactive elements, such as navigation.

Accessibility Guidelines

Although we will defer more specific guidelines until the chapters that discuss the related design elements, some overall suggestions are in order here:

- Design the site to accommodate adaptive technology such as screen readers. Test your site with at least one popular screen reader, such as JAWS or IBM Home Page Reader.

- Provide choice and adaptability in methods of use. For instance, one person might prefer to use a mouse, another visitor the tab key, and yet another visitor the access keys (function or control keys). The more choices we can provide, the more visitors we can accommodate.

- Any time an image, animation, audio file, or video carries information content (as opposed to just entertainment value), provide the information in an accessible text-based format as well, either with captioning or by linking to a text-only page.

- Design the site to be simple and intuitive. Eliminate any unnecessary complexity.

- Separate structure from format. For instance, use HTML to identify structural elements such as headers, using standard header tags (<h1>, <h2>, and so on). Move content formatting to CSS, where it can be overridden by visitors. Format a document so that it's still legible (though not necessarily as visually appealing) even if the style sheet is disabled.

- Ensure that pages are still usable when scripts, applets (small programs, usually written in the Java programming language), or other programmatic objects are turned off. If impossible to do that, provide equivalent information on an alternative page.

- Be cautious about creating an Adobe Flash-only page. Although more recent versions of Flash can render a page more accessible than prior versions, some accessibility support is still incomplete. Additionally, the visitor cannot override visual settings like she could with an HTML-based page. If you do build a Flash-only site, you should provide a link to a text-based alternative.

- Clearly identify the language of the page in the <html> tag, like this:

```
<html lang="en">
```

- If, after best efforts, you cannot create an accessible page, provide a link to an alternative page that uses W3C technologies, is accessible, has equivalent information and functionality, and is updated as often as the original (inaccessible) page.

Accessibility Resources

For further accessibility information, refer to any of the following:

- The official U.S. Government site explaining the Americans with Disabilities Act (ADA), www.usdoj.gov/crt/ada/adahom1.htm as well as www.section508.gov.

- *Access by Design: A Guide to Universal Usability for Web Designers*, by Sarah Horton. Berkeley, California: New Riders, 2006. An excellent reference.

ACCESSIBILITY OVERRIDES IN THE BROWSER

Newer browsers permit the visitor to override CSS settings on a web page, thereby allowing each visitor to make his or her own decisions about how to render the site accessible. Still, you must be cautious when using CSS, because older browsers didn't always support such overrides.

- AIS's Web Accessibility Toolbar, www.visionaustralia.org.au/info.aspx?page=614. An invaluable plug-in for Internet Explorer that includes tools for checking a wide range of accessibility issues. It includes commands to view a page at different resolutions and in grayscale, both of which are useful for site design in general.

- JAWS screenreader, www.freedomscientific.com/fs_products/software_jaws.asp

- IBM Home Page Reader, http://www-03.ibm.com/able/solution_offerings/ hprtrial3.html

Accessibility validators and/or further accessibility information:

- www.validator.w3.org

- http://bobby.watchfire.com

- www.vischeck.com/vischeck

- http://diveintoaccessibility.org

- www.usablenet.com

- Adobe Dreamweaver (provides accessibility validation)

Summary

This book, along with every other web design book you will ever encounter, will hold forth on lots of rules for design. Do this, don't do that. But for every rule, there is some problem best solved by breaking that very rule. It depends upon the situation: upon whether it's the organization's CEO telling you to break the rule; upon whether adhering to one rule entails breaking another, more crucial, rule; upon the problem being solved. Always keep in mind that "rules" aren't laws—they are only guidelines.

T.S. Eliot stated, "It's not wise to violate rules until you know how to observe them." Picasso followed the rules at the beginning his career; his early drawings and paintings were realistically rendered. Only after he had fully mastered the rules did he have the skill level it took to break the rules to great effect. Only such a master can successfully break rules. As a result, the remainder of this book is devoted to teaching you the rules so that, later on, you may have the skill to break them—appropriately.

Design Checklist

The following checklist serves two functions: to summarize the major points and "rules" presented in the chapter, and to help you ensure you've done all you should before finalizing any web site you are creating.

Usability—*Did you:*

- Keep in mind browser inconsistencies, and test against your target browsers?

- Try to use HTML for structural identification and CSS for visual formatting?

- Consider the usability guidelines of self-evidence, speed, feedback, and accuracy?

- Aim to satisfy the usability factors that make a site functional as well as create a visual design that makes a site memorable?

Visual Design—*Did you:*

- Create a site that is aesthetically appealing, a unique experience, and evocative?

- Make sure the web site has a coherent visual identity that supports the branding of the product or organization?

- Consider using an organizing metaphor?

- Simplify whenever appropriate?

- Apply restraint in using gratuitous features?

- Analyze competing sites?

- Keep in mind that design isn't "art for art's sake," but instead must solve a user's problems?

Accessibility—*Did you:*

- Provide identical content for people with impairments whenever possible, or equivalent content in a different format when not?

- Consider visual, aural, and physical impairments?

- Design the site to accommodate adaptive technology?

- Provide choice and adaptability in methods of use?

- Provide alternative access to images, animation, audio, or video that carry information content?

- Separate structure from format?

- Ensure that pages are still usable when scripts, applets, or other programmatic objects are turned off?

- Clearly identify the language of the page in the `<html>` tag?

- If, after best efforts, you could not create an accessible page, provide a link to an alternative page that is accessible?

CHAPTER TWO

Site Analysis

ANONYMOUS:

"There's never enough time to do it right, but there always seems to be time to do it over."

There's an old, old joke about an airplane pilot who comes on the loudspeaker to assure the passengers, "I have good news and bad news. The good news is that we are making marvelous time. The bad news is, we're lost." Silly, yes, but the scenario is relevant because it isn't always so far off from reality when applied to software design. The point we can take away from the anecdote is that spending time and effort up front determining exactly where we are going avoids wasting time building the wrong system— one that does not satisfy our visitors' needs. Money spent early on, deciding precisely what to build right the first time, is money well spent.

Analysis, then, is the process of determining exactly what is needed before we start building anything. Essentially, we must think before we build, because we cannot hit a target if we don't have a clear view of it first. We ask a lot of questions of all stakeholders—managers, technical people on the project, and potential site visitors—before doing anything else.

In the first chapter, we looked at the system life cycle and how analysis fit into it, as shown again here in **FIGURE 2.1**. You might recall that we discussed how we must do overall site analysis at the inception of a project, but that we also go through a mini life cycle (including analysis, design, and construction and testing) for each individual page as well, as shown again in **FIGURE 2.2**. Thus, analysis is tightly integrated to all other tasks of the life cycle, rather than existing as a totally independent process. Additionally, the process is iterative; content and design changes must be incorporated throughout the entire life cycle. For instance, we often backtrack to prior stages and pages as we get feedback from users and potential visitors. Regardless, the tasks of analysis must be completed at some point: site-wide analysis at the inception of the project and page-specific analysis throughout the project.

FIGURE 2.1 Overall System Development Life Cycle

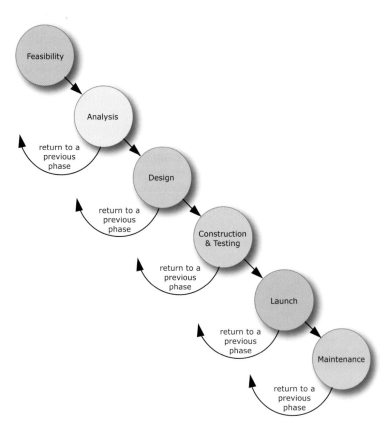

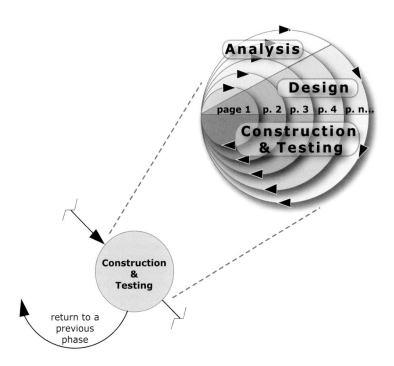

FIGURE 2.2 Web Site
Construction as a Spiral

Site-wide analysis consists of the thinking and planning that goes into a site before a single page is designed or constructed. It essentially determines what will be included on the site, while the later stages of visual design determine how the elements of the site will be presented visually. We will examine in turn the six major tasks of site-wide analysis:

1. Clarify the organization's goals for the site.

2. Identify the target audience, the site's potential visitors.

3. Identify visitor goals.

4. Determine site constraints.

5. Determine site content.

6. Analyze site architecture.

Clarify the Organization's Goals

First, we need to form a clear picture of the organization goals for the site. What is its mission, its purpose, its objectives? For example, is the site intended to generate sales leads? To sell directly to customers? To build product awareness but not actually sell anything? To inform visitors about a political issue? To provide information?

Once our goals are defined, we must identify which of these goals are mandatory and which are optional. For instance, Amazon would consider closing as many sales as possible to be a mandatory goal. Encouraging visitors to sign up for notification of forthcoming DVD releases might be a desirable yet optional goal that could be abandoned if necessary.

We must also determine the scope of the project. That is, how extensive will it be? For example, Target would probably choose to offer only a small selection of its typically vast store inventory on its web site, thereby limiting the scope of the project. A retailer of large appliances might choose not to sell online at all, but instead only offer product specifications and service information.

• • •

SOME OPTIONAL GOALS ARE MANDATORY

Keep in mind that if the CEO wants it, it's mandatory, regardless of whether or not it makes good business sense.

In all cases, the scope needs to be explicitly defined. Otherwise, we run the risk of *scope creep*: the process of adding more and more unplanned features on the fly. The most insidious words in web design (not to mention new home construction) are, "Well, while we're at it…"

A *mission statement* that prioritizes goals will aid in maintaining focus in this cacophony of competing demands. Keep in mind that different business units— marketing, customer service, techies, and management—will all be clamoring for space on the site. A mission statement will help the organization to be able to say "no" when some stakeholders must be told that not everything they want can be included on the site.

Let's look at the three basic categories of organizational goals for commercial web sites:

- Increasing profits

- Disseminating information or opinions

- Serving as the user interface for a standard business application

As we look at these three goals, keep in mind that most web sites are "selling" something, even if the site doesn't involve monetary currency; a web site might well be "selling" opinions or information instead.

Increasing Profits

Most e-commerce sites fall into this category by selling a product or service, as do Amazon, Dell, and E*TRADE. Web sites can also increase profits in ways other than just selling products directly, such as by boosting brand awareness or by decreasing the costs associated with a high incidence of customer service calls.

In any case, we design a sales web site to provide the information and ambiance that persuades visitors to open their wallets. These days, such factors include not only showing our products and services in the best light, but also in convincing the visitor that our site is reliable (will deliver a satisfactory product or service, as promised) and trustworthy (will not use our credit card or personal information inappropriately). As we saw in the prior chapter, the visual design of our web site can go a long way toward convincing visitors that we are both reliable and trustworthy.

Keep in mind that among the fastest growing moneymaking businesses on the web today are B2B (Business to Business) sites. A B2B site sells supplies and services to other businesses.

Disseminating Information

Some sites are not primarily sales sites but are instead intended to inform, educate, persuade, or entertain. For instance, a corporate site might post "white papers" on best practices in the software development industry, as a way of contributing to the industry and thus increasing the organization's status. A news organization like CNN might post the latest news updates. A political organization might publish political opinion pieces. A rock band's site might provide a concert schedule and free MP3 samples of the band's latest CD.

Although these sites are not primarily concerned with selling something, that doesn't mean there isn't money involved. For instance, a news organization might sell ads that bring in revenue to fund the site. A political organization hopes to convince visitors of their wisdom and sincerity so that visitors will donate money to the cause. Even though a rock band might not be actually selling their CDs directly from their web site, they are certainly hoping that visitors purchase those CDs from retail stores.

Serving as the User Interface for a Business Application

A *user interface* (the screen display that accepts user input and displays system output) is needed for any computer system that communicates with people. Every time we visit a web site, we are interacting with that site's user interface, also called the *front-end*.

A traditional computer business application, such as for entering customer charges or keeping track of inventory, typically uses a *graphic user interface*, or GUI (pronounced "goo-ee"). The interface is built in to the application software that actually processes transactions, and is usually hand-built by the programmers along with the rest of the application.

A *browser user interface*, or BUI (pronounced "boo-ee"), communicates with the user through the browser while the *back-end* business application (business logic on the server) uses standard programming languages like Java, C++, or even COBOL to interact with the underlying databases. The significance of a BUI is that a business application not typically delivered through the web can still use a browser to provide its user interface.

In the future, the most ubiquitous deployment of web technology may well be in BUIs, not for public-access web sites, for good reasons:

- A browser has all sorts of built-in facilities—for buttons and forms and such— that can make coding a user interface easier and faster than in the typical GUI environment.

- Browser-based technologies such as HTML are fairly easy to learn. That ease of learning is not necessarily true for the programming languages and environments used to build GUIs.

- Web sites must be as agile as the business itself, so that they can be updated quickly and easily for competitive advantage. Again, because HTML is relatively straightforward, HTML-based interfaces are easier to update than standard GUIs.

- BUIs are portable. If we code a site wisely, its pages will display properly in all of our target browsers, on any operating system. On the other hand, most programs written in standard programming languages must be at least recompiled and perhaps even rewritten to run in each different computing environment.

- BUIs don't need to be downloaded and maintained on every user's PC, as many standard applications require. Instead, only a single copy is required—the copy on the web server that all users access.

Identify the Target Audience

Let us not forget the most important stakeholder of all, our potential visitors. All communication events, whether in print, on television, or on the web, should be aimed at a *target audience*. Identifying the target audience is second in importance only to defining the goals of a site. After all, you can't meet the needs of an audience if you don't know who that audience is.

Accordingly, we now must ask, who are the people most likely to frequent the site? Identifying a target audience isn't necessarily easy in the worldwide, heterogeneous universe of the web. Sometimes it's hard to ascertain even the country our audience resides in, much less more specific data. Still, it can be done, as any marketing guru would be happy to tell you. Sometimes it's just common sense, while at other times it requires extensive research.

Let's say we are an organization selling electronics: computers, stereos, and appliances. It's not sufficient to say, "Our audience consists of people who want to buy computers, stereos, and appliances." We need to be more specific.

What are the demographics of the target audience, in terms of income, age, education, family status, and health conditions? What problems do they have? What appeals to them? What do they need? Unless you have a very clear definition of the audience, you cannot design a site to appeal to that audience.

Here are the characteristics to define during the process of nailing down your target audience:

- **Physical demographics**—Gender, age range, health status. Females and males tend to prefer a different look for a web site. If you need to satisfy both, you will need to create a design that appeals to both. Age and health status have implications for issues like vision impairment and mobility. Additionally, older folks might well be less computer-literate because they didn't grow up with computers as younger generations have.

- **Cultural demographics**—Economic status, employment, education level, social group, nationality, language, values. Economic status and employment might dictate whether a visitor accesses the web from a high-end home computer, an intranet at the office, or a low-end computer at the public library. Education level, social group, nationality, and language dictate the level of writing you can use. Values can dictate everything from the language that won't offend the audience to the products that are appropriate to sell on the site.

- **Computer experience**—Knowledge of technology, usage patterns, favorite sites, web surfing patterns and frequency. Computer experience is an important factor in determining the characteristics of such elements as navigation and search methods.

- **Findability**—Will your visitors find your site from a search engine, a banner ad, a link on another site, printed promotional materials, or from a friend's referral?

- **Computer equipment profile**—Operating system, system speed and power, connection speed. You will be making design decisions based upon this knowledge. For instance, bandwidth (speed of the connection) is less of a concern if most of your visitors are on high-end systems within a corporate intranet, but a major concern if some of your visitors are on low-speed, dial-up lines.

- **Frequency of visits**—Repeatedly or infrequently? Infrequent visitors in particular need sites that are exceedingly easy to use, because they will have to re-learn how to use the site each time they visit.

- **Location of access**—From home, a business, a public-access location. For instance, an office worker who might enjoy background sound at home will be more than mildly irritated if your site blares "noise" when he's surfing the web from his cubicle at work. After all, that sound tells everyone in the surrounding cubicles that someone is goofing off.

- **Competing sites**—What other sites do your visitors patronize? When you know what these are, you can assess the bar that has been set for the visitor experience.

- **Internal or external**—Are they internal (for example, doing back-end data entry using a BUI application) or external (as they would be for most public-access web sites)? Security issues can be important in either case. For instance, not all employees are typically granted access to every page on the company intranet. Another site might need to protect the security of credit card numbers from both internal and external visitors.

- **Design expectations**—What do visitors expect your site to look like? This information will be critical when you progress to the visual design of the site.

When characterizing one or more target audiences for your site, the more specific and vivid you can be, the better. Create a *persona* (an imaginary person or character) to symbolize each of the main types of people you expect to use the site), and give each one a name, a personality, and a brief biography. You might even associate a picture with the persona, to make him or her more memorable. As you work through the design of your site, call up the persona in your mind and ask yourself, "What would this person like to see on the site? How can I make this person's task easier to accomplish?"

The target audience and their needs must be the central focus in every decision you make. If you understand your target audience, you can determine what they want, design for them, and test with them. Satisfy their needs, and you have earned repeat visitors.

Keep in mind that the importance of your site to the target audience has great bearing on what that audience will tolerate. Fans of a popular rock band might be more than willing to wait for an interminably long download just to get their hands on a short MP3 clip of the band's newly-released single. In contrast, a visitor who is only mildly interested will have little tolerance for such a long wait.

Identify Target Audience Goals

A visitor doesn't drop in on a web site simply because it's cool, or looks attractive, or has terrific navigation. Instead, a visitor hopes the site will help him or her to accomplish a goal. If the tasks necessary to achieve that goal become at all difficult to complete, the visitor is likely to abandon the site and search for a competing site that is easier to use. Thus, we must determine the needs of our visitors and do whatever we can to make those tasks seem effortless. If we can meet the visitor's needs, we will have established a long-term relationship with that visitor, and our site has the potential to be a success on the web.

Consequently, the best way to support an organization's goals is to consider how best to support our visitors' goals. How do we go about sustaining a business goal, such as to sell lots of products, while at the same time supporting visitors' goals to buy something? What works for both of us? Well, of course we need to demonstrate to visitors that our site is reliable and provides the best value, or the best quality, or the best service. Then we allow the visitors to make purchases easily and quickly. Anything that interferes with visitors' goals is ultimately counterproductive to a site's goals as well, because visitors will be disinclined to use the site.

We define or identify our visitors' goals by getting feedback from current customers, interviewing potential visitors, and analyzing competing web sites. Visitor goals might include:

- Purchasing products or services online, as economically and efficiently as possible.

- Researching products or services for future purchase, either online or at a retail store.

- Obtaining service for a product that he or she already owns.

- Obtaining information about a topic of interest.

A *use case* is a step-by-step documentation of a sequence of interactions that must be completed for a visitor to accomplish a task, presented from that visitor's point of view. (This is where the personas come in handy.) Normally, there is one main scenario for successful completion of the basic task, plus additional scenarios for alternate paths when things go wrong or for when the task has an unusual component. Put all the scenarios together, and you have a complete use case for a typical user interaction. See the sidebar for an example of a use case that includes two alternate scenarios.

USE CASE FOR PURCHASING A PRODUCT

1. The customer browses the on-line catalog and adds desired items to the shopping cart.

2. When done shopping, the customer clicks the "checkout" button.

3. The customer enters the shipping information.

4. The system presents full order details, including shipping costs.

5. The customer enters credit card data and clicks "place order."

6. The system verifies the credit card.

7. The system confirms the sale immediately.

8. The system sends a follow-up email to the customer.

Alternative: Authorization Failure

6. The system fails to authorize the credit card.

7. The system allows the customer to re-enter credit card information up to two more times.

8. Upon third failure, the transaction is terminated with an error message.

Alternative: Repeat customer

4. The system displays the full order details, including the customer's standard shipping option and the last four digits of the credit card.

5. The customer may accept or reject the standard shipping and credit card information.

6. The customer clicks "place order."

7. See Steps 6-8 in the primary scenario.

We also need to analyze how often a visitor might perform each task. Those that are performed often should take priority and have the most visibility on the site. For example, Amazon sells more books, music, and movies than it does gardening tools or jewelry. As a result, books, music, and movies are the most visible navigation tabs on the site, while gardening tools might be buried under an "Other" tab. Such menu visibility facilitates visitors' most frequent tasks.

▨ DESIGN PATTERNS

One way of analyzing any task is to see how it might fit into a *design pattern*, a common, recurring problem that can make use of a standard solution. This technique relies on the belief that almost anything that anyone might want to do has been done already. We can leverage the "been there, done that" designs of the folks that came before us. For example, think of typical shopping-cart applications. Only rarely does a site do something radically different from that recognizable metaphor. When it does happen, it's usually an unpleasant surprise. The point is that we can re-use the patterns of the web pages that we have been visiting ourselves—patterns that have already been proven to work. We need not reinvent the wheel with every site. In fact, it's not just a waste of time, it's likely to be a failure!

Design patterns can include not only a sequence of visitor interactions but also a recommended layout for the necessary pages and specific guidelines for designing those pages. Such design patterns proliferate on the web. We have already mentioned shopping carts, but also consider standard patterns for:

- Horizontal, tab-based navigation

- Vertical menu navigation

- Privacy policies

- "About Us" pages

- "Contact Us" pages

- Quick checkout

- Return instructions

- Simple and advanced searches

- Login screens

- Creation of a new account

- Verification of order status

- Wish lists

Note that some companies have actually patented some software patterns, such as Amazon's "One Click" design pattern. In fact, several court cases ensued over rights to use such patterns, with ambiguous results. The legal controversy seems to have subsided over the last few years, but it remains possible that closely copying a design pattern from another web site could result in patent issues and legal battles.

● ● ●

MORE ABOUT PATTERNS

For further information on design patterns as they relate to web sites, see *The Design of Sites*, by Douglas K. Van Duyne, James A. Landay, and Jason I. Hong.

By identifying target audience goals, we can support visitors' decisions and actions, not only the best-case scenarios (the user completes his or her intended task) but also the worst-case scenarios (the user doesn't complete a task or encounters an error). We are always searching for ways to expedite the entire process.

Determine Site Constraints

Site analysis results in a list of constraints as well as a list of requirements. In particular, a budget and time schedule must be met. For instance, a tax-preparation web site must be completed in time for the visitors to prepare their taxes by the due date. Although it might be ideal to limit costs by using a small project team, the realities of this particular situation are such that there must be a staff and budget adequate to complete the project within the given time constraint.

Ideally, there are three goals we strive for in the development of a web site:

- The finished product should provide value proportional to the incurred costs.

- The site should be completed in an appropriate time frame.

- The site should be of high quality.

Unfortunately, we can usually choose only two of those three goals; the third one, whichever of the three it is, always suffers. That is, perhaps we can build the site cheaply and fast, but then the quality will be compromised. On the other hand, if we are willing to increase the budget, we might be able to create the site quickly and still deliver high quality. In a nutshell, the site can be cheap to build, fast to build, or of high quality, but usually not all three.

Cost-benefit analysis (deciding if the benefits provided are worthy of the attendant costs) plays a big part in the process of identifying constraints. Obviously, we want the benefits to exceed the costs. When the benefits are lower than the costs, however, that doesn't automatically mean we need to abandon the project. Perhaps we should first attempt to sniff out any "gold plating" in the requirements: those bells and whistles that are not absolutely required but that increase the budget dramatically. These, then, are the areas we might trim in order to complete the project on time and within budget.

One thing to keep in mind is that we are not necessarily required to deliver the entire system at once. Often a phased rollout/launch, with critical areas of the site going online earlier than areas of lower priority, can relieve a tight development schedule or budget.

There may be other constraints beyond budget and time schedule, including legal, operational, technical, and design constraints. For example:

- A corporate site attempting to attract investors has legal constraints as to what it is allowed to say to those investors.

- A site accessing a database that is updated by several discrete corporate units has operational constraints that are not an issue if the database were centrally maintained.

- We might be limited in the number of people available to work on the development team or by the skill set of that development team.

- We might need to use an existing logo and branding, thereby dictating numerous design decisions, especially color scheme.

- There are any number of things that we might like to do on a web site that just are not technically possible in today's web environment.

And of course, all such factors are best identified early in the project.

Determine Site Content

FIGURE 2.3 shows again how Content relates to the rest of site design. As mentioned in Chapter 1, content is king; if a site does not have good content, it will have few visitors. Or perhaps the site will have visitors initially, but, finding nothing of value, they never return.

FIGURE 2.3 Web Content

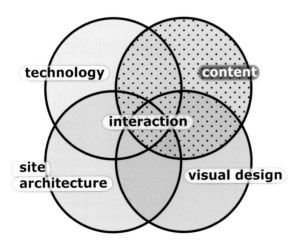

Failing to retain visitors is a costly mistake. The marketing rule of thumb is that it costs five times as much to sell to a new customer as it does to sell to a returning customer. Obviously, then, once we have a visitor, we want to keep her. We are trying to minimize *churn*, which is the number of visitors who are not converted to customers, or who are converted just one time, never to return. Churn is inversely proportional to the *conversion rate*, the percentage of visitors who purchase something before leaving a site. Providing compelling content and presenting products in the very best light can increase conversion rates and minimize churn.

● ● ●

WEB CONVERSION RATES

The average web site conversion rate hovers at only 1–2%, whereas a few sites (notably Sephora.com, Lands End.com, and Drugstore.com) can have conversion rates in the 10–20% range. See *Computerworld* February 5, 2001, page 50, http://www.computerworld.com/softwaretopics/crm/story/0,10801,57260,00.html.

Of course, purpose and target audience drive content; every bit of content on a site should support its purposes and be geared toward its audience. We need to slant our content toward what the visitor values. For instance, a potential customer for a site selling organic products is of course concerned with finding the product she is looking for, and whether it's a good value, and whether or not she'll purchase it, but perhaps also with determining if the company follows her guidelines for organic products. In such a case, a mission statement about the company's policy for organic products would probably be very useful, while a win-loss report on the company's (organic, of course) softball team would not.

Of course, the potential customer needs to accomplish her tasks as quickly and efficiently as possible, while we also need to also convince the visitor that she should choose our products and services over those of another web site. Anything we can do to distinguish one product or service from another, thereby facilitating the visitor's decision-making process, will make our site more attractive. Essentially, we are trying to be more than just easy to use; we are trying to be persuasive as well—as if we were in the store with her. Accordingly, we need to demonstrate the value of our site to the customer as soon as possible.

Creating Content

Web designers don't usually have to provide the content for a site. If the site is data-driven—such as Amazon with its product database—records from the database comprise the majority of the content. If the site is informational, *subject matter experts* (SMEs) most likely provide the content, just as physicians provide the content for a site like WebMD.com. If the site is primarily for marketing, the organization's advertising staff generates most of the copy.

Nevertheless, there may be times when you, the designer, may be called on to suggest content, write the content yourself, or critique and edit content you have been given. Keep the following in mind:

- The employed writing style should match the voice of the site, whether formal, hip, humorous, chatty, or stilted. You wouldn't use a formal, academic writing style on the Disney site any more than you would use a casual, chatty style on a site that posts the latest physics research for college professors.

- Carefully inspect all content for correct grammar and spelling. If possible, hire a professional copyeditor for the task. If that is not possible, employ two copyeditor tricks:

  - Read the content aloud. Reading aloud forces you to look at every word, something that many of us don't do when reading silently. Additionally, your ear can often catch grammatical problems that your eye misses.

  - Read the content backwards, which forces you to look at each word for correct spelling.

- Consider employing a descriptive, one-sentence-or-less tag line that succinctly summarizes what the site does, something that is particularly enlightening to our visitor if our organization isn't well known. The tag lines on the examples below are italicized:

  - Dive Into Accessibility: *30 days to a more accessible web site*

  - IMDb: *Earth's Biggest Movie Database™*

  - Dr. Dobbs: *Software Tools for the Professional Programmer*

- You may not use any content (text, images, or multimedia) from other sources without written permission from the copyright owner, or you will be risking legal penalties. Many copyright owners are happy to grant permission as long as credit is given.

- Aim for a clear, concise, and vigorous writing style. Vigorous writing uses strong, descriptive, and evocative words. Contrast the following two sentences:

  - "She walked down the street."

  - "The young lass trudged through the dingy alley."

The first sentence is bland, while the second sentence conjures a memorable image as a result of its colorful and specific language. Vigorous writing engages the visitor, as long as it doesn't become too wordy.

• • •

TACT

Sometimes, editing content we've been given presents a situation that must be handled with delicacy; "If average citizens are bad writers, clients are bad writers with egos." –From *Taking Your Talent to the Web*, by Jeffrey Zeldman.

• • •

VIGOROUS WRITING

"Vigorous writing is concise. A sentence should contain no unnecessary words, a paragraph no unnecessary sentences, for the same reason that a drawing should have no unnecessary lines and a machine no unnecessary parts." –From Strunk and White's *The Elements of Style.*

Creating a Sticky Web Site

What can we do to create a *sticky* site, one that keeps visitors browsing for a long period of time and returning again and again? Of course, the quality of the primary content has much to do with a site's stickiness. In general, the content should emphasize what our site offers that is of value to users and how our services differ from those of key competitors. For example:

- Don't just talk about how impressive the company is—give the visitors something they value *right now*.

- Update the content regularly, making sure visitors know when it will be updated.

- Offer discount coupons or run special promotions, preferably on a regular schedule so that visitors check back often.

- Run a contest. Be careful, however, because there are legal ramifications as to what you can and cannot do with a contest.

- Provide *value-added content*, content that goes above and beyond the original purpose of the site. Examples:

  - Williams-Sonoma (www.williamssonoma.com) suggests recipes that use the cooking utensils and specialty foods sold on the site.

  - At www.photo.net, shutterbugs can contribute their own photos to the gallery and request critiques from other visitors. Encouraging visitors to contribute to a site is termed *building community*. Amazon's (www.amazon.com) visitor-submitted book reviews are another example.

  - Rand-McNally (www.randmcnally.com) provides not only maps (its primary content) but also can suggest the names of restaurants and hotels in a specified location.

- As your high-school composition teacher drummed into your head, be sure to answer the "who," "what," "when," "where," "why," and "how," as appropriate.

- Be careful with humor; extreme cleverness can be extremely irritating on subsequent iterations of the joke. Just think of those television ads that we find amusing only on the first viewing; from then on, we fumble for the remote control when those commercials pop up on the tube.

- Avoid displaying a visitor counter. Most visitors don't trust them, and they are passé to boot.

- Don't explicitly welcome visitors to your site, as in "Welcome to Bill's Bicycle Shop." Such a welcome is unnecessary and a waste of good browser real estate. The only exception would be if you expected a large audience from the Orient, in which case a welcome message is required good manners.

- Consider formatting longer content as Adobe Portable Document Format (PDF) files if you expect visitors to print the content before viewing it.

- If the date of content creation is relevant, explicitly indicate that date. For instance, a news article should display a date, while a page showing the solution to a complex mathematical equation need not.

- When newer content replaces older content, you might want to *archive* (make available, but not so prominently on the site) the old content if you think some-one would still be interested in it. Archiving has the advantage of avoiding *linkrot* (broken links) from other sites that are linking to your (older) content, as long as you keep the document in the same location on the server.

- When appropriate, include photos and biographies of key figures in the organi-zation. For instance, a medical clinic would be well-advised to include pictures and biographies of their physicians. After all, a potential patient might well be interested in seeing a photo of the person he is trusting with his life. In a case like this, personality wins out over anonymity.

In summary, you should ask yourself why anyone would want to return to the site a second time, a third time, or, even better, a 97th time. If you can't come up with a good answer for that question, you need to brainstorm ways to enhance the content.

Define Site Architecture

We are in the throes of an information explosion; we are all susceptible to infor-mation overload. The challenge today is not in collecting information—our world already has more information than it knows what to do with—rather, it's making that onslaught of information *findable*. The cacophony of data available on the web has both enhanced and frustrated our ability to find what we need. We've all Googled a phrase only to have thousands of web sites show up on the results pages. How do we sort out which pages have value to us, and which don't? We can, and *should*, sort out the structure of our own web site so that the information it contains is findable.

Information architecture refers to the organization, labeling, and presentation of data in any context, from the appearance of a graph in a corporate newsletter, to the format of a recipe in a cookbook, to the organization of a card catalog in a library. The main tasks of information architecture are categorizing, labeling, and organizing fragments of information in such a way that humans can comprehend the framework and use it to retrieve the desired fragments. The whole point of information architecture is to manage complexity, which means to render it usable by making its structure visible.

In the physical world, a well-designed building is no accident. If it's strong, functional, easy to navigate, and aesthetically pleasing, it's because an architect put a lot of thought and effort into discovering the user's needs and designing the building to fulfill those needs. Similarly, in the web world, a strong, functional, and aesthetically pleasing web site is the result of thoughtful information architecture.

For the purposes of this chapter, we will narrow our terminology to *site architecture*—the organization and navigation of information within a web site. **FIGURE 2.4** illustrates how site architecture relates to the rest of site design.

FIGURE 2.4 Site Architecture

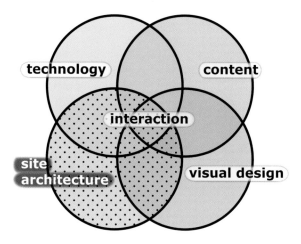

Site architecture is a fuzzy blend of information architecture and interaction design. It involves:

- The content, or the fragments of information, buried in the site.

- The relationship of individual fragments to one another; that is, the logical structure that ties those fragments together in a way that intuitively makes sense to visitors.

- The navigation that visitors use to traverse the logical structure.

Site architecture is the glue that holds the entire site together. Because a site must grow and change along with the evolution of business needs, the site architecture must be scalable and flexible.

Notice that we haven't mentioned visual design yet. Site architecture is how the *mind* views the information, while visual design is how the *eye* sees it. Visual design is important, obviously, and we will examine that in the chapters to come, but it can be implemented only after the site architecture is defined. Function must come before form; site architecture is the framework on which the visual elements hang.

An ironic reality of site architecture is that the simpler, the more obvious, and the more elegant the site navigation appears to the visitor, the messier, more complicated, less obvious, and more difficult the site architecture probably was to construct. Essentially, our purpose as designers is to absorb complexity and render it simple so that visitors don't see it or feel it. We expend huge amounts of effort, skill, understanding of human needs, and (don't forget) common sense to transform complexity into apparent simplicity, all in order to deliver the simple version back to our visitors in a highly palatable form. The more straightforward the navigation is for the user, the more work it probably took for us to craft.

Let's begin the whole process by looking first at how we go about labeling and logically categorizing the content on our site, just as a library categorizes its books by topic.

Labeling

Ever since humans invented language, they have been labeling things as a way of organizing and understanding their world. It's something we do naturally. That said, it's not something we always do *well*. The more thought we put into the labels and the more we consider how visitors will interpret them, the more straightforward the site will be for our visitors to navigate.

Labeling for a web site includes not only obvious navigational labels, such as links on menus, but also page titles, headers, and keywords for searching and browsing. All of these labels are components in the site architecture, and all of them help the user to find what he or she is seeking. Think of web site labeling as analogous to creating both an index and a table of contents for a book.

The words that comprise labels are often ambiguous, and that ambiguity is further exacerbated by the need for brevity on web-based labels. In a conversation, we augment our words with gesture, facial expression, or tone of voice; we gauge if our conversation partner understands by interpreting the other person's facial expression; and our conversation partner can ask us to clarify what we mean. None of this normal conversational interaction is available to a web site visitor. Consequently, web site labels must be clearer and less ambiguous than our everyday spoken language if they are to be truly useful.

Devising labels is a process of first doing a content inventory and then brainstorming for every possible label we can imagine. To come up with an initial list of labels, we can:

- Extract meaningful labels from the content for the site, especially from headers and subheaders.

- Peruse competitors' sites for ideas.

- Consult the online thesauri with which some industries are blessed. Here, industry-specific terminology that just might make good labels is consolidated, defined, and cross-referenced. For instance, there are any number of online thesauri for the computer industry, as well as for other content domains including medicine, education, and the sciences.

- Check existing server logs to see what search terms your visitors used to find content on the current site, if one exists.

When brainstorming for labels, consider synonyms, abbreviations, acronyms, alternative spellings (yes, even misspellings), and associated terms. An example of an associated term for the word "pepper" might be "salt." Associated terms are opportunities to provide additional relevant information or to expand a sale. For instance, an airline reservation site might present hotel and car rental links on the page confirming a visitor's airline reservation, or a women's clothing site might suggest a pair of red shoes if the visitor purchases a red dress.

Preferred Labels

The next step is to focus the list in order to pinpoint the most concise, precise, descriptive, and familiar (to our visitors, that is) term as our *preferred label*. Both screen real estate and the visitor's "cognitive space" are far too valuable to be wasted with vague or unnecessary words. By choosing an obvious term as a preferred label that we use consistently throughout the site, we are effectively constructing a controlled vocabulary.

A preferred label is ideally a single word, although sometimes phrases are unavoidable. The preferred label should be one that would serve as a good trigger for your audience, one that they would be likely to recognize. For example, a site designed for experienced gardeners could safely use labels like "annuals," "perennials," and "biennials" without explanation. Those labels might need explanation, however, if the site were for brand-new gardeners.

If your site has a mixed audience, don't use technical and non-technical terms in the same context. For instance, don't use "annual" and "plants that return every year" (that would be a "perennial" to experienced gardeners) in the same menu. If your navigation system must accommodate both novices and experts, then it's better to present separate targeted menus for each audience. Alternately, use the technical term but elaborate by displaying the non-technical description or definition next to the term.

Be careful with overly clever labels. Although they have the potential to be amusing and engaging and can add appeal to a web site, cleverness can also sabotage navigation. For example, if an auto dealership labels a link "Wheels," is it referring

● ● ●

QUIPS AND QUOTES

"A good label is so obvious it's dull as dirt."
–From *Information Architecture: Blueprints for the Web*, by Christina Wodtke.

to its inventory of automobiles (because "wheels" is a slang term for auto), or is it referring to actual specialty *wheels* that can be ordered for any automobile? If the visitor has to pause for even a moment to figure out the navigation or has even a slight possibility of guessing wrong the first time, the labeling system has failed. In a choice between clever and clear, you should almost always choose clear.

After you have identified your preferred labels, test them with potential visitors; have them tell you what they think the labels mean, just by reading them. There should be strong concurrence between what the visitors think the labels mean and what you intended them to mean. If not, the disconnect needs to be fixed.

Most web site visitors aren't willing to read in depth when they're online. Instead, they scan labels—navigation labels, heading labels, subheading labels—for any content that interests them. We'd best deliver clear, interesting, and relevant labels if we want to engage our visitors. The point is that labels, along with the site architecture, should help visitors find what they need, not erect roadblocks.

Categorizing Topics

Information architecture in general is concerned with grouping and organizing labels into a *taxonomy*—a hierarchical and cohesive vocabulary of categories and subcategories. The topics belong together, and any attempt to break them apart into different categories would only muddle the hierarchy structure. Categorizing, the first step in creating a logical and intuitive hierarchical navigation system, is all about finding patterns and relationships. The information we gather here is termed *metadata*—data about data. We are determining what data we have and how it's all related in an overall schema.

Choosing appropriate categories is, to some extent, plain old common sense. Still, categories aren't always obvious. Some labels may seem not to belong in any category except "miscellaneous stuff." Other labels might belong under multiple categories. And some categories are so large that they beg to be broken down into subcategories and sub-subcategories. Such categorization is indeed both a science and an art.

Many designers find it helpful to put all possible labels on index cards and then perform a card-sorting exercise to group them by category. It can even be helpful to ask two or more designers to sort the cards independently to compare the similarities and differences in their groupings.

Some possible types of category groupings, as well as examples, are shown in **TABLE 2.1**.

● ● ●

"DON'T THROW IT AWAY!"

Don't discard any of the labels that didn't pass muster as a preferred label. Instead, save them to use later, as HTML <meta> tag keywords, alternate search keywords for internal searches, and alternate search keywords and terms in any site index.

TABLE 2.1 CATEGORY GROUPINGS

This kind of business:	Using this category system:	Might group labels by:
News portal group	Topic	• World News • Local News • Sports • Weather • Entertainment
Computer retailer	Product grouping	• Desktop Computers • Laptop Computers • Accessories
Corporation	User	• Customers • Investors • Employees
Tool retailer	Task	• Order Tool • Order Replacement Parts • Get Technical Specs • Contact Us
Corporation	Department	• Sales • Marketing • Manufacturing • Human Resources
Corporation's internal phone directory	Alphabet (which works well only if the user knows the precise name)	• Names of employees • Departments
Web site doing majority of its business in Italy	Importance or frequency (with the most important or frequent items first)	• Italy • Great Britain • Ireland • Scotland • United States
Newspaper's article archive	Chronology (either normal or reverse order)	• 2008 • 2007 • 2006 • 2005
International company	Location	• France • Great Britain • Ireland • Scotland • Spain
Hotel (starting with a picture of a front lobby)	Metaphor	• Reservation desk (hotel reservations) • Entrance to the restaurant (restaurant reservations) • Concierge desk (other attractions)

Categories can provide context for our content. Let's say we see a menu item labeled "Trains." If that item falls under a "Vehicles" category on the menu, it's safe to assume the trains weigh many tons and go very fast. If it's under a "Toys" category, it's going to be small, cheap, durable, and appealing to children. If it falls under a "Hobbies and Models" category, it's still going to be small, but now it's likely to be fragile, very expensive, and appealing to model railroad aficionados. Without knowing the context of the "Trains" link, visitors could very well be led astray. This overlapping of categories is one of the reasons they are tough to develop and often somewhat ambiguous.

Let's look next at a bad example of categorization. A large retail photography site breaks its products down by "amateur" and "professional." Well, what about the "amateur" who is perfectly willing to spend big bucks on professional equipment? Will that visitor tolerate going through the entire amateur line before discovering that the equipment offered there just isn't powerful enough? Perhaps it would have been better to group the products by price point, say "under $1000" and "over $1000." Most people, amateur or professional, have some idea of how much they are willing to spend before they hunt for a product. Consequently, categorization by price would have a better chance of hooking the buyer up with an appropriate product. The problem with the aforementioned photography web site is that the designers chose categories based upon the way *they* viewed the categories, not on the way a *visitor* might view the categories.

After the categories and their associated labels are chosen, we can start arranging the site into a hierarchical site plan, with major categories at the top, subcategories underneath, and sub-subcategories and labels under that. What we are designing is essentially a multi-level table of contents for the site. For instance, a site that's selling computers might have the following categories and labels:

- Desktops
  - Under $1000
  - Over $1000
- Laptops
  - Under $1000
  - Over $1000
- Accessories
  - Printers
  - Scanners
  - Networking

Chapter 3 will examine how to build upon this preliminary structure to create an intuitive navigation system.

Organizing Site Structure for the Developers

· · ·

QUIPS AND QUOTES

The canon of skilled programmers, probably based on hard-won experience: "The sooner you start coding, the longer the project will take. Take the time to plan it first."

The more thought you put into planning the structure of the site from the developer's point of view, the less likely you will be to have to reorganize the structure later. "After the fact" reorganization of directories and file names is not only time-consuming, but it also runs the risk of breaking links. That is, if visitors have bookmarked pages on your site before the reorganization, or external sites have included links to your pages, those bookmarked and linked pages won't be found after the reorganization (so-called *linkrot*). Links from search engines to your site will also be broken until the engines have discovered the changes.

Creating a site structure involves organizing files and directories on the server, establishing standard naming conventions for directories and files, and using relative instead of absolute addressing.

Organizing Files and Directories on the Server

As soon as a site exceeds just a few pages, it becomes unmanageable to cram all site files into a single directory (also called a folder). Instead, create a directory structure that follows your carefully crafted site-architecture hierarchy. Just as you have a home page with several main pages underneath it, so too can you create a home directory with a subdirectory under it for each of the main pages. For larger sites, you might want subdirectories under main page directories, just as you have sub-pages under main pages. It's become standard practice to provide high-level CSS, JavaScript, and image directories for elements that are reused throughout the site. Additionally, each main subdirectory might have its own subdirectories for those elements that are unique to just that area of the site, as shown in the example in the sidebar.

SAMPLE DIRECTORY STRUCTURE FOR A RETAIL SITE SELLING COMPUTERS

root folder (includes `index.html`**)**

- `images`
  - `webImages` **(includes all site-wide, web-ready images)**
  - `originalImages` **(includes all site-wide, original editable images)**

- `css` (includes all site-wide CSS files)
- `javascript` (includes all site-wide JavaScript files)
- `beta` (for maintaining test files, before they're ready to implement)
- `desktopSystems` (includes `desktop.html`)
  - `webImages` (includes any web images specific to desktop computers)
  - `originalImages` (includes any original images specific to desktop computers)
  - `css` (includes any CSS specific to desktop computers)
  - `javascript` (includes any JavaScript specific to desktop computers)
- `laptopSystems` (includes `laptop.html`)
  - `webImages` (includes web images specific to laptop computers)
  - `originalImages` (includes original images specific to laptop computers)
  - `css` (includes CSS specific to laptop computers)
  - `javascript` (includes JavaScript specific laptop computers)
- `accessories` (includes `accessories.html`)
  - `etc....`

Developers have many tools at their disposal to help manage site structure. One such tool is the site-mapping feature in Adobe Dreamweaver. **FIGURE 2.5** illustrates how Dreamweaver organizes site files into a hierarchy, how different documents link to each other, and which links are broken.

Yet another useful tool is Link Checker, which can check for broken links site-wide, as shown in **FIGURE 2.6**.

If you rename or move a file from within Dreamweaver, it offers to update all links site-wide that refer to that file, as we saw in Chapter 1. If you attempt to delete a file, Dreamweaver warns you if there are still links in the site pointing to that file.

"DON'T LEAVE HOME WITHOUT THEM"

Obviously, these features are such huge timesavers and error-avoidance aids that you should never move, rename, or delete a file from outside of your development tool.

FIGURE 2.5 Site Map in
Dreamweaver

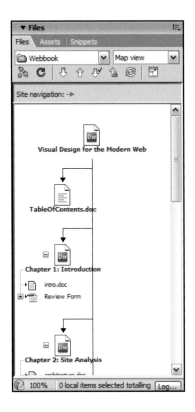

FIGURE 2.6 Checking Links
in Dreamweaver

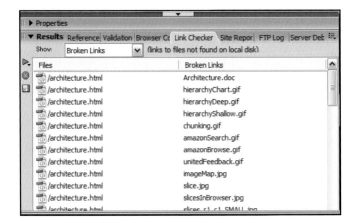

Establishing Standard Naming Conventions

You must also set up a standard format for directory and file names. All lowercase? Mixed lowercase and upper case? If mixed case, do you capitalize the first letter of each word ("NavShoppingCart.gif") or just the words that follow that first word ("navShoppingCart.gif")? Or should you instead use underscores to separate words ("nav_shopping_cart.gif")? It may seem like a big decision at the moment, but actually, the convention you choose is much less important than your consistency in following it. Many web servers are not tolerant of spaces and special characters in folder and file names, so stick to letters, numbers, hyphens, and underscores.

Folder and file names should be chosen to mean something to the developers who are trying to wend their way through the maze. A file name like "aa123" is worthless in that respect, while one like "navBar" is helpful. You might want to use a prefix, based on general purpose, for each type of file, such as prefacing all navigation images with "nav" or all logo images with "logo." As a result, all files with a related purpose are grouped together on any listing of files in the subdirectory.

It's tempting to name images by visual attributes, like "navBlueButton.gif." The downside here is that visual attributes might very well change as the site evolves. For instance, "navBlueButton.gif" becomes an inappropriate and confusing name if you later decide to recolor all the buttons red. Better to name images by function, not by visual attributes, because the function of a graphic usually remains constant. "navGoButton.gif" is valid regardless of the button's current (or future) visual characteristics.

It's equally important to use similar standards for CSS `class` and `id` names. As with files, don't choose names that refer to visual attributes of color or position. For instance, "blueBox" and "topNav" are names that can become outdated with even minor visual adjustments to the page. Instead, use names with structural meaning, names that reflect what the element does, like "mainNav," "localNav," "mainContent," or "sidebar."

Choosing Relative versus Absolute Addressing

Relative addressing means the link paths are set up to be relative to the directory where the current page resides. For instance, "images/gif/myButton.gif" exhibits relative addressing, in which the file is in the subdirectory "gif," which is under the "images" subdirectory, which is in turn under the directory in which the current HTML document resides. Furthermore, using "../" at the beginning of the reference sends the browser up a level, so that "../../gif/myButton.gif" sends the browser up two levels from the location of the current page, and then down to the "gif" directory where the file is located.

Absolute addressing, conversely, means that each page is accessed independently, via the full URL. The absolute address for the aforementioned image might be "http://www.whatever.com/root/someSubCategory/images/gif/myButton.gif."

The problem with absolute addressing is that if you move the site, either from your local machine to the web server or to an entirely new web server, all the links break. Such moves necessitate updating every absolute address to point to the new location, often a time-consuming and error-prone task. On the other hand, relative addressing should work flawlessly regardless of where the site happens to be located, as long as the site's directory and link structure remain unchanged.

Although you have no choice but to use absolute addressing for links to pages outside of your site, make sure to use relative addressing for all links to pages within your own site.

Summary

Site analysis is the thinking and planning that goes into a site before you so much as choose a color scheme or code a single line of HTML. Spending time and effort on analysis means we can design and construct the right site the first time. Our task is to identify the site goals, the target audience and their goals, and the time and budget constraints. All of those things determine the content we will present on the site and the way we organize the site architecture.

Design Checklist

The following checklist serves two functions: to summarize the major points and "rules" presented in the chapter, and to help you ensure you've done all you should before finalizing any web site you are creating.

Overall Site Analysis—*Did you:*

- Perform analysis to determine exactly what is needed before you started building anything?

- Determine primary and secondary site goals?

- Identify primary and secondary target audiences?

- Identify the tasks the target audience will want to perform?

- Identify time and budget constraints?

• • •

DO-IT-YOURSELF CHECKLIST

For a "fill-in-the-blanks" document that might be used to detail the results of overall site analysis, go to the web site.

Content Analysis—*Did you:*

- Make sure that every bit of content on the site supports the goals of the site?

- Provide all of the information the visitor needs to choose your products and services over those of another web site?

- Distinguish one product or service from another, thereby facilitating the visitor's decision-making process?

- Demonstrate the value of your site to the customer as soon as possible, possibly by including a descriptive, one-sentence-or-less tag line?

- Include humor only with great care?

- Include the "who," "what," "when," "where," "why," and "how," as appropriate?

- Avoid using a visitor counter?

- Avoid welcoming visitors to your site?

- Use Adobe PDF files only if you expect visitors to print the content before viewing it?

- Explicitly indicate dates on time-sensitive content?

- Consider archiving, rather than deleting, old content?

- Include photos and biographies, if appropriate?

Site Architecture Analysis—*Did you:*

- Devise strong and logical categorization, labels, and underlying structure for the site, based upon the way visitors will view the information?

- Extract meaningful labels from content, competitors' sites, and online thesauri, and/or check server logs?

- Consider alternate labels including synonyms, abbreviations, acronyms, alternative spellings and misspellings, and associated terms?

- Determine preferred labels?

- Be careful with overly clever labels?

- Test labels with users?

- Save rejected labels for later use as synonyms in search functions, the site index, and HTML `<meta>` tag keywords?

- Devise a logical structure for directories and files on the server?
- Standardize file naming conventions, based on function rather than visual characteristics?
- Employ relative addressing to reference files within the site?

Navigation

JAKOB NIELSEN, WWW.USEIT.COM/ALERTBOX/991003.HTML:

Jakob's Law of the Web User Experience: "Users spend most of their time on other sites, so that's where they form their expectations for how the Web works."

The greatest site architecture is irrelevant if no one can figure out how to access the pages in that architecture. Web surfers are impatient—they want to get to the good stuff effortlessly. They rarely expend any time figuring out unwieldy navigation; it's so much easier to ask Google to suggest another site. As a result, navigation must help visitors to find what they want easily. If, as a side benefit, you can expose them to what *you* want them to discover, so much the better.

In this chapter, we will look first at principles and guidelines for navigation, including the overall navigational structure of the site, types of links, link states, and link *affordances* (visual cues). We will then go on to examine the specifics of both navigational text and navigational images, and finally, we will organize both types of navigation into structures such as menus and site maps.

Introduction to Navigation

Navigation should do the following:

- Provide a conceptual map of the site. A visitor should be able to make a mental model of the site structure.

- Give feedback as to current location: "You *are* here." In other words, show visitors where they are currently located in relation to the entire site. Psychologists call this *grounding*: locating a known reference point in a foreign information space. Page titles, color-coded sections of the site, a disabled link for the page that is currently loaded, and breadcrumbs (more on all this later) serve as current location markers.

- Remind the visitor how he or she got there: "You *were* there." Breadcrumbs as well as a disabled current link (but left intact in the menu system) give the visitor some idea of how he or she got to the current page.

- Help the visitor find what he or she wants: "You *want to go* there." After all, that's the point, isn't it? A logically-structured hierarchy with clear categories and labels, along with secondary navigation aids such as a search function and site map, help to render the visitor's quest painless.

- Make the visitor aware of other offerings on your site: "You *could go* there, if you're interested." The navigation should point out other intriguing content on the site. Think of the navigation as serving the same function as a table of contents of a magazine; both provide an introduction to what is available on the pages—the stuff you were looking for, and the stuff you might be happy or surprised to find as well.

All of these considerations facilitate *wayfinding*, the process visitors use to find what they need. We all use the same general wayfinding techniques whether we're navigating a web site or the Mall of America.

Navigation Principles

We are going to look at several general principles that underlie every decision in designing navigation:

- Create simple, visible, consistent navigation.

- Take advantage of what visitors already know.

- Orient visitors with "You Are Here" markers.

- Minimize visitor effort.

- Provide multiple ways to access information.

- Provide for visitors with varied skill levels.

- Provide feedback.

- Make sure the navigation is flexible and expandable.

Create Simple, Visible, Consistent Navigation

Navigation should be instantly recognizable as navigation—don't force visitors to "scrub" the cursor all over the screen to find an unidentified hotspot (link). It might be intriguing on an artsy "experience" site, one designed just for entertainment, but it's not at all acceptable for a more mainstream ecommerce site.

Don't vary the look, feel, and placement of navigation from page to page unless you have some overwhelmingly good reason to do so. The number and order of links shouldn't be altered, because menus with links that appear on one page but disappear on another page are confusing to users. For instance, the link to the current page shouldn't disappear from that page's menu, because changing the structure from page to page confuses visitors. After all, the link to the current page serves as the grounding "you are here" marker on the site structure. However, you should *disable* the current link (simply remove the <a> tag) and somehow alter it visually (for example, gray it out) so that it's obviously no longer clickable.

Navigation labels should be consistent as well. For instance, don't call a person who belongs to a health club a "member" on one page, a "participant" on another page, and a "visitor" somewhere else. Pick a preferred term and stick to it. Also be consistent in punctuation, spelling, capitalization, and grammar usage (all labels starting with either a verb or a noun, for instance).

Finally, remember that the label within the <a> tag is a promise, really, and we shouldn't make misleading promises. We need to be very clear to visitors where they are going before they get there.

• • •

QUIPS AND QUOTES

In *Web Pages That Suck*, Vincent Flanders and Michael Willis term unidentified links as "mystery meat navigation."

Take Advantage of What Visitors Already Know

If we unexpectedly changed all stop signs in the United States to blue triangles, the most likely result would be uncountable nasty collisions. If we instead erected red circle signs, the results would probably be less disastrous—drivers would leverage their knowledge of red octagons and perhaps figure out that the very similar red circles had a similar meaning. The point this story tries to make is that we have a better shot at making unusual navigation elements understandable if they have at least some characteristics in common with the tried and true standards.

Keep in mind that the greater the obvious benefit to any new standard, the more willing users will be to retrain themselves. For example, would you be willing to learn a completely new computer keyboard layout if it eventually provided you with a 10% increase in typing speed? No? What if it doubled your speed? Quadrupled it? Yes, it would have to provide quite a bit of benefit before any of us would be motivated to invest the time and effort required to learn the new system. The same holds true for navigation systems on web pages. Try to leverage what the visitors already know and assume, even if you do choose to change things somewhat.

Orient Visitors with "You Are Here" Markers

The visitor needs to know his or her position in the site at all times. Imagine being dropped into the middle of Kansas, without signs telling you where you are. Visitors can be similarly baffled when dropped into a lower-level page from a search engine results page. They need a sense of place—a sense of where they are located in the hierarchy of the site and where they can go next within that hierarchy. "You are here" indicators, like the site logo, page title, page header, and a disabled menu link to the current page, can provide this guidance.

Minimize Visitor Effort

If you force visitors to log in or download a special plug-in to enter a site, you might just lose them. Visitors will endure such extra exertion only after they've been convinced there is some compelling personal benefit. Until then, they would rather bail out of the site.

Just as importantly, visitors don't want to click through endless pages to get where they want to go. However, clicks that are unambiguous, that lead them to information of high personal value, or that somehow reassure them that they are close to goal are usually tolerated.

The "Poorly Designed Workflow" sidebar shows a site that required numerous clicks and separate page loads just to buy a set of matching bedsheets.

POORLY DESIGNED WORKFLOW

Note that every <click> below represents a new page load. (Yes, this process actually did exist on a major bedding retailer's site, just a few years ago.)

Home décor <click>

  Bedding <click>

    Top sheet <click>

      Twin size <click>

        Green <enter quantity>

        Add to cart <click>

        <back>

      <back>

    <back>

    Bottom sheet <click>

      Twin size <click>

        Green <enter quantity>

        Add to cart <click>

        <back>

      <back>

    <back>

    Pillowcases <click>

      Twin size <click>

        Green <enter quantity>

        Add to cart <click>

Let's think about how we could redesign this process. Let's say that analysis of customer purchases shows that customers usually buy an entire set of bedding in the same color and size—not an unrealistic assumption. Sometimes they buy additional items to match, like an extra pair of matching pillowcases, while at other times they buy individual items, perhaps only a pair of pillowcases. What if we used the navigation structure in the "Well Designed Workflow" sidebar? Now, several items (including a complete set) can be purchased all at the same time. The benefits of minimized visitor time, effort, and annoyance are obvious.

WELL DESIGNED WORKFLOW

Home décor <click>

    Bedding <click>

        The following is all on one page:

        Bedding size <click on one>

            Twin ☐

            Standard ☐

            Queen ☐

            King ☐

        Color <click on one>

            Red ☐

            Green ☐

            Blue ☐

        Products <enter quantities>

            Complete bedding set ____

            Bottom sheet ____

            Top sheet ____

            Pillowcases ____

        Add to cart <click>

Provide Multiple Ways to Access Information

We need to provide users with multiple ways to find things, based upon different ways of thinking and different tasks that need accomplishing. The classic example of multiple ways to find things is a library card catalog, in which a visitor can search for a book by title, author, or subject keywords. Likewise, Amazon understands that web site visitors want to search for books on the web using the same categories. A visitor to Amazon can further filter the search by new or used books, different formats (hardback, paperback, audio book, and so on), reader age, language, and publication date (see **FIGURE 3.1**). She might read through a few pages of a book, skim reviews and check out other books recommended by the reviewers, or browse the other books that Amazon thinks might be of interest. She might choose to save a book in her wish list, for quick recall later.

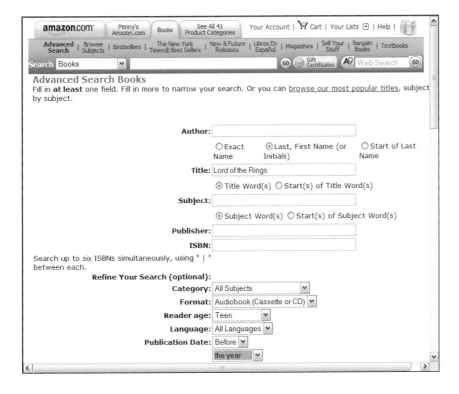

FIGURE 3.1 Advanced Search (© Amazon.com, Inc. or its affiliates. All Rights Reserved.)

Amazon also understands that sometimes visitors know exactly what they are looking for, as when they enter an exact book title ("The Return of the King"), and sometimes they don't, as when they enter a general subject instead ("fantasy fiction"). The first method is based on *known item searching*. If all users knew what they were looking for, it would be much easier to design navigation systems.

The alternative to known item searching is more exploratory. Amazon supports the exploration method with its "Browse Subjects" page (see **FIGURE 3.2**). Further browsing options include "Best Sellers," "New York Times Best Sellers," "Bargain Books," and "Used Books." Sometimes, the first exploratory foray serves merely as a springboard to send visitors down yet another path. This exploratory method is messier, more ambiguous, and more difficult to support.

FIGURE 3.2 Browsing (© Amazon.com, Inc. or its affiliates. All Rights Reserved.)

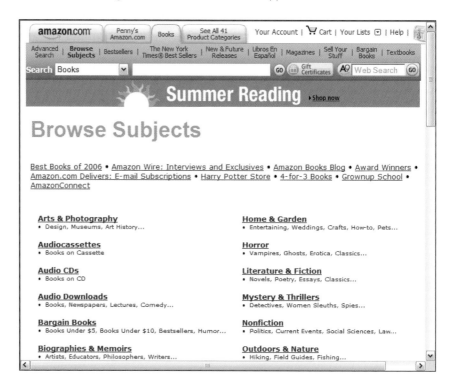

Notice that although Amazon's site is structured hierarchically by categories such as books, music, and movies, visitors can bypass the hierarchy entirely by using the generic search function. The lesson here? Even though we need to make the structure apparent to visitors, the structure shouldn't hamper non-hierarchical access to information.

We can also allow our visitors to tailor the navigation as they see fit, using a technique termed *personalization*. We provide the means for each visitor to customize the site to see only the links he or she has requested, in the format requested. For instance, a visitor might choose to see only local news, sports news, and entertainment news when opening a news portal site.

Provide for Visitors with Varied Skill Levels

Experienced web surfers can often figure out even confusing navigation systems. Web "newbies," though rare these days, may not even be familiar with the convention of using an underline as a way of indicating links. The vast majority of visitors fall somewhere in between. The good news is that a clear and elegant navigation system does indeed support everyone, regardless of skill level. Still, if the newcomers need additional support such as instructions or help pages, make sure those support features don't hinder the more experienced visitors.

Provide Feedback

We should provide some sort of feedback any time a visitor must wait for an extended period of time after clicking a link. For instance, if a visitor is downloading a large file, we might offer a small animation that proves to the user that the download is progressing. For instance, United Airlines shows an animation of an airplane flying across the page as the site takes a few moments to search for flights. Without such an animation, a long wait might convince the visitor that the web site is locked up. User perception is critical here; a long wait in which something, *anything*, appears to be happening is often perceived to be shorter than an uncertain wait of the same duration.

Make Sure the Navigation is Flexible and Expandable

Site flexibility and expandability aren't important to visitors, but they certainly are to those of us who must maintain the site. When our industry talks about *web time*, it's referring to the fact that web sites must be nimble enough to adjust quickly and with little warning to changing business needs. Our navigation system must be flexible enough to accommodate such adjustments. For example, a menu consisting of navigational text is very easy to update (whether adding, altering, or deleting links). On the other hand, an impressive Flash animation that consists of five links, slowly rotating in a circle, is not; adding or deleting a single link would mean that everything else on the graphic would need to be rearranged, and all of the animation must follow suit. Always consider ease of future maintenance when evaluating a particular navigation scheme.

Required Navigation

At the very least, every page should include the following navigation aids to facilitate wayfinding:

- **Site identification** (logo, name, etc.) and page identification (title line and page header). You simply can't depend on the home page to orient your visitors, because they don't always come in through that front door. A search engine or another site might have sent the visitor directly to a lower-level page (called *deep linking*), or the visitor might have entered via a bookmark to a subsidiary page. You should display site and page identification on *every* page in the site, so that visitors aren't lost or bewildered, stuck on some unidentified lower-level page.

- **Contact information**, or an obvious link to the page containing contact information. Contact information should include not only email contacts but also phone numbers and postal address. Even though *we* might prefer to deal with electronic communication from our visitors, many of the *visitors* have come to distrust sites that refuse to reveal a physical presence in addition to a virtual one.

- **A link to the home page** (unless the page in question *is* the home page). Although the site identification/logo can serve as a link to the home page, there should still be an explicit "Home" link as well. In any case, the user should always be able to return to the home page in a single click, regardless of where he or she is on the site.

- **Links to the main pages under the home page**. These links, along with the link to the home page, are termed *persistent global navigation* because they are on every page in the site. The global navigation serves to do more than just link to main pages; it also provides the visitor with a conceptual map of the site structure and scope.

As appropriate, some pages might also include:

- *Local navigation* for subsections under the current page. This navigation evolves from the subcategories and labels that were identified for the site architecture. This is also called *cross-over navigation* because it links sideways to sibling pages, rather than up or down the hierarchy.

- A search function, which is obviously more important for larger sites than for smaller ones.

- Site-wide utilities, such as "Store Locator" or "Checkout."

Organizing Navigational Structure to Match Site Structure

In the previous chapter, we examined creating the site architecture based upon a taxonomy and its preferred labels. Once we have determined these categories and subcategories and assigned labels to them, the underlying structure of the site itself becomes apparent to us. Now we employ navigation to make that underlying architecture apparent to our visitors. Navigation, then, is the site architecture made visible.

There are three basic models for organizing the navigation of a site: random-access navigation, sequential navigation, and hierarchical navigation.

Random-access Navigation

A random-access scheme requires visitors to pick individual, unrelated topics randomly from a menu. A random access model isn't truly organization—it's chaos. Without a visible structure of some sort, visitors have trouble finding what they are looking for, instead becoming overwhelmed and giving up. Random access "organization," or lack thereof, might be acceptable in entertainment or experience sites, where the challenge of figuring out the navigation is considered to be part of the entertainment, but it's rarely suitable for mainstream web sites. It's just too difficult to find anything, and visitors can't build a mental map of the site.

Sequential Navigation

A sequential navigation scheme is designed to be read one page after another. An example would be a long article spaced over several pages, with a "next" link at the bottom of all but the final page in the series. Navigation might look something like **FIGURE 3.3**.

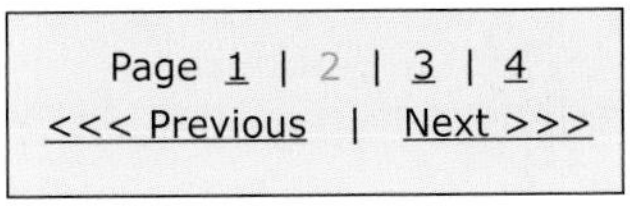

```
┌──────────────────────────────┐
│    Page  1  |  2  |  3  |  4   │
│    <<< Previous  |  Next >>>   │
└──────────────────────────────┘
```

FIGURE 3.3 Navigation — a familiar navigation scheme for a multi-page situation.

Although we are comfortable with this structure—after all, books have been organized on a "next page" structure for rather a long time now—it's rarely appropriate for an entire web site. Most of the time, visitors aren't reading our entire web site from "cover to cover." As a result, sequential navigation is usually implemented only for selected pages within a site.

Hierarchical Navigation

Hierarchical navigation schemes, the most pervasive, require following links up and down a hierarchy. Humans have a natural affinity for hierarchical organization in all areas of our existence, whether it's categorizing genera and species in nature, depicting our family tree, setting up a corporate management structure, or organizing a web site. Ideally, hierarchies are structures that we understand intuitively, making them the perfect framework upon which to hang a navigation system.

A text outline portraying a hierarchical site might look something like this:

Home Page

- Desktops
  - Under $1000
  - Over $1000

• • •

HIERARCHICAL MINDS AND THE BACK BUTTON

Our intuitive under-standing of hierarchical structures could well be why we often use the "Back" button instead of clicking on a direct "sideways" link from a lower-level page; we are tracing back up the hierarchy in our mind, too, so that we don't get lost. Must be some kind of homing instinct.

- Laptops
  - Under $1000
    - Under 5 pounds
    - Over 5 pounds
  - Over $1000
    - Under 5 pounds
    - Over 5 pounds
- Accessories
  - Printers
  - Scanners
  - Networking

Dreamweaver and other development environments can create graphical hierarchy charts (see **FIGURE 3.4**). In Dreamweaver, you have two workflow options:

- Draw the hierarchy chart and then allow Dreamweaver to create the skeleton HTML documents depicted on the chart.

- Create the HTML pages and ask Dreamweaver to display the resulting chart.

FIGURE 3.4 Hierarchy Chart from Dreamweaver

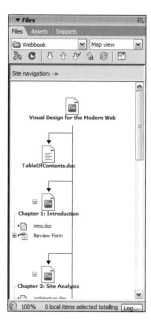

Creating a graphical hierarchy chart manually, outside of a development environment, is usually more trouble than it's worth, and adding new pages later can be a rearrangement nightmare. It's much easier and usually just as effective to use a text outline, as shown just a bit ago.

The menu system in a hierarchical scheme usually mirrors the hierarchical structure of the site architecture that we identified earlier. Still, links that disregard the structure can be valuable as well. For instance, a lower-level content page might actually fit under two separate categories in the hierarchy. Computer buyers visiting Dell's site might locate a laptop computer by clicking on "laptops," or they might navigate to the same page by clicking on "home users." Fortunately, the *hypertext* (that is, linkable) nature of the web allows us to link to and cross-reference pages from within multiple categories, without redundantly storing multiple physical copies of those documents. On the web, one thing can indeed seem to be in two places at once.

Mixing Navigational Models

Many sites mix models: hierarchical access for the majority of the site but sequential or even random access for selected subsections. Regardless of the model or models employed, visitors should be able to make a mental map of the site.

Link Functions

We can classify links within a navigation system by function:

- Internal hyperlinks
- External hyperlinks
- Download links
- Auto-email links
- Note links

Internal Hyperlinks

Standard *internal hyperlinks* link to other HTML pages within our own site. See the sidebar for a review of the HTML for internal hyperlinks.

▨ HTML REVIEW: INTERNAL HYPERLINKS

Internal text link:

```
<a href="info/furtherInformation.html">Further Information...</a>
```

Internal image link:

```
<a href="images/imageLarge.html" target="bigPicture">
   <img src="images/imageSmall.jpg" height="100" width="130"
      border="0" alt="Clifden Castle" />
</a>
```

Included in the internal hyperlink category are action/command links, which initiate or complete some sort of action. Common action links include Submit, Reset, Back, Print, Go, and Search. Such actions are often indicated by some type of a graphic button, even when the rest of the navigation system uses navigational text.

An *internal anchor* is a "domestic" link that jumps to a location deep within a page. If that location is within the current page, the page repositions to that location but doesn't reload. If the location is within a different page, the new document loads, positioned so that the indicated location is at the top of the browser window. We often see this on FAQ pages, for instance.

▨ HTML REVIEW: INTERNAL ANCHORS

There are two pieces to an internal anchor: the clickable link that points at the desired location, and the "bookmark" anchor, placed at the desired location.

Here's an internal anchor pointing to a bookmark within the *current document*:

```
<a href="#destination">
   More information...
</a>
```

And here's an internal anchor pointing to a bookmark within a *new document*:

```
<a href="path/mypage.html#destination">
   More information...
</a>
```

This is the destination location "bookmark":

```
<a name="destination" id="destination"></a>
```

The main advantage to providing internal anchors is that visitors can bypass content that doesn't interest them, making them more likely to stick around for content that does. One popular use of an internal anchor is to provide a link at the bottom of a long page, quickly returning visitors to the top of the page.

External Hyperlinks

External hyperlinks take the visitor outbound to sites that don't belong to us, outside of our control. With selective use of external links, we can leverage content produced by others, as long as that content supports our goals.

HTML REVIEW: EXTERNAL HYPERLINKS

External text link:

```
<a href="http://www.yahoo.com" target="_blank">Yahoo!</a>
```

External image link:

```
<a href="http://www.yahoo.com" target="_blank">
   <img src="images/yahooLogo.jpg" height="100" width="130"
      border="0" alt="Go to Yahoo" />
</a>
```

Note that we must include the "http://" at the beginning of any external address, or the browser assumes we are looking for a page somewhere within our own site.

We have to be careful with external links, however. We don't want our visitors to be so enamored of the external site that they forget to return to our own. What, then, are the alternatives?

- Avoid external links entirely, an option that is often counterproductive.

- Employ frames, leaving your identification and navigation persistently on view in one or more frames and opening the external page in a separate frame. Unfortunately, the use of frames is controversial; see the frames discussion later in this chapter.

- Open each external link in a new window, so that your site is waiting patiently in the original window when the visitor closes the new window. Opening new windows is also a controversial alternative, though, because they violate accessibility rules (see the accessibility discussion near the end of the chapter). New and unrequested windows also rudely clutter the visitor's screen. Even so, visitors often don't want to lose where they were in your site—for many of them, an unrequested window might be a fair tradeoff for not getting lost.

● ● ●

BACK TO THE TOP

Although it could be argued that a "Back to Top" button at the bottom of a page allows the visitor to return to top navigation menus quickly, it could also be argued that a better alternative on long pages would be to provide redundant navigation at the bottom as well.

- Open each external link in the same "new window." That is, you open a new window the first time a visitor clicks an external link but from then on continue to reuse that same window for all future external page requests. You thereby avoid cluttering the screen with a multitude of windows. Simply assign the same target name to all external links:

```
<a href="http://www.amazon.com" target="myChosenWindowName">
<a href="http://www.yahoo.com" target="myChosenWindowName">
```

Download Links

Download links let visitors download files that are not typical web files. For instance, visitors might be able to download MP3s (music), DOCs (Word documents), PDFs (Adobe Portable Document Format), PPTs (PowerPoint presentations), or even executable programs. Since these files are going to be stored on the visitor's computer upon download, it's helpful to display the file name next to the link so that visitors can locate it on their computers later. Additionally, it's a good idea to warn users of the file size if the file is large. A typical download link might look like this on a web page:

Penny Lane (pennyLane.mp3, 3.2 MB)

Here, the file name (pennyLane.mp3) is listed after the song title, followed by the file size (3.2 MB) that serves as a "Just how patient are you?" warning for visitors with slow connections. The HTML for a download link is identical to a standard hyperlink.

Auto-email Links

Auto-email links format a blank email, addressed as specified in the href attribute of the <a> tag, as shown in the sidebar. Note that you have two options for the text displayed for the visitor: Provide the actual email address, or provide a text description of the destination. Showing the real email address has the advantage of being easily copy-able into the visitor's address book or into an email manually if the auto-email errors off. Conversely, a text-based description is easier for visitors to understand. Neither option is the "better" one; it depends on your audience and their expectations.

▬▬▬ HTML REVIEW: AUTO-EMAIL HYPERLINKS

An auto-email link brings up an empty email in the visitor's email program. The email is directed to the address specified in the href attribute of the <a> tag.

Auto-email link displaying the actual email address:

```
<a href="mailto:support@somedomain.com">
    support@somedomain.com</a>
```

Auto-email link displaying a text description:

```
<a href="mailto:support@somedomain.com">
   Email Customer Support</a>
```

Auto-email link displaying a conflicting email address (often used by spammers and certainly *not* recommended):

```
<a href="mailto:JimBob@IWantYourCreditCardNumber.com">
   support@BankOfAmerica.com</a>
```

Note that although the displayed address can be different from the actual address for the email, it's generally inadvisable. In these days of unsafe computing due to viruses and phishing for personal data, visitors who notice the discrepancy will distrust your site.

Note Hyperlinks

A *reference link*, the most common type of link on the web, merely brings up a new page, often (though not always) in the same window as the originating link. In contrast, a *note link* can be viewed as the Web equivalent of a footnote, end-note, or sidebar; it is peripheral information that would interrupt the flow of the main content if included within that content. Note links are often used to show larger versions of thumbnail pictures as well. Accordingly, a note link is usually opened in a new window, often deliberately set to a specific size and with user controls disabled. In such cases, the only action permitted the visitor is to dismiss the window, which returns control to the originating window. See the sidebar for the JavaScript needed to open a note window.

USING JAVASCRIPT TO OPEN A NEW WINDOW

While we can open new windows using `target="_blank"` in an `<a>` tag, we can't thereby control window characteristics such as size and whether or not the user controls the display. For that, we must use JavaScript. Include the following JavaScript somewhere within the `<head>` of the document:

```
<script language="javascript">
function openWindow()
{
   newWindow=window.open("http://www.niu.edu",
   "windowName",height=600,width=800,status,menubar,toolbar");
   newWindow.focus();
}
</script>
```

To tailor this script to your needs:

- Replace the URL above with the URL of the page to load into the new window.

- Replace "windowName" with the name you might possibly want to use as the target in other <a> tags.

- Replace height and width with the pixel dimensions for the new window.

- Remove status, menubar, and toolbar if you want to remove user controls and browser chrome (toolbars and such). Do this only after careful consideration, however, because web surfers often resent it when a web site overrules their preferences or robs them of their familiar navigation tools.

Here is the code for the <a> tag that executes the JavaScript:

```
<a href="#" onclick="openWindow()">Display larger image</a>
```

Be aware that some *pop-up blockers* (browser plug-ins intended to block unrequested advertising windows) could prevent the display of the new window, and that tricky bugs can arise when using window.open. Consult a good JavaScript reference if you have problems.

Navigation Affordances

We have all learned to recognize hyperlinks on web sites. The characteristics that clue us in to a link are called *perceived affordances*, or just *affordances* for short. For example, the underline affordance on text is a pretty reliable clue (or at least, it should be) that a link is present. If we click on underlined text and nothing happens, we feel duped. The point is that we should apply link affordances *only* to links. We'll look at specific navigational affordances for text and graphic links in a bit.

No matter which affordances we use, we should be consistent; for instance, the size, color, and style of text links should be constant throughout the site. It's usually appropriate to change affordances only if meaning is attached to the change. For instance, a site might use green links and page backgrounds for all "Products" pages, with blue links and page backgrounds for all "Services" pages.

Whatever affordances we use, we walk a fine line when designing the visual appearance of navigation. Of course, we want visitors to notice the navigation as enticement to explore the site. At the same time, content is the very heart and substance of the site, and it should be given primary focus. Just as page numbers and headers in a book are readily apparent but don't need to be in bright colors and huge fonts, so too must navigation be apparent but shouldn't distract the visitor from the content.

Link States

Possibilities for link state include:

- Available/at rest

- Available/rollover

- Active

- Visited

- Current

We will look at an overview of each state in the sections that follow. Later in the chapter we will see exactly how to use affordances to indicate state in both navigational text and graphic links. Note that you don't necessarily need to indicate all link states, but be consistent from page to page to avoid bewildering visitors.

Available/At Rest State

Available/at rest links exhibit the default state, shown as the page is initially rendered, without a mouse positioned over the link. The default color for text links and image link borders is blue in most browsers. This color can be changed in the <body> tag with the link attribute, and virtually all link attributes (color, underline, etc.) can be styled with CSS's a:link pseudo-class.

Available/Rollover State

Available/rollover refers to the state of a link when the mouse is positioned over it. Rollover effects can't be rendered with HTML alone, but the CSS pseudo-class a:hover can specify text-link rollovers, and JavaScript can implement image rollovers (essentially image swaps).

Active State

An *active link* is one that was just immediately clicked. The latter effect shows only briefly, while the new page is loading, but it does give useful feedback to reassure the visitor that the click was recognized. Red is the default active color for text links and image link borders in most browsers, but it can be changed in the <body> tag with the active attribute, and virtually all link attributes (color, underline, etc.) can be styled with CSS's a:active pseudo-class.

● ● ●

VISITED LINKS

If visited links are those that have been visited recently, how long is "recently"? It varies between browsers, but typically, visited links stay marked for longer than just the current browser session. In fact, the visitor might return days later to find that visited links are still flagged.

Visited State

A *visited link* is one that has been recently visited. Purple is the default visited color for navigational text in most browsers, but it can be changed in the `<body>` tag with the `visited` attribute, and virtually all link attributes (color, underline, etc.) can be styled with CSS's `a:active` pseudo-class.

Indicating visited links is most important for larger sites that visitors want to explore systematically, such as a list of articles on a particular subject. In contrast, indicating visited links on sites where visitors are more likely to return to the same link repeatedly would seem to do little more than add visual clutter.

Avoid using a glaringly obvious color for visited links, because too much contrast adds even more visual clutter to the page. Instead, the color should be subtly but noticeably different from the standard link color. A less saturated (less bright) version of the standard color is usually appropriate, as long as the text is still legible against the background color.

Current State

The *current link* isn't truly a link, because it shouldn't actually be clickable. That is, we keep the item on the menu, but we remove the link affordances and the surrounding `<a>` tag, thereby disabling the link. We are saving our visitors from needless page reloads due to accidental clicks.

Why, then, don't we just remove the link from the menu structure entirely? Because the disabled link serves as a placeholder for the current page; a "you are here" marker, if you will, and also ensures that the menus on all pages look exactly alike. Otherwise, we would risk muddling our visitor's mental model of the site structure.

Navigational Text

You've seen, and used, this kind of construction all over the web:

Purchase this book at Amazon.

That's a text link—useful words that take you somewhere specific without displaying the actual URL. Here's the ubiquitous and simple HTML for it:

```
<a href="http://amazon.com">Purchase this book at Amazon</a>
```

Text links are the navigational workhorse of web sites. This technique has several key advantages over navigational graphics like buttons:

- Text links present a compact, clean, and simple visual effect.

- Text links download quickly, while navigational image files are much larger and thereby slower to download. Multiply that download delay by the number of unique navigational images, and multiply that by two if rollover effects are required, and the delay, of course, becomes even more exaggerated.

- Rollover effects can easily be implemented site-wide by simply modifying the site-wide CSS.

- Links on text-based menu systems can be added, deleted, and modified easily, while some navigational menu systems (notably sliced images and image maps) are much more difficult to update.

- Individual links are easy to update. Just type the text in the HTML file, and FTP the file to the server. Navigational images such as buttons, on the other hand, are more tedious to update. Such an update might involve:

  - Opening the graphics program and the image file.

  - Making the desired change(s).

  - Exporting the image for the at rest link.

  - Exporting the image for the rollover effect.

  - Updating the HTML file (if either the name or the size of the image has changed).

  - FTPing the image files to the server.

  If there are 50 different buttons on a site, each with unique wording, we'll need to go through this process for 50 different images.

Because text links have so many advantages over navigational graphics, the button images that were so popular just a few years ago seem to be much less common these days.

Text Link Wording

Much of what we need to know in order to choose the wording for text links was discussed in reference to creating labels in the "Site Architecture" topic of Chapter 2. Still, we should also remember the following hints:

- Be concise, precise, and descriptive. (Yes, this has already been mentioned, and yes, it bears repetition.) Ideally, labels should be just a single word, although short phrases are sometimes unavoidable.

- Don't label any link "Click here." A throwback from the early days of the web, "Click here" adds nothing to a visitor's understanding and therefore still requires an adjacent description of some sort. Instead, just make the description of the link "clickable:"

Unacceptable: Click here for Bob's Bicycles, which offers racing bikes at discount prices.

Acceptable: Bob's Bicycles offers racing bikes at discount prices.

- If the label needs further elaboration, the `title` attribute on the `<a>` tag can provide a longer rollover description that's viewable in newer browsers.

Affordances for Text Links

Virtually all web users recognize an underline and the standard link colors as the most common text link affordances. Usability experts often claim that we shouldn't muck around with these affordances, because doing so interferes with the visual cues that users have come to expect. After all, making our pages user-friendly is more important than making them color-coordinated.

Still, these days web surfers are much more sophisticated than they were just a few years ago. They seem to recognize several text-link affordances, including the following:

- **Underline.** Today we have multiple underline options. The underline itself can be:
  - Always present, for all link states.
  - Visible on the link at rest, but disappears on rollover.
  - Visible on rollover, but disappears on the link at rest.
  - Removed entirely, with links indicated by other affordances such as color and styling changes.
- **Style change.** Links might be indicated with boldface, italic, or a different typeface.
- **Text or background color change.** Everyone is familiar with the default link colors of blue, red, and purple. Unfortunately, these colors don't show up well on dark web page backgrounds, and they certainly clash with many color schemes. For instance, standard link colors would look positively garish on a page of subtle brown and gold earth tones.

As long as you provide at least one recognizable affordance, you don't necessarily have to provide *all* of them. But whatever text link affordances you choose, avoid using those same affordance characteristics for elements that aren't intended to be links.

CSS Pseudo-classes for Indicating Link State

Of course, we can specify the color for at-rest links, active links, and visited links using attributes in the `<body>` tag. With CSS formatting, we can do even more, using pseudo-classes to change the underline, border, background color, and rollover effects. Examples of the four CSS link pseudo-classes are shown in the sidebar.

> ### ▰▰ CSS REVIEW: LINK STATE PSEUDO-CLASSES
>
> **For CSS link styles to work as expected, they should normally appear in the order below in the stylesheet.**
>
> ```
> <style type="text/css">
>    a:link    {color:#ff0000; text-decoration:none;}
>    a:visited {color:#00ff00; text-decoration:none;}
>    a:hover {color:#0000ff; text-decoration:underline;}
>    a:active {color:#ff00ff; text-decoration:underline;}
> </style>
> ```
>
> **Rules later in the pseudo-class sequence always override rules earlier in the list. Here, a:active overrides all others, and a:hover overrides a:visited and a:link. Violating the order above can result in breaking some effects. For instance, the result of moving a:hover to the second item on the list would be that rollover effects will not work on any links that have been visited. On the other hand, that could be effective if you *don't* want visited links to show rollover effects.**
>
> **What if you don't want all of the link states to be visible? Perhaps, for example, you want to avoid the visual clutter of different affordances for visited links. If you omit a:visited from the style sheet, the browser's default visited color might appear anyway. The remedy is to explicitly specify a style for the visited link that is identical to the standard at-rest link style. For instance:**
>
> ```
> <style type="text/css">
>    a:link    {color:#ff0000; text-decoration:none;}
>    a:visited  {color:#ff0000; text-decoration:none;}
>    a:hover {color:#00cc00; text-decoration:underline;}
>    a:active    {color:#00ff00; text-decoration:underline;}
> </style>
> ```

Whatever effects we specify, we should be cautious when using any effect that changes the size of the text, as does boldface, italic, or a different font size. Altering size characteristics can force any subsequent page elements to shift position on the page, an undesirable and potentially very messy consequence.

Disabling the Current Link

As we've already discussed, we should disable the current link but keep it in the menu structure. To disable the link, simply remove the <a> tag. Also style it with some visual affordance that makes it clear that the text is no longer clickable. To do this, surround the text with a <span> tag (see sidebar for a review of <div> and <span> tags) to associate the text with a CSS class. For instance, the HTML might look like this:

```
<span class="disabledLink">Contact Us</span>
```

The CSS styling to "gray out" and remove the underline from all such disabled links might look like this:

```
.disabledLink {color:#999999; text-decoration:none;}
```

HTML REVIEW: <DIV> AND <SPAN>

<div> and <span> tags are wrappers that permit treating areas of content as a whole for styling reasons. For example, Paragraphs 1 and 2 in the following example are red. Paragraph 3 reverts to the default text color.

```
<div style="color:#ff0000">
    <p>Paragraph 1</p>
    <p>Paragraph 2</p>
</div>
<p>Paragraph 3</p>
```

<div> tags are considered to be block tags; that is, they usually force a line break when the </div> tag is encountered. <div> tags can wrap other block tags, such as the <p> tags in the example above.

<span> tags are used for in-line content; that is, when a line break isn't desired. For example:

```
<p>Here's a <span style="color:#ff0000">red </span>word.</p>
```

Unfortunately, there are some circumstances in which you can't easily disable the current link. If you are using templates or server-side includes (a way to copy boilerplate HTML into a page) to copy identical navigational HTML into every page, there is no easy way to disable the current link automatically. Fortunately, there is a CSS "hack" that can disguise a *hot* (i.e., clickable) current link by removing link affordances, as explained in the sidebar.

MAKING A HOT CURRENT LINK APPEAR TO BE DISABLED

When navigation is automatically copied into a page (using templates or server-side includes), it's not practical to disable the current link. Instead, we *disguise* the current link to make it look disabled so that visitors are unlikely to click on it.

To accomplish this, first define a standard external CSS file for the default characteristics of all link states, just as you would normally. Next, uniquely identify each menu item in the *boilerplate* menu (that is, the copied-in menu) using the id attribute, as shown in the sample menu below:

```
<!-- Standard navigation copied into each page -->
    <a href="homepage.html" id="homeLink">Home</a><br/>
    <a href="products.html" id="productsLink">Products</a><br/>
    <a href="services.html" id="servicesLink">Services</a><br/>
    <a href="contact.html" id="contactLink">Contact Us</a><br/>
```

Now you can use the id designator to override the standard link styling for *just* the current link on each page. In the <head> of every page, create a global style that references the id for the link for just that the current page. For example, on the "Products" page, include the following:

```
<style type="text/css">
    #productsLink {color:#666666; text-decoration:none;}
</style>
```

On the "Services" page, include this:

```
<style type="text/css">
    #servicesLink {color:#666666; text-decoration:none;}
</style>
```

The specifically targeted style in the <head> grays out the color and removes the underline, so that the link appears to be disabled. Although the link is, unfortunately, still clickable, visitors are unlikely to actually click it.

Enhancing Text Links

Text links have been accused of being boring, even with styling and rollover effects. We can jazz up text links easily using bulleted lists with custom bullet images, rollover bullets, background button images, or CSS borders that mimic buttons.

Bulleted Lists with Custom Bullets Images

Menus are ideal candidates for employing bulleted lists, since what is a menu but a list of links? We can enhance a bulleted list menu by specifying custom images as the bullets, like the stars on the menu in **FIGURE 3.5**. The downside is that the bullets don't change on rollover. The HTML and CSS for this menu is shown in the sidebar.

FIGURE 3.5 Custom Images
as Bullets

▓▓▓▓ CSS FOR CUSTOM BULLETS

```
<ul style="list-style-image:url(star.gif);">
    <li><a  href="home.html">Home</a></li>
    <li><a  href="products.html">Products</a></li>
    <li><a  href="services.html">Services</a></li>
    <li><a  href="contact.html">Contact Us</a></li>
</ul>
```

This example assumes that the text link rollover effects were formatted with external CSS.

Rollover Bullets

As mentioned above, a downside to custom bullets in a `<ul>` is that the bullets themselves cannot exhibit rollover effects. You can, however, format a bulleted list manually, incorporating a rollover effect on both the text link and the bullets, as shown in **FIGURE 3.6**, in which the mouse is positioned over the "Products" menu item.

FIGURE 3.6 Manually
Formatting a Bulleted List

To create a rollover bullet, float a small image or icon to the left or right of the link text. Wrap *both* the text link and the image in the same *<a>* tag. Use Dreamweaver to create a rollover effect for the bullet image (more on that technique in a bit, under Navigational Images) and use CSS to style the text rollover effect. The result is that a mouse rollover activates a rollover effect on both the text and the image. Note that you need only two bullet images for the entire navigation system—one for at rest and one for rollover. See the sidebar for the HTML.

▬▬ HTML FOR ROLLOVER BULLETS

This example used Dreamweaver (Insert > Image Objects > Rollover Image) to insert the HTML for swapping the bullet on rollover as well as to insert JavaScript in the head to support the swap. The original bullet is openStar.gif, while the rollover bullet is solidStar.gif. The text link rollover effects would be formatted as desired with external CSS.

Here's the resulting *<a>* tag for just the "Products" menu item:

```
<a href="products.html"
   onMouseOut="MM_swapImgRestore()"
   onMouseOver="MM_swapImage('navBullet'," ",'images/solidStar.gif',1)">
   <img name="navBullet" id="navBullet" src="images/openStar.gif"
     border="0" width="15" height="15" alt="Products" />
   Products
</a>
```

Yet another variation on this same technique is to use a transparent image as a bullet placeholder for the link at rest, and use an arrow of some sort for the image rollover, as shown in **FIGURE 3.7** again (with the mouse over "Products"). The code is identical to the previous example; the only difference is that the original image is a transparent placeholder, while the rollover image is an arrow.

FIGURE 3.7 Using a Different Image for Rollover

Background Button Images

A text link can look just like a button if it's floated in front of a background image that looks like a generic, text-free button. That is, the button isn't really a part of the link, just the background to it. The HTML for this technique is shown in the sidebar. Note that it can be a bit tricky to get the text to line up precisely where you want it on top of the background image.

HTML AND CSS FOR BACKGROUND BUTTON IMAGE

```
<td width="98" height="27" align="center"
    style="background-image:url(backgroundButton.gif);">
  <a href="http://www.products.mysite.com">Products</a>
</td>
```

CSS Borders that Mimic Buttons

Another way to mimic a button is to employ CSS 3-D border styling (see **FIGURE 3.8** and **FIGURE 3.9**) using border-style: outset and border-style: inset properties. The sidebar illustrates the CSS.

FIGURE 3.8 Text Rollover
with border-style:outset CSS

FIGURE 3.9 Text Rollover
with border-style:inset CSS

▬ CSS BORDERS THAT MIMIC BUTTONS

CSS can mimic a rectangular rollover button. Just include border-style:outset (for a normal button) and border-style:inset (for a depressed button) on the link styles:

```
a:link    {border-style:outset; border:5px inset; borderpadding:6px;}
a:visited  {border-style:outset; border:5px inset; padding:6px;}
a:hover {border-style:inset; border:5px inset; padding:6px;}
a:active {border-style:outset; border:5px inset; padding:6px;}
```

The extra padding ensures that the text doesn't crowd up against the edges of the button.

Navigational Images

As we've seen, navigational graphics are more difficult to maintain and take substantially longer to download than text links. At times, though, only navigational graphics can provide the required visual impact. Sometimes we might compromise, using text links for most of the navigation but images for generic *actions* (Go, Search, Submit, Clear, Back, Reset) so that critical actions such as these stand out from the page more clearly.

REUSE IMAGES THROUGHOUT THE SITE

Remember, an image is downloaded to the visitor's cache the first time it's referenced on the site, and then reused from the cache. Therefore, the download price is paid only once, even though the image might be referenced by many discrete pages. As a result, generic navigational images for actions such as "go" can be used multiple times with only a single download.

WORDING ON NAVIGATIONAL IMAGES

Text associated with a navigational image must be terse. While a text link that stretches across 200 pixels might be acceptable, a button that does so in order to accommodate a long text description would look both clunky and amateurish.

• • •

<ALT> TAGS

Always use the alt attribute to repeat the wording of an image-based link, because screen readers for the visually impaired cannot read the text on images.

In Chapter 6, we'll look at graphics in general, irrespective of their various uses. In this section, we will look only at issues specific to navigational images such as buttons, icons, image maps, and sliced images.

Affordances for Navigational Images

We recognize immediately that a rounded rectangle with a bevel effect and a text label is a link because it uses several of the following affordances:

- Symmetrical shapes, particularly circles, rectangles, ovals, and rounded rectangles (shown in **FIGURE 3.10** in order by increasing degrees of "button-ness").

FIGURE 3.10 Navigational Graphic Affordances

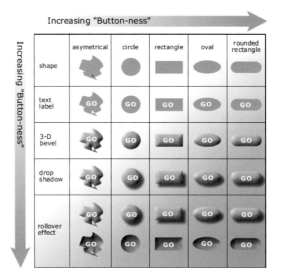

- Labels that seem to be navigational.

- 3-D bevels, such that the element looks like a raised or depressed button.

- Drop shadows, which further enhance the real-world look of the button.

- Rollover/mouseover effects.

- A picture or icon that shows a real-world object, such as a picture of a printer for a "print page" icon.

- Autonomy (isolation from non-navigational content) as well as grouping of the symbol. An example of such autonomy would be a vertical row of buttons down the left side of a window; the isolation of the cluster implies that the cluster is some sort of a menu.

One of these characteristics alone might not make an object appear to be a navigational graphic. For instance, we might add a drop shadow to a header without visitors assuming that it's navigation. But start layering multiple affordances, as is the case in the lower right corner of Figure 3.10, and visitors would be surprised (not to mention annoyed) if the image were not clickable. Therefore, avoid layering navigational affordances on non-navigational elements.

Image Rollovers

Rollover/mouseover effects are an expected feature of navigational images these days. An image rollover effect uses JavaScript to swap the original image with a new image. Common rollover effects include the simulation of movement (such as the depression of a button), a text or background color change, a surrounding glow, increasing or decreasing the size of a drop shadow, brief animation, or…well, you get the idea. The good news is that we don't need to write the JavaScript for the rollover; Dreamweaver and other development environments can do it for us.

In any graphic rollover, the original image and the swapped-in image should be exactly the same size (make sure to specify `height` and `width` attributes on the image HTML). Also, don't change any characteristics on the rollover image accidentally. For instance, if the only thing that is *intended* to change on rollover is the color of the button, then neither the text nor the button itself should accidentally shift by so much as a pixel. The resulting bobble would look amateurish.

Navigational Icons

Navigational *icons* (small, stylized pictures or symbols) are by their very nature designed to take up minimal screen real estate. Some web icons seem to be universally understood these days, such as a shopping cart icon, a printer icon, or the question mark as a symbol for "Help!" Apart from a few standard symbols such as these, icons can be ambiguous and mysterious, rendering them better as complements to, rather than replacements for, text links. The irony of icons is that if they need a text description to make them clear, they no longer conserve space on the screen, or, indeed, serve their purpose at all. Still, they provide a quick shortcut, an "eye catcher" if you will, for repeat visitors who are familiar with the icons and who therefore don't need to bother reading the descriptions.

Creating clear, understandable icons is incredibly challenging because they need to be so tiny. Check out symbol-based fonts, such as Webdings and Wingdings, for symbols that can be used as icons.

BONUS TOPIC: Creating Graphic Rollovers

See the web site for a tutorial on using Fireworks in conjunction with Dreamweaver to create a rollover button and insert it into an HTML file.

BONUS TOPIC: Keyboard Equivalents for Common Symbol-based Fonts

See the book's web site for a Word document that provides the keyboard equivalents for the most common symbol-based fonts.

Image Maps

An image map is a single image with areas designated as *hotspots* (links). Hotspots can be specified as rectangles, circles, or irregular polygons. **FIGURE 3.11** shows an image map with hotspots indicated by colored overlays.

FIGURE 3.11 Image Map with Hotspots

HTML REVIEW: IMAGE MAPS

```
<img name="fruitBowl" id="fruitBowl" src="fruitBowl.jpg" border="0"
    width="392" height="500" alt="Fruit Image Map"
    usemap="#fruitImageMap" />
<map name="fruitImageMap" id="fruitImageMap">
    <area href="/apple_info.html" shape="circle" coords="251,146,31"
        title="Nutritional Data for Apples"
        alt="Nutritional Data for Apples" />
    <area href="/apple_info.html" shape="circle" coords="219,203,35"
        title="Nutritional Data for Apples"
        alt="Nutritional Data for Apples"  />
    <area href="/grape_info.html" shape="rect" coords="14,154,97,333"
        title="Nutritional Data for Grapes"
        alt="Nutritional Data for Grapes" />
```

```
<area href="/grape_info.html" shape="rect" coords="290,156,373,335"
    title="Nutritional Data for Grapes"
    alt="Nutritional Data for Grapes" />
<area href="/lime_info.htnl" shape="poly"
    coords="114,110,107,144,131,171,156,167,165,149,155,122,138,110,114,
110"
    title="Nutritional Data for Limes"
    alt="Nutritional Data for Limes" />
</map>
```

The <img> places the image itself, while the usemap attribute links that image to the <map> tag. Think of the map as a clear plastic overlay that lies on top of an image. On the overlay, an area tag outlines each hotspot. <area> tags should include both title and alt attributes, for a rollover explanation that is cross-browser compatible. The shape attribute determines the shape of the hotspot—circle, rect(angle), or poly(gon). The coords attribute identifies where the defining points of the shape are located within the map:

- A circle hotspot is defined by the x,y coordinates of its center point and the radius, in pixels (three coordinates).

- A rectangle hotspot is defined by the x,y coordinates for its upper left and lower right corners (four coordinates).

- A polygon is defined by the x,y coordinates of each point on the polygon (an even but variable number of coordinates).

The coords attributes (inside the quotes) cannot be interrupted by any line formatting, such as spaces or line breaks, which is why the formatting is awkward for the last <area> tag above.

Photoshop, Fireworks, and Dreamweaver all provide support for easily creating image maps; we merely click and drag to create shapes on the image, while the program calculates coordinates and writes the HTML. In general, an image map requires more complicated HTML than would several independent image links. For that reason, use an image map only when you can't get the desired effect using separate navigational images.

Sliced Images with Hotspots

Image maps can't provide true graphic rollover effects on the hotspots, unfortunately. In order to accomplish multiple discrete rollovers on what starts out as a single image, we break the image apart into *slices* (rectangular pieces) that are seamlessly reassembled into an HTML table. Then each piece can be manipulated independently, including adding rollovers to selected table cells.

Luckily, image editors like Photoshop and Fireworks help us to slice and reassemble an image. Here are the steps, illustrated:

1. Slice the image into rectangular pieces in any graphics-editing program that supports slicing. **FIGURE 3.12** shows a fruit bowl image with a rectangular slice drawn around one of the limes, in preparation for making that rectangle a hotspot. The image-editing software extends the rectangle's line segments to the edge of the image in order to cut the image apart into table cells.

FIGURE 3.12 Slicing an Image

2. Export the image to an HTML table and populate the table cells with all of the pieces of the image. When rendered in the browser, the whole shebang looks like a single image, as shown in **FIGURE 3.13**. Here, table borders are turned on so that we can see the table structure, but normally they would be invisible. **FIGURE 3.14** shows the individual slices. The HTML for this table is complex, even though the image contains only a single requested slice (the original rectangle around the lime). Imagine how complicated it would be if it contained the same number of hotspots as the image map we looked at in Figure 3.11.

FIGURE 3.13 Sliced Image Re-assembled in an HTML Table

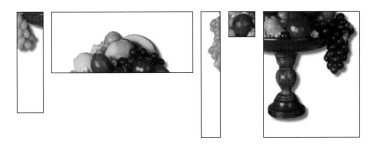

FIGURE 3.14 Individual Slices

3. Wrap the `<img>` tags requiring rollovers in `<a>` tags, complete with the desired rollover effects, just as you would for any other graphic rollover.

HTML REVIEW: SLICED IMAGES

Here's the HTML for the assembled, finished table, complete with the automatic image slices:

```
<table border="0" cellpadding="0" cellspacing="0" width="392">
    <tr>
        <td>
            <img src="spacer.gif" width="55" height="1" border="0" alt="" />
        </td>
        <td>
            <img src="spacer.gif" width="71" height="1" border="0" alt="" />
        </td>
        <td>
```

```
                <img src="spacer.gif" width="266" height="1" border="0" alt="" />
            </td>
            <td>
                <img src="spacer.gif" width="1" height="1" border="0" alt="" />
            </td>
        </tr>
        <tr>
            <td colspan="3">
                <img name="slices_r1_c1" id="slices_r1_c1"
src="slices_r1_c1.jpg"
width="392" height="170" border="0" alt="" />
            </td>
            <td>
                <img src="spacer.gif" width="1" height="170" border="0" alt="" />
            </td>
        </tr>
        <tr>
            <td rowspan="2">
                <img name="slices_r2_c1" id="slices_r2_c1"
                    src="slices_r2_c1.jpg"
                    width="55" height="330" border="0" alt="" />
            </td>
            <td>
                <img name="slices_r2_c2" id="slices_r2_c2"
                    src="slices_r2_c2.jpg"
                    width="71" height="61" border="0" alt="lime" />
            </td>
            <td rowspan="2">
                <img name="slices_r2_c3" id="slices_r2_c3"
                    src="slices_r2_c3.jpg"
                    width="266" height="330" border="0" alt="" />
            </td>
            <td>
                <img src="spacer.gif" width="1" height="61" border="0" alt="" />
            </td>
        </tr>
        <tr>
            <td>
                <img name="slices_r3_c2" id="slices_r3_c2"
                    src="slices_r3_c2.jpg"
                    width="71" height="269" border="0" alt="" />
            </td>
            <td>
```

```
        <img src="spacer.gif" width="1" height="269" border="0" alt="" />
      </td>
   </tr>
</table>
```

As we just saw, sliced images can result in lengthy and complicated HTML. Not surprisingly, future modifications to a sliced image and its HTML can be challenging. It's often best to go back to the original image and regenerate all the HTML code, rather than trying to modify the existing HTML directly.

Navigation Organization Tools

Navigation organization tools at our disposal include menus, embedded links, frames, teasers, search, breadcrumbs, and sitemaps. We will look at each in turn.

Menus

Menus are the "meat and potatoes" of navigation. They serve not only as navigation but also as illumination of the underlying architecture of the site; a clear menu structure helps visitors build a mental map of the site.

Mutually Exclusive Menus

Although we saw earlier that multiple means of navigation are helpful, the elements within a *single* menu shouldn't be allowed to overlap. Instead, they should be *mutually exclusive.* The easiest way to understand this is to look at an example. Let's say that a computer retailer found it useful to offer navigation by both user type (corporations, small businesses, home users) and by product type (desktops, laptops, accessories). Consequently, a home user who wants to purchase a laptop could click on either "home user" or on "laptops." Under such circumstances, what would be wrong with the menu in **FIGURE 3.15**?

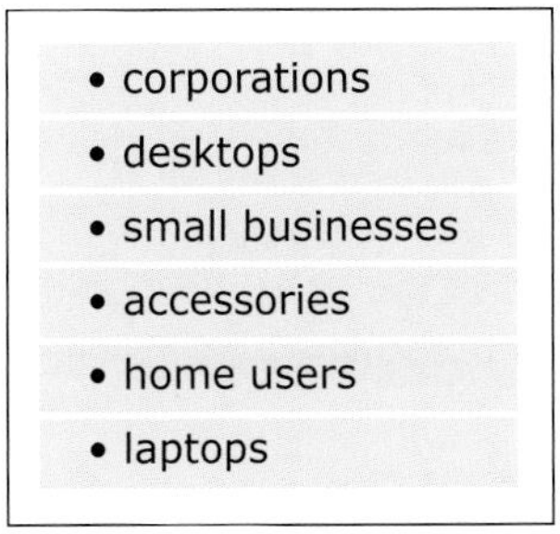

> • • •
>
> **NAVIGATION AIDS IN DREAMWEAVER**
>
> In Dreamweaver, choose Window > Snippets > Navigation to build a variety of simple, single-level text menus quickly and easily.

- corporations
- desktops
- small businesses
- accessories
- home users
- laptops

FIGURE 3.15 What's Wrong with this Picture?

The problem is that the two different categorization schemas ("user type" and "product type") are combined into a single menu. Visitors have a hard time making a mental model of the site when a single menu presents multiple ways of performing the same task.

In a case such as this, the different categories should be presented in two discrete menus, so that each independent menu contains only items that are mutually exclusive. Take a look at the resulting menu structures in **FIGURE 3.16**:

FIGURE 3.16 Mutually Exclusive Menus

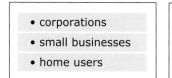
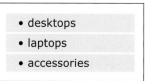

Notice that, in this simple case at least, each menu is intuitively clear, even though the words "users" and "products" don't appear as menu titles. For that, we can thank our innate human propensity for discerning hierarchies.

Menu Location

Placement of menus should be consistent from page to page. **FIGURE 3.17** shows several alternatives. Chapter 4 will discuss menu placement further, in the context of the layout for the entire page.

Here's a quick description of the basic types of menu placement we've just seen:

- **Inverted-L layout** with main navigation typically across the top of the "L." Local navigation, which changes depending upon where the visitor is in the site, is then aligned down the left side, as in Figure 3.17A. (Alternatively, Figure 3.17B features prominent main links down the left side, with less-frequently-used links like "History" "About Us," and "Employment" featured across the top.)

- **Horizontal main menu** with a sub-menu bar for local navigation just below, as in Figure 3.17C. The contents of the local navigation bar change depending upon which main link has focus.

- **Drop-down menus** for local navigation, as in Figure 3.17D.

In any case, there must be an obvious logic to the menu groupings, because links that are clustered are considered to be somehow related. The visitor should be able to grasp the purpose/category grouping of each menu intuitively.

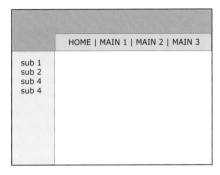

A. Main menu across top,
sub-menu down the left.

B. Main menu down the left,
menu of lesser importance across the top.

FIGURE 3.17 Menu
Placement

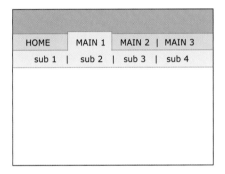

C. Main menu across top,
sub-menu horizontally just below.

D. Main menu across top,
drop-down sub-menu

Menu Appearance

A menu that appears on multiple pages in the site should be structurally identical from page to page. That is, every page should present the same links, in the same order, and in exactly the same place on the page. The menu items shouldn't move, not even a single pixel, and we should never remove or change the order of menu items as the user moves from page to page. A menu on which things seem to magically appear, disappear, or flit around only serves to baffle visitors.

A menu should stand out from the page just enough that the visitor can easily identify it while at the same time not stealing focus away from content. Menus can be indicated by:

- Containing the items within a border or a block of a different background color.

- Placing text links in a vertically aligned list. Any icons or bullets accompanying the links should usually be aligned directly above one another as in the menu on the left in **FIGURE 3.18**. Menu items that are centered, with icons landing wherever they land, look amateurish, as shown on the right in Figure 3.18.

FIGURE 3.18 See What a Difference Vertical Alignment Makes?

Acceptable, Bullets Left Aligned   Unacceptable, Bullets Not Aligned

Menu Size

Menu hierarchies can be narrow but deep, with only a few choices on each menu (**FIGURE 3.19**), or broad but shallow, with numerous choices on each menu (**FIGURE 3.20**).

FIGURE 3.19 Narrow But Deep Hierarchy

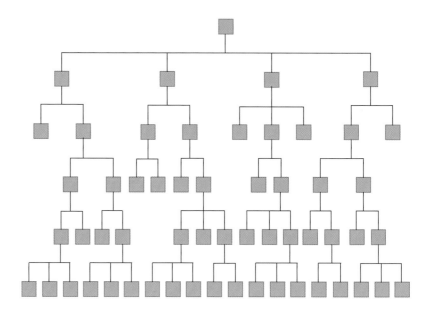

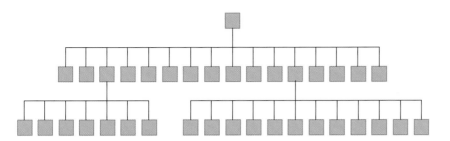

FIGURE 3.20 Broad But
Shallow Hierarchy

Traditional non-web user interface designers have always tried to follow *The Rule of Seven*, which states that the average person can remember or comprehend only seven discrete elements (plus or minus two) at a time. As a result, menus on non-web interfaces usually exhibit small menus in a narrow-but-deep hierarchy, with seven or fewer choices on each menu. If we trace our way down the hierarchies in Figures 3.19 and 3.20, we can see that the relatively small menus on the narrow-but-deep hierarchy take more user clicks to get to the bottom. In a real system, each of those clicks would be followed by yet another page refresh. Such page refreshes aren't a problem with a non-web application; since all of the pages normally reside on the same computer, not on a remote server, the time delay is negligible.

For more information about The Rule of Seven, see George A. Miller on "The Magical Number Seven, Plus or Minus Two: Some Limits on Our Capacity for Processing Information," at http://www.well.com/user/smalin/miller.html.

However, the web is a different environment entirely; visitors have the choice to move to another site if they are annoyed by too many clicks or too many additional page loads. Thus, we often ignore The Rule of Seven and instead create broad-but-shallow hierarchies. We can minimize any inherent comprehension problems by *chunking* (grouping or categorizing) the menu items appropriately. For instance, MSN.com chunks its main menu into categories such as "News and Sports," "Look it Up," "Living and Finances," and "Entertainment." Visitors aren't expected to comprehend *all* of the links on the page; instead they can quickly scan for relevant categories and comprehend only those categories. Longer (though chunked) menus also allow us to use more precise, less vague wording on each link.

By chunking menus, we are once again using the human propensity for intuitively grasping hierarchies, this time to eliminate the cognitive clutter of long, undifferentiated menus.

● ● ●

THE RULE OF SEVEN

There is controversy, about whether *comprehending* is the same as *remembering*. It may very well be true that we can *comprehend* far *more* than seven items at a time, thereby releasing us from The Rule of Seven when *remembering* isn't required. In fact, rigidly following the rule may increase human error.

Expandable Menus

For larger sites, consider using multi-level, expandable, interactive menus, often called *drop-down*, *fly-out*, or *cascading menus*, depending upon their visual characteristics. Whatever the terminology, the sub-menus appear only on rollover or on click, thereby conserving screen real estate and reducing visual clutter on the page. At the same time, multi-level expandable menus reduce the need to load *drill-down pages* (pages whose only function is to display menus).

There are two basic types of multi-level menus: *jump menus* created with HTML <select> boxes, and dynamic HTML menus that use CSS and JavaScript to show and hide <div>s.

Jump Menus Using Select Boxes

A drop-down menu using a <select> box looks like a standard select box, except that the choices presented are link descriptions. We use JavaScript to open a new document based upon the chosen <option>. **FIGURE 3.21** shows a jump menu after the drop-down arrow is clicked. To create a jump menu in Dreamweaver, choose Insert > Form > Jump Menu. Use the "+" to add each new menu item, and type the text and the URL for each. Click the box that inserts a "Go" button, and click "OK" when done.

FIGURE 3.21 Jump Menu Using HTML's <select> Tag

Dynamic HTML Menus

Dynamic HTML menus use CSS positioning and JavaScript to show and hide sub-menus and sub-sub-menus over the top of the existing page content. Keep in mind that drop-down menus are notoriously finicky in some of the older browsers, because they depend on CSS positioning.

FIGURE 3.22 shows a very simple drop-down menu created automatically (well, almost) by Dreamweaver. Figure 3.22A shows the menu at rest, while Figures 3.22B and 3.22C show the drop-down menus that appear when the first and second menu items are clicked. See the sidebar for more about creating dynamic menus.

A. Menu at rest.

FIGURE 3.22 Simple Yet
Dynamic DHTML Drop-
down Menu Created in
Dreamweaver

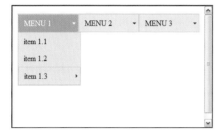

B. First level drop-down menu appears when
the first-level menu is clicked.

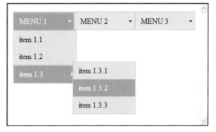

C. Second-level drop-down menu appears when
the second-level menu is clicked.

CREATING A DYNAMIC MENU

Both Dreamweaver and Fireworks provide support for creating dynamic menus, called "pop-up menus" by Adobe. For instructions in Dreamweaver, search Help for "Spry menu." In Fireworks, choose Help > Contents > Creating Buttons and Pop-up Windows. After the menu system is created, you can tweak the resulting CSS files to get the visual effects that you desire.

Another alternative is to download menu code from such sites as www.javascriptsource.com (free) or www.macromedia.com (some free, some for a fee). Entering "drop-down menu" into a search engine will provide you with dozens more such sites.

Keep in mind that even menu systems that claim to be cross-browser often aren't, so be sure to test the resulting code in all of your target browsers. If the menu system breaks in an obvious way in some of the browsers, the easiest way to fix the problem (even if you know JavaScript) is to simply delete what you have and start over with a completely different script from another source.

Sequential Menus

Sometimes pages are meant to be read sequentially, such as for a long article that spans multiple discrete pages. In such cases, sequential menus are often placed at the bottom of a page, as in **FIGURE 3.23**:

FIGURE 3.23 Sequential Menus

Page 1 | 2 | 3 | 4 | 5 | 6 | 7 | 8 | 9-16
<<< Previous Page | Next Page >>>

Here, the visitor can click on any page number other than the disabled current link, shown here as Page 2. When there are too many pages to access directly from a single menu, a link like the "9-16" shown at the end of the top line can furnish the visitor access to the next group of pages. It also shows visitors how many pages remain, so that they can decide whether or not to keep going. Finally, "Previous Page" and "Next Page" allow visitors to navigate all of the pages in order easily.

Drill-down Menu Pages

Drill-down pages (also called *click-through pages*) contain mainly menus, with very little or no content. Portal sites like Yahoo or MSN are good examples of drill-down pages. It's perfectly acceptable for a portal page to be only a drill-down page; that, after all, is its purpose. But we usually try to avoid unnecessary drill-down pages within content sites because they force visitors to download still more pages without yet reaching any real content. It's better to consolidate a couple of pages, so that each page has some useful content as well as navigation.

For instance, it's conceivable that Amazon's home page could contain nothing but links to its major categories (books, music, movies, and so on) and a search box, but that would be a deplorable lack of marketing imagination. Such a home page would hardly lure visitors into buying something more than what they came looking for. As a matter of fact, Amazon's home page (**FIGURE 3.24**) displays suggestions personalized to the visitor, in addition to providing the main menus and a prominent search feature. A visitor doesn't feel quite so used when there is at least some content of value on what would otherwise be just a click-through page.

Avoiding drill-down pages benefits us as well as our visitors, because it decreases page loads, thereby decreasing the load on our servers. Nonetheless, sometimes there can be advantages to retaining drill-down pages:

- A focused but tantalizing menu can entice visitors to look more closely at all of our offerings. Consider how grocery stores always put the dairy section at the far back of the store; every customer intending to buy a single gallon of milk must walk past a long aisle of other tempting products. So, too, can a focused menu lure visitors into further exploration.

- When a site displays paid advertising, each page load generates ad-impression revenue. Thus, more clicks mean more revenue.

Frames

Frames are highly controversial, to the point where many designers rant that they are inherently evil and refuse to use them, ever. Although this book won't go quite that far, it's fair to say that frames should be avoided unless you have some over-whelming reason to use them.

HTML REVIEW: FRAMES

```
<frameset rows="100, *" title="Web Design Aesthetics">
   <frame src="logo.html" name="logo" id="logo" title="Logo Area" />
   <frameset cols="120, *" title="Web Design Aesthetics">
      <frame src="navigation.html" name="navigation" id="navigation"
         title="Navigation Area" />
      <frame src="content.html" name="content" id="content"
         title="Content Area" />
   </frameset>
</frameset>
```

This specification creates a web page divided as in FIGURE 3.25.

FIGURE 3.25 Three Frames.
Table borders are turned on
for illustration.

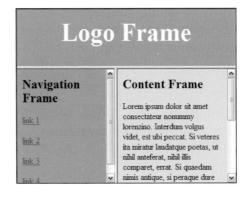

Let's look first at the myriad disadvantages of frames:

- A page with multiple frames must load multiple HTML documents, which of course takes extra time.

- When navigation is in one frame and content in another, it takes quite a bit of custom work with JavaScript to disable the current link so that users aren't confused or inconvenienced by accidentally reloading the current content frame.

- The location bar reflects the frameset URL, not the URL of the content frame, which can confuse visitors.

- Frames disrupt indication of visited versus unvisited links as well as bookmarks/favorites in the browser.

- The browser's "Back" and "Forward" buttons no longer function as visitors might expect.

- Although a visitor can print an individual frame, he or she might not get the expected content if the cursor isn't positioned properly on the page.

- Search engines have problems indexing "framed" sites.

- Frames have unique security issues; each frame can potentially have different permission levels, which is complicated to manage.

- If the page is designed with all of the navigation in one frame and all of the content in another, the visitor might be unable to move around the site if the navigation frame errors off in some way.

Of course, there must be some advantages to using frames, or they would have disappeared long ago. Here are a few:

- We have more control over what is always on display on the page; for instance, we can make sure the identification banner, page header, and menu system are always visible. Consequently, the user doesn't have to scroll all the way back to the top navigation to move on. Arguably, though, a simple set of text links at the bottom of the page instead could solve this navigation issue without frames.

- When the document in the content frame changes, only that content is down-loaded. This content document is smaller because the identification banner and menus have been stripped out to a separate frame or frames. Thus, the content document downloads faster.

  We can duplicate many of the effects of frames by using CSS to position <div>s so that the <div>s containing the page identification and menus are always present, with another scrolling <div> containing the content. The debugging for this kind of layout is usually more involved than debugging a table-based layout.

The bottom line is that we should make use of frames only if there is an over-whelmingly good reason to do so. Determine whether frames would make the site easier to navigate, which may be a good enough reason to rely on them. If all that is required is partitioning the page off into chunks, then tables or <div>s are far better choices.

If you feel you must use frames, there are some hints that will make them more user-friendly:

- If you set up a vertical frame for navigational images, be sure that the frame is an exact pixel count wide, large enough to hold each image. If you use a percentage instead, the navigation might be cut off on smaller windows.

- Avoid turning off scrolling. Removing scrolling can render some of the page completely inaccessible for people with smaller or lower-resolution monitors, particularly disastrous if the inaccessible area contains the navigation. Instead, leave scrolling on automatic, so that a scrollbar appears only when needed.

- Turn off frame borders, which are just plain ugly, and anachronistic to boot.

- Each content page should have at least some minimal backup navigation, in case the navigation frame errors off or a search engine delivers the visitor directly to the content page without the enclosing frameset.

- Consider including `<noframes>` if there's a chance that some of your visitors have ancient browsers that don't recognize frames (although such visitors are a minuscule percentage of today's web surfers).

Local Search Functions

Including a well-designed internal search function on your site can give users speedy access to the information they need. For instance, the fastest way to locate a web design book on Amazon is to enter the title or author name in Amazon's search box. Finding a specific book by browsing the "web design" category on the hierarchical site map would be a daunting task, given the 8,176 books in that category on Amazon as of this writing.

An effective search function can be expensive to develop. Although there are plug-in search engines that can be tacked on to a site and then chug away indefinitely with little input from developers, they deliver only mediocre results unless tailored to the content on a site. You'll get the most pertinent results when a skilled indexer, with knowledge of the domain, configures the search engine with categories, keywords, and keyword synonyms. Such hand-crafted search configuration doesn't come cheaply. So it's a classic cost-benefit decision: is this site worthy of a search function? Is the bang worth the bucks? It might be, if several of the following are true:

- The site is quite large, such that browsing isn't a reasonable way to find something.

- The site is complex, with interrelated information and many cross-references.

- The site is fragmented, with ambiguous and overlapping categories.

- The target audience would expect a search function.

- The target audience would use the search function frequently enough to justify the cost.

- The site has highly dynamic content. For instance, a site map for CNN.com couldn't be maintained fast enough to keep up with ever-changing news content.

In tailoring a search engine to our site, we return to the extensive lists of labels we compiled when researching our site architecture in Chapter 2. At that time, we worked to narrow our choices to only the most perfect, most precise, and most succinct preferred terms. Now, however, we include *all* of the terms that were on the original, unedited lists, as well as any and all terms that our users might come up with, including likely misspellings of popular search terms.

We need to look at the site from radically different viewpoints now, to come up with categories that perhaps weren't required for the original site architecture. For instance, perhaps the site's hierarchical structure organizes technical articles by the general subject category, but we know that visitors need access by author, exact title, date, or geographical location. The list of possible search terms that we will feed to the search engine continues to expand.

Search Interface

In most cases, the search interface on each page should be as simple as possible, consisting primarily of a text input box for entering the search query. Research shows that 27 or so characters seems to be an optimal size (www.useit.com/alertbox/20020512.html) because it's large enough that most search terms fit without scrolling.

You might pre-populate the search text box with brief instructions. For instance, the search box on www.redenvelope.com initially states, "description or item #," to give the searcher some idea of the type of search phrases that are allowed. (See Chapter 8 for the pros and cons of displaying instructions like this in a form field.)

Visitors often expect that the search process should be activated simply by hitting "Enter" on the keyboard while still within the search text input box. That is automatically the case as long as two things are true:

- The "Search" action button is a standard HTML `<submit>` button.

- The search text input box is the only user-entered field within the form that surrounds it.

In all other cases, more extensive JavaScript will be needed for "Enter" to be recognized properly.

We should initially present the simplest search interface possible, but we can also offer an advanced search page for users who need it. Advanced search options may include:

- Choice of search zones: the entire web, just our site, or specific sub-areas within our site. For example, on Amazon.com, visitors can choose to search all of Amazon, or just books or movies or music or whatever. Figure 3.1 presented Amazon's Advanced Search function, with the search narrowed to just books, as indicated by the "Search Books" header.

● ● ●

KEEP IT TOGETHER

The "Search" action button should be adjacent to the text input box.

- Filtering of search criteria: elimination or inclusion of elements based upon speci-fied characteristics. Again looking back at Figure 3.1, we see how Amazon can filter a search based upon media format, reader age, language, and publication date.

Search Engine Results Pages

The results of a search query are displayed on a search engine results page (SERP). The SERP should repeat the search terms somewhere on the page, display the domain that was searched (the entire web, just this site, or specific sub-area within the site), and indicate the number of matching pages found.

Each individual result should include enough information about the destination page that visitors can make an informed decision about its relevancy. Google's SERP in **FIGURE 3.26** is an excellent example (and probably the one that came to mind as you read this description); it shows the page title, relevant content, and URL of each resulting page.

FIGURE 3.26 Search
Engine Results Page
(www.google.com)

The `<title>` tag from the found page dictates the clickable headline that displays on the result, and it's the very first thing the searcher sees. Because of this, we should formulate page titles that are both accurate and enticing. But that's another topic for another book.

There are two schools of thought for creating good page titles. One is to start with the site identifier, followed by the unique page title. For instance, pages for the site that accompanies this book might be titled as such:

```
<title>Visual Design: Chapter 2, Site Analysis</title>
<title>Visual Design: Chapter 3, Navigation</title>
```

All of the pages in the site contain the initial phrase "Visual Design," while "Chapter 2" and "Chapter 3" uniquely identify individual pages. This naming convention certainly provides the most information, albeit resulting in long titles. The primary disadvantage is that, if the visitor has multiple pages open in our site at the same time, the taskbar at the very bottom of the user's display screen shows only the first few title words, which are identical for all pages. Unfortunately, there simply isn't a good compromise.

The `<meta name="description" content="…" />` tag provides the description that shows on some SERPs, right after the title, instead of the content surrounding the search term. If ever there were a place to be engaging, to pique interest, this is it. Use all of your writing and marketing skills to make this sing!

In what order should the results appear on the SERP? The options include sorting by:

- **Relevancy:** the most relevant items are displayed first. The engine can make a judgment of relevancy based on such indications as whether or not the query term was in the page title and URL and how often the query term appears in the content. It also looks at whether the words of a query term are in close proximity. For instance, if the search phrase were "*George Washington Carver*," the phrase "Biography of *George Washington Carver*" would rank higher than "*George* Smith, a *Washington*, D.C. Meat *Carver*," because the requested terms are not physically adjacent in the latter. Realtor.com shows the results of a search sorted by relevancy, depending upon how closely the properties match the requested features from the advanced search query.

- **Date:** either the most recent items are displayed first (as on news sites) or the oldest items are displayed first (as for any site presenting pages from an historical perspective).

- **Alphabetical order:** for anything naturally organized alphabetically, such as telephone book entries or titles of articles.

- **Geography:** displayed by region or proximity. An example would be a retail store locator utility, with the closest stores at the top of the list.

- **Popularity:** based on how many visitors the pages have had, how those visitors ranked those pages (if visitor ranking is encouraged), and how many other pages link to them.

• • •

BE BRIEF

Search engine results typically show around 66 characters of the title, so don't waste precious space on an initial "The" or "Welcome to…" Make the first few words the most salient and information-dense.

• • •

SERP CONTENT DISPLAY

Some SERPS show the content from the description <meta> tag, while others display the content surrounding the search term instead.

The best search functions allow visitors to choose what *they* consider to be the most important ranking characteristics. For instance, searchers on Realtor.com can choose between results ranked by square feet, by how closely the home matches requested features, or by price.

It's also helpful to present a choice of how many results display per page. For instance, www.nordstrom.com initially displays 21 results per page but offers the option to display 99 results per page instead.

Search engine results pages should offer the visitor the opportunity to alter or refine the search if the results aren't satisfactory. The initial results can serve as a springboard, helping a visitor decide how to construct a more focused query.

Search Logs

Log files from your local search engine can show you which terms visitors entered into your search function. These logs can help you to refine both your navigation and the search system itself, since the terms that surprise you are often the terms where the "scent" of information has been lost for the visitors. For instance, if the same unexpected phrase turns up in the search logs repeatedly, perhaps you need to feature that phrase more prominently on your main navigation.

Embedded Links

Embedded links (also called *contextual* or *inline links*) are text links set within normal body text and indicated only by some formatting change, such as underlining and a color change. For example, *this phrase* could be an embedded link if it were on a web page. Embedded links are pretty much like footnotes in a book; they provide secondary elaboration that supplements the main content without interrupting the flow of that content. At the same time, the context of the surrounding content helps to clarify exactly what information will be presented if the visitor clicks the link.

Embedded links shouldn't be used as the sole navigation on a page, because they don't offer the mental site mapping cues that menus provide. Moreover, numerous embedded links can overwhelm the page with visual noise, just as they are doing in this paragraph. Use such links judiciously.

Teasers

A teaser is an "aside" designed to grab the visitor's attention. Teasers are commonly used for announcements of sale items or news flashes. Even banner ads could be considered teasers. Teasers are often set off to the side of the main content, in an area of their own. Sometimes they instead appear at the end of a summary paragraph, offering the visitors the opportunity to read more information. For instance, a news site might provide a one-paragraph news brief, with a More >> link to the longer article.

Site Maps, Tables of Contents, Site Indexes, and Directories

For larger, more complex sites, a *hot* (linked) site map, table of contents, index, or directory can help users who can't find what they need in any other way. A traditional site map exposes the site's hierarchy, while an index or directory is usually only a single level deep. A simple text-based outline format (**FIGURE 3.27**) is ideal for its clarity, fast download, and ease of maintenance, while still visually reinforcing the site's organization.

FIGURE 3.27 Google Site Map (www.google.com)

Breadcrumbs

Breadcrumbs are a simply a trail of standard text links that illustrate where the visitor is in the site hierarchy and provide an easy way to traverse back up the hierarchy. For instance, if the visitor is attempting to purchase bedding, the breadcrumbs for the page selling bedsheets might look like this:

Home Décor > Bedding > Sheets

Both "Home Décor" and "Bedding" are clickable text links that take the user back up the hierarchy. "Sheets" isn't a hyperlink because it refers to the current page.

Although breadcrumbs might well be overkill on smaller sites, they can be a lifesaver to visitors on larger, more complex sites, just as they were intended to be for Hansel and Gretel.

• • • •

BREADCRUMBS IN DREAMWEAVER

To build the skeleton for breadcrumbs in Dreamweaver, choose Window > Snippets > Navigation > Breadcrumb, and then select either ">" or ":" as the separator between levels.

Keyboard Shortcuts

In web parlance, *keyboard shortcuts* (key combinations that perform the same as clicking on a link) are particularly valuable for frequent visitors (although occasional users typically won't bother with them) and for visitors who are physically unable to use a mouse. A link with an associated keyboard shortcut might look something like this:

Northern Illinois University (Alt+N)

In some browsers, the keyboard shortcut puts focus on the element but doesn't actually activate it. In such cases, the visitor would still need to press the "Enter" key to trigger a link.

To create a keyboard shortcut, add accesskey="N" to the <a> tag, if "N" is the key being assigned:

```
<a href="http://www.niu.edu" accesskey="N">
Northern Illinois University</a> (Alt+N)
```

Splash Pages

A splash page is a page that loads before or while the home page loads (**FIGURE 3.28**). Most of the time, a splash page is intended for nothing more than entertaining the visitor. Sometimes, though, it actually has a real purpose, which is to stall while the site gathers the visitor's system specifications (browser and version, available plug-ins, cookies, etc.). Because splash pages take time to load and delay visitors in their mission to accomplish a task, they are another controversial issue. Many designers as well as web surfers adamantly oppose their use.

FIGURE 3.28 Splash Page
(www.PandaExpress.com)

If you have to use a splash page, make sure that it has an artistic sense such that it:

- Adds to the character of the site enough to justify the extra download time.

- Downloads as quickly as possible.

- Can be easily bypassed if the visitor chooses to do so, as illustrated with the "Skip" link on Figure 3.28. Even if the page is incredibly entertaining on the first visit, it's usually just an unnecessary aggravation on the fifteenth or fiftieth visit.

Favorites Menus

If a visitor bookmarks a page in your site, the page title is the default name for the "Favorites" entry. Consequently, it's critical that the title be concise and descriptive, because "Favorites" descriptions are usually smaller than even the descriptions allowed for SERPs.

A *favicon* is a custom icon that appears next to the site name on favorites menus, on the desktop, and on the taskbar. **FIGURE 3.29** displays a portion of a favorites menu showing several such icons.

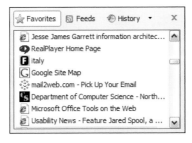

FIGURE 3.29 Favorites Menu with Favicons

You can create a custom favicon using special icon software. Favicons are most reliable at 16 x 16 pixels and should be saved under the name favicon.ico in the same directory as the home page. Keep in mind that the favicon won't appear retroactively if the site was bookmarked prior to the favicon's creation. That is, the favicon must be present at the time the site is actually bookmarked for it ever to appear on the visitor's computer.

• • •

CREATING A FAVICON

See www.webdevelopersjournal.com/articles/favicon.html, www.favicon.com, or www.irfanview.com.

Link Reliability

Navigation is worthless if it doesn't take the visitor somewhere. Jakob Nielson, a usability guru, warns against *linkrot*, a terminal web disease with the presenting symptom of dead links. Linkrot is one of the fastest ways to convince your visitors that your site is unreliable. Make sure your links are functional before you implement the site (Dreamweaver has a utility to check links sitewide), recheck every link after you deploy the site on the server (because links that work locally during development may very well break on the server), and recheck all links (particularly external links) periodically after that.

Even though development environments like Dreamweaver make it easy to reorganize a site's structure, be exceedingly cautious about doing so if your site is already up on the web. Reorganizing or renaming means that users who have already bookmarked your site and search engines who have already indexed it will be presented with the dreaded "404: File not found" page, as shown in **FIGURE 3.30**.

FIGURE 3.30 Error 404: File Not Found

If you simply must reorganize, you can override the standard 404 page with your own custom 404 HTML page that displays the organization's name and logo, a link to the home page, any other discernable information about the bad URL, and an email link for help. **FIGURE 3.31** shows a non-technical, reassuring, and tongue-in-cheek custom 404 page that plays off a site's sailing theme. Although one could argue that it should also include the site's logo, the page still serves its purpose: to entice a lost visitor back into the site with links to the site index, site map, and search area.

FIGURE 3.31 Rerouting a Moved Page (With kind permission from Diederik Willemsen of www. sailingissues.com.)

Not all web servers support custom 404 pages; check with your web server administrator. If allowed, you'll have to follow the rules of your server as to the name and location of the 404 page. In some cases, you'll have to edit an existing server utility file to point to the error page.

Once you've uploaded the required files, test the new error page by typing in a URL that includes your valid domain name but with a nonexistent path or file name. You should see your custom page, ready to help any lost and confused visitors who might otherwise give up on your site.

Navigation and Accessibility

Some users will be unable to take advantage of your site unless you design the navigation for maximum accessibility. There are, of course, guidelines for making site navigation accessible:

- Use a consistent layout style on all pages, so that visitors can find what they are looking for more easily. Of course, *all* visitors, not just those with physical impairments, benefit from a consistent layout style.

- Include `alt` attributes on all navigation images. Both the text on the image and the `alt` attribute should state the link destination with consistency and brevity; screen readers articulate every word, even the unnecessary ones, which can delay visitors. References to the image from elsewhere on the page should refer to the `alt` text rather than to any visual attributes of the image:

  - *Unacceptable:* "Click the green button."

  - *Acceptable:* "Click the 'Go' button" (if "Go" is the label on the button as well as the value of the `alt` attribute).

- Use client-side image maps as shown in this chapter, not server-side image maps. Also offer equivalent text links, because screen readers can't help the visually impaired find the appropriate hotspot on an image map.

- If you're using frames, include a descriptive `title` attribute on the frameset and each frame. For instance:

```
<frameset cols="30%, 70%" title="Web Design Aesthetics">
    <frame src="navigation.html" name="navigation" id="navigation"
        title="navigation area" />
    <frame src="currentPage.html" name="content" id="content"
        title="content area" />
</frameset>
```

- Make sure that navigation would still be obvious if all color were removed. Text links in bright red and content text in bright green, for instance, might look identical to a visitor with red-green color blindness. Include other navigational affordances such as underline, boldface, or italics to ensure that color is not critical to recognizing navigation.

- Drop-down menus that display only on rollover are particularly challenging for screen readers. One alternative is to make the link that triggers the drop-down clickable as well. Such a click delivers an alternative menu-only page displaying the same links as the drop-down menu.

- Include some kind of visual and readable content between two adjacent text links; spaces alone aren't enough. Something as simple as the "|" symbol from the keyboard is adequate. For instance:

  Not acceptable: Home   Products   Job Opportunities

  Acceptable: Home | Products | Job Opportunities

- Provide as many alternative navigation methods as possible, including a search utility, a site map, a site index, breadcrumbs, and keyboard shortcuts/access keys.

• • •

**SERVER-SIDE
IMAGE MAPS**

Since image maps originating on the server are discouraged for several reasons, not the least being a lack of accessibility, we won't examine them at all in this book.

- Provide a "skip navigation" link so that vision-impaired visitors don't have to wait for a screen reader to read through the same repetitive navigation system on every page. The link bypasses the navigation entirely, jumping straight to the content on the page. To implement the link, place a 1x1-pixel transparent GIF image just prior to the navigation menu. The *alt* text on the image should read "Skip navigation" or "Skip to content." Wrap the image in an <a> tag that links to a standard internal anchor at the beginning of the content.

- Avoid opening new windows, but if you do, notify the visitor first.

- Provide HTML pages as alternatives to Flash-only pages. (See Chapter 4 for a brief discussion of Flash-only web site construction.)

Remember, many features that are recommended for navigation accessibility are of benefit to all users, not just the disabled. Prime examples include tables of contents, site maps, navigation flexibility, keyboard shortcuts, and consistent navigation.

Summary

The bottom line of navigation is that visitors want their on-line experience to be easy, intuitive, predictable, and fast. The only way you can design a site that supports all of this is to look at the site from the point of view of the visitors: will they understand your site structure, labels, and navigation? In short, the site architecture should support the navigation elements, and the navigation should reveal the site architecture.

Design Checklist

The following checklist serves two functions: to summarize the major points and "rules" presented in the chapter, and to help you ensure you've done all you should before finalizing any web site you are creating.

Navigation Principles—*Did you:*

- Employ navigation to provide a conceptual map of the site?

- Provide feedback as to the current location?

- Remind the visitor how he or she navigated to the current location?

- Help the visitor find what he or she wants?

- Make the visitor aware of other offerings on the site?

- Provide site and page identification, contact information, a link to the home page, and global navigation on every page?

- Display local navigation, a search function, and site-wide utilities on appropriate pages?
- Avoid changing window size or deleting chrome if opening a new window?
- Adhere to the principles of navigation:
  - Make navigation simple, visible, and consistent?
  - Take advantage of what visitors already know?
  - Orient visitors with "You Are Here" signs?
  - Avoid requiring any extra effort from the visitor?
  - Provide multiple ways to access information?
  - Provide for visitors with varied skill levels?
  - Provide feedback?
  - Construct the site to be flexible and expandable?

Text Links—*Did you:*

- Use text links (as opposed to graphic navigation) whenever possible?
- Design appropriate text link affordances so that users are always clear as to what is and is not a link?
- Avoid underlining text that isn't a link?
- Display link states (available/at rest, available/rollover, active, visited, and current) by using affordances that visitors will recognize?
- Choose text link wording to be concise, precise, and descriptive, usually based on the terms discovered during the discovery process for labeling site architecture?
- Avoid saying "Click here"?
- Use the `<title>` tag to provide a longer description of the text link?
- Disable the current link?

Navigational Images—*Did you:*

- Use navigational images only when their impact enhances the site enough to make the download hit and the increased maintenance worthwhile?
- Design appropriate navigational graphic affordances so that users are always clear as to what is and is not a link?

- Avoid using these affordances on non-navigational images?
- Specify the `alt` attribute for every navigational image?
- Use rollover effects appropriately?
- Clarify non-standard icons with a text description?
- Employ image maps and sliced images with hotspots appropriately?
- Disable the current link?

Menus—*Did you:*

- Locate menus consistently from page to page, with each menu structured identically?
- Cluster links that are somehow related?
- Identify menus visually?
- Consider using bulleted lists (both custom and manual) to structure text menus?
- Choose drop-down menus, sequential menus, and drill-down pages appropriately?

Frames—*Did you:*

- Avoid using frames unless there is some overwhelming justification to do so?
- Set navigational frames to an exact pixel count wide?
- Avoid turning off frame scrolling?
- Turn off frame borders?
- Include backup navigation on content pages?
- Consider including `<no frames>` for visitors who don't have frames enabled in their browsers?

Local Search—*Did you:*

- Include a local search function if users expect it, if the site has highly dynamic content, or if the site is large, complex, or fragmented?
- Expand preferred terms to include synonyms and even misspellings?
- Make the main search interface as simple as possible, while offering advanced search for the visitors who need it?
- On the SERP, display the search terms, the domain that was searched, and the number of matching pages found?

- Display relevant information about the destination pages, sorted appropriately?
- Offer the visitor a chance to refine the search criteria?

Other Navigation—*Did you:*

- Include embedded links, teasers, site maps, directories, breadcrumbs, keyboard shortcuts, and splash pages when they would enhance the visitor's experience?
- Create a favicon?
- Make absolutely certain your site contains no broken links?
- Consider creating a custom 404 "page not found" document?

CHAPTER FOUR

Page Layout

FROM *THE WEB DESIGN WOW! BOOK*,
BY JACK DAVIS AND SUSAN MERRITT:

*"Information can't be left to simply float about on the screen.
It has to be put in context, framed in windows and panels
that are tied consistently and clearly to an underlying grid."*

Page layout has always had to contend with certain
aesthetic issues. But modern—that is, electronic—page
layout has to deal with technical issues every bit as much
as with aesthetic ones in order to be successful. The
technical issues include how large our files can be and
how many *pixels* (single points, or dots, in a graphic image)
we can expect to use for our page display. The aesthetic
choices are similar to those that have been used in other
artistic media for centuries: how we arrange text, images,
and empty space on the page to create areas of focus. In
web design in particular, the technical and aesthetic issues
are tightly coupled. We simply cannot design an appealing page layout without first understanding the technical
limitations of the medium.

● ● ●

**TWELVE POPULAR
WEB SITES**

See Chapter 1 for more
information about the
twelve popular web sites.

Accordingly, we will examine first the technical issues, and then the aesthetic issues of designing an effective, visually consistent, and well-organized web page. When controversy exists on a recommendation, we will examine how our twelve popular web sites are handling the issue as of this writing.

Technical Considerations

To address the technical issues, you must first determine everything you can about your prospective visitors' systems, as discussed in Chapter 2:

- How speedy are your visitor's computers and internet connections, and how fast is your server?

- What display resolutions are they using?

These factors are going to determine how large the site's files can be as well as the display size and resolution we should use for our site.

File Size Concerns

● ● ●

**CSS: CASCADING
STYLE SHEETS**

Note that for the sake
of ease and clarity, the
examples in this text
use inline styles rather
than the more preferred
external CSS files.

The larger the total size, the longer a page will take to download and display. Keep in mind that total file size refers to *all* of the files that make up a web page, including HTML, external CSS, external JavaScript, images, sound, and video. Of these files, HTML, CSS, and JavaScript files are simply text, and therefore often fairly compact. It's usually the image, sound, and video files that are large enough to cause download problems.

Even the so-called experts disagree widely on exactly how large a total page size should be, from less than 20K per page to more than 100K (including all the graphics files for the page) for public web sites. The 20K rule is virtually impossible to follow if you need professional-quality graphics on the site. But if you are targeting an audience with slow internet connections or limited patience, you might well have to forego the killer graphics and abide by that limit.

On the other hand, if you can determine that the majority of your visitors are on high-speed broadband connections like DSL or a corporate intranet (internet technologies used on an internal network), then larger file sizes may be acceptable. You also have less to worry about if your audience is so fascinated by the site's content that they are willing to wait an interminable time to download the page, as would be fans of a particular rock band, anxiously waiting to download the prerelease of a new tune.

• • •

FYI: STATISTICS FOR HOUSEHOLDS WITH BROADBAND ACCESS

We will not look at general statistics for broadband access here, because they are of only limited use. For one thing, the statistics are changing rapidly. For another, they usually list only total numbers of households rather than more useful statistic for percentage of broadband users versus percentage of slow connection users. The statistics also don't account for the fact that many users take advantage of broadband connections at work rather than using slower connections at home. And finally, generic statistics may well have little bearing on the statistics for your particular target audience—there is simply no substitute for understanding that target audience.

When considering whether or not to allow larger files, realize that it's likely you will lose at least some portion of your audience. Make sure that you understand what percentage of visitors you are losing, and also that the level of loss is acceptable before proceeding.

Planning for Limited File Sizes

How do you plan ahead for limited file sizes? Although we will look at specific guidelines relating to issues like optimizing graphics in later chapters, a few hints are helpful now, at the inception of a project:

- Pull out most of the CSS and JavaScript into external files. These are downloaded only the first time they are referenced on a site. From then on, they can be reused by all other pages in the site, without further download hits.

- Reuse graphics, audio, and video from page to page, because they, too, are downloaded only the first time they're referenced.

- Don't use gratuitous graphics, animation, or sound. Each file should have a clear reason for being on the site, whether for utilitarian purposes or for enhancing the site's appeal. A large, attractive image map used for navigation has both practical and aesthetic purposes, as would pictures of products for sale. On the other hand, a graphic that is just filling space should be eliminated.

- Use small images rather than larger ones whenever possible, because, all other factors being equal, small images download faster than large images. For example, you might use a small image that *tiles* (repeats) across the background instead of a single, large background image.

- Minimize the number of unique navigation buttons. For instance, a site with 50 different navigation buttons, each with unique wording and a rollover effect, will require downloading 100 different images. In contrast, 50 text links (with rollovers provided by CSS) carry only a small download price. As we saw in Chapter 3, text links don't have to be boring.

Display Size and Resolution

One of the more challenging aspects of designing web pages is taking into account a myriad of display sizes and resolutions. Display resolutions are measured in pixels. Even so, the term "resolution" can refer to two very different measures:

- The height and width dimensions of the entire display screen, in pixels. There are standard dimensions for computer displays, such as 800 x 600 resolution or 1280 x 1024 resolution.

- PPI (pixels per inch, analogous to DPI/dots per inch for print media). We commonly use 72–100 PPI as the rule of thumb, but the true PPI measurement is determined by the interaction of the display property settings on the computer with the size of the monitor. This interaction means that PPI is not as straightforward as it might seem—certainly not a set measurement from system to system.

As an example, let's assume that we have two different computer systems that are currently using identical monitors (**FIGURE 4.1**). One system displays 800 x 600 pixels on the monitor, while the other is set to a resolution twice as high, 1600 x 1200 pixels. Therefore:

- The pixels must necessarily be smaller and more closely spaced on the *higher* resolution, 1600 x 1200 pixel system, since it displays twice as many pixels on the same monitor.

- It follows, then, that a given web page and all of its components will look *smaller* on that higher-resolution system, because the pixels are smaller and packed in tighter. For example, in Figure 4.1, since the pixels are smaller on the 1600 x 1200 resolution image, so too will be the text and images. Keep in mind that since the pixels are larger on the lower-resolution system, individual pixels are also going to be more obvious.

Now let's look at a similar problem but from a different angle. Instead of changing the *resolution* between our two systems, let's instead hold the resolution constant but change the *monitor size*. Let's say that both of our systems are configured to display at the same width-by-height resolution (the actual pixel dimensions are irrelevant for this discussion). One of the systems uses a 19" monitor, while the other uses a 15" monitor. Since both systems display the same number of pixels, those pixels must necessarily be larger and spaced further apart on the larger monitor. The upshot is that given the same width-by-height resolution, every element on the page appears larger on a larger monitor. **FIGURE 4.2** displays the difference.

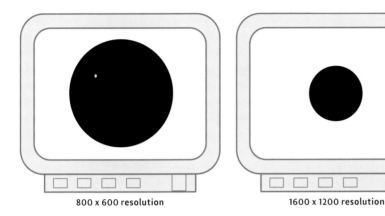

800 x 600 resolution · 1600 x 1200 resolution

FIGURE 4.1 Effect of Display Resolution on Element Size

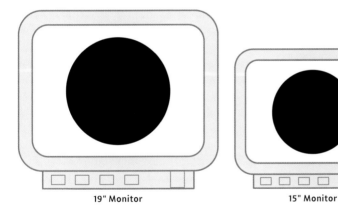

19" Monitor · 15" Monitor

FIGURE 4.2 Effect of Monitor Size on Element Size

As we have seen, both the resolution settings on the system and the monitor size dictate how large given elements of a web page appear, and how much of the page actually fits on the screen. As width-by-height resolution increases, pixels get smaller, as do the all of the elements on the screen that are made up of those pixels. As monitor size increases, pixels get bigger, as do all of the elements on the screen.

TABLE 4.1 illustrates how screen size and resolution interact, resulting in varying text and graphic sizes (demonstrated with relative, not absolute, element sizes). Note again how the text and graphics look largest at low resolution on a large display, and smallest at high resolution on a small display.

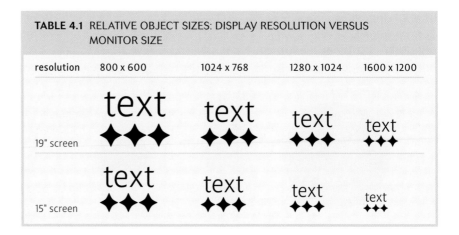

TABLE 4.1 RELATIVE OBJECT SIZES: DISPLAY RESOLUTION VERSUS MONITOR SIZE

To summarize the general interaction of resolution and monitor size:

- Lower-resolution systems and/or larger display screens result in larger text and images. The disadvantage is that the pixels on the display can be blown up to the point where they become pixelated, that is, the individual pixels are large enough to be easily visible—an undesirable effect.

- Higher-resolution systems and/or smaller display screens result in smaller text and images such that the elements can end up being too tiny to read easily.

As you can see, the 72–100 PPI mentioned earlier is little more than a rule of thumb, since the actual number of pixels in an inch on the screen depends upon the interaction of display resolution and monitor size. Again, a web inch is a relative inch, not an absolute inch.

Other factors also affect how many pixels display on a user's screen:

- Older systems or less expensive newer systems generally sport lower width-by-height resolution than newer (and more expensive) computers and monitors.

- When computer systems arrive on their buyers' doorsteps, most are "dialed down" a notch or two from the highest width-by-height resolution they are capable of displaying. That is, a system capable of displaying 1280 x 1024 may very well be set to only 1024 x 768 when the user receives it.

- Many users, perhaps even most, don't know that width-by-height resolution can be changed, much less know how to do it.

- Visitors with vision impairment, age-related or otherwise, might deliberately turn down the resolution so that everything on the screen is larger and easier to see.

- Many visitors rarely size their browser windows up large enough to fill the entire screen. Instead, they often have multiple programs open and partially visible all at once.

- Laptop computers, not to mention web-enabled cell phones and PDAs, often support lower resolution than equivalent desktop computers.

- Liquid crystal displays (LCDs), like those on laptops and flat-panel computer displays, support only a single resolution well. That is, if the visitor changes the resolution to something other than the default, the display quality can degrade dramatically.

Various web sites provide statistics on the popularity of the possible resolutions, some with stats for free, many for a fee. But be aware: These stats are gathered from web sites that may very well have completely different user demographics than the demographics for your site. For instance, stats from a web site like Webmonkey.com, which caters to web developers (who usually work on souped-up computer systems), have little relevance for a site designed for teachers at public elementary schools (who have notoriously prehistoric systems). Again, you must identify your audience and try to ascertain the type of computer systems they are most likely to have before you make resolution-dependent decisions.

Horizontal Page Size

We have seen that display size and size of elements on the page vary, depending upon the visitor's system. Nonetheless, we must still decide on a standard size for the pages in our site. Keep in mind that if a page is too wide to fit on the visitor's display, the browser automatically provides a horizontal scroll bar so that visitors can access the hidden areas. Visitors generally dislike horizontal scroll bars; no one wants to scroll repeatedly from the end of one line on the right side back to the beginning of the next line on the left side.

As a result, we need to choose our page size so that our visitors don't need horizontal scroll bars. An 800-pixel-wide display is the safest for most public-access web sites. In fact, that is the resolution chosen for 50% of the twelve representative sites shown in **TABLE 4.2**.

● ● ●

WINDOW DIMENSIONS FOR VARIOUS SYSTEMS

See http://hotwired.lycos.com/webmonkey/templates/print_template.htmlt?meta=
/webmonkey/99/41/index3a.html for the definitive listing of how many pixels are available for the various browsers and versions. 744 pixels is the safest recommendation, although 750 pixels works just fine for the vast majority of systems.

TABLE 4.2 PAGE WIDTH OF THE TWELVE REPRESENTATIVE SITES*

	Fixed width at 800 pixels wide	Fixed width at 1024 pixels wide	Variable width (expands & contracts to fit the browser window size)
adobe.com	X		
amazon.com			X
cnn.com		X	
ebay.com	X		
imdb.com			X
mapquest.com	home page		lower-level pages
microsoft.com	some lower-level pages	home page and most lower-level pages	
msn.com	X		
msnbc.com	X		
randmcnally.com	X		
ticketmaster.com	X		
yahoo.com		X	

*as of June 9, 2007

We will be using 800 pixels as the horizontal target size for all examples created for this book, for the following reasons:

- It's the most common page size on the web today, if we are to believe our representative web sites.

- It's accessible to almost everyone.

- It caters to the users who want to have multiple windows open simultaneously.

You cannot use all 800 pixels, unfortunately, because you must allow some pixels for the *browser chrome*—the pixels that the browser itself uses. Subtract chrome, and subtract a few more pixels in case the user has not adjusted his or her monitor properly, and you end up with about 744–750 pixels horizontally. The examples in this book will use 750 pixels.

Some web sites create a horizontal page size larger than 800 x 600 pixels but provide a notice that the site is best viewed at that higher resolution. The problem is that, as we have seen, many visitors either cannot or don't know how to alter their resolution. To boot, the visitors who can change their resolution have usually set it to a particular size for good reason. It also seems impolite to require visitors to change their settings just because we are too lazy to make our layout usable at multiple resolutions. Accordingly, consider the potential annoyance factor before asking your visitors to change their computer settings.

Pages for Printing

If you want to be certain that visitors can safely print the entire page in the browser's portrait orientation, you should cut down the page size even further, to only 535 pixels horizontally. Unfortunately, 535 pixels leave us very little room. A better alternative might be to use a separate "Print Page" link that delivers a 535-pixel-wide version of the page optimized just for printing. Visitors particularly appreciate it when the "Print Page" link combines a multi-page article into a single printable page.

Yet another solution uses CSS styling that kicks in only when a page is directed to the printer. See the sidebar for the specifics on how to do this.

▓▓▓ USING CSS TO FORMAT A PAGE FOR PRINTING

There are two ways to isolate the print directions in CSS:

- Link to two CSS files, one with the CSS file for display on the screen, and the second one with formatting rules targeted just for printing. Simply use the attribute media="print" on the <link /> to the CSS file for print styling, as in the second line below:

```
<link href="mediaScreen.css" rel="stylesheet"
   type="text/css" />
<link href="mediaPrint.css" rel="stylesheet"
   type="text/css" media="print" />
```

- Use a global style sheet, including media="print" to specify printing characteristics:

```
<style type="text/css">
body
{
    font-size:10px;
    color:#d8a79b;
```

```
        background-color:#333333;
    }
    </style>
    <style type="text/css" media="print">
    body
    {
        font-size:12px;
        color:#000000;
        background-color:#ffffff;
    }
    }
    </style>
```

Unfortunately, neither form of `media="print"` works in older browsers.

Vertical Page Size

Although visitors may dislike horizontal scrolling, vertical scrolling is usually well-tolerated. While some visitors would prefer to scroll through one long page than to wait for several separate pages to download, others seem to dislike scrolling more than two or three screensful. There doesn't seem to be a consensus in the industry over which alternative is kindest to visitors. Keep in mind that every time a visitor reaches a "next" button, he or she must make a conscious decision whether or not to continue, whereas continuing to scroll might not trigger such an obvious "Should I or shouldn't I?" consideration. As a result, there's a chance that we might keep the visitor browsing longer with one long page than with several sequential pages.

Tools of Page Layout

If all we need is text that runs from the left side of the page to the far right edge, we don't need any special tags or CSS to place the elements on the page. That is generally not the case, however. Most of the time we want to line things up in a grid or place elements precisely on the page. For now, we will look at the tools for such placement. Later, we will see how to use those tools to create an aesthetically pleasing page.

The major tools of page layout are `<frame>`, `<table>`, and `<div>` (all in conjunction with CSS), and Flash files. We will look at each.

Frames

Frames are highly controversial, to the extent that many designers view them as inherently evil and refuse to use them, ever. Although this book will not go quite that far, it is fair to say that frames should be avoided unless you have some overwhelming reason to use them. We have already looked at frames in the Navigation chapter, so we won't review them here. Nonetheless, since the subject of this chapter is page layout, it is worth mentioning that it is certainly *not* appropriate to use frames merely to section the page off into a grid; that purpose is better served with <table>s or <div>s.

Tables

A table is nothing more than a two-dimensional grid on which we can arrange elements. For instance, we might put objects in an invisible table (borders turned off) just so that the objects line up the way we want them to. **FIGURE 4.3** shows a simple two-row by two-column HTML table, with the first line designated as a header line. See the sidebar for a review of the relevant HTML.

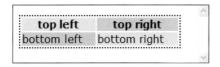

FIGURE 4.3 A Simple Table

▊▊▊ HTML REVIEW: TABLES

Here is the HTML that makes up the table you see in Figure 4.3:

```
<table style="border:2px dotted #000000; width:250px;
   background-color:#ffffff;">
   <thead>
     <tr>
        <th style="background-color:#dde7e9;">top left</th>
        <th style="background-color:#c2d7db;">top right</th>
     </tr>
   </thead>
   <tbody>
     <tr>
        <td style="background-color:#c2d7db;">bottom left</td>
        <td style="background-color:#dde7e9;">bottom right</td>
     </tr>
   </tbody>
</table>
```

> • • •
>
> **NOTE**
>
> Throughout the chapter, HTML and CSS content irrelevant to the topic at hand has been omitted for the sake of brevity.

Here are some hints about building tables:

- Cells are stacked one above another, forming columns. If you have an unequal number of cells in the rows, or if the cells in a column are of unequal width, your table displays unpredictably.

- A table row or cell cannot be sized any smaller than the largest element it contains.

- If you are having trouble trying to get a single table to accommodate the layout for an entire page, stop trying. Use multiple independent tables instead, ending one before starting the next, with each table managing a different layout section.

- Tables nested within tables are notorious for breaking, and can be difficult to troubleshoot. Nest tables only if you cannot come up with an easier way to accomplish your goal.

- Place cell widths on only a single row of the table. Other rows will be forced to obey those widths anyway, but now there is only a single row that needs to be updated if column widths change.

- For cross-browser compatibility, make sure that every table cell has some type of content, even if it is invisible content such as an   or a 1x1 pixel transparent image.

The <div> Tag

A <div> tag is merely a box that surrounds content so that we can treat that content as a unit for placement and formatting reasons. For instance, we could wrap an image and its accompanying text in a <div> in order to surround the unit with a common border and a common background color, or in order to place the entire container at a specific location on the page. See the sidebar for a review of the <div> tag and its attributes.

▨▨▨ **HTML REVIEW: THE <DIV> TAG**

A <div> tag can be used for formatting a block of content as well as for positioning that content on the page. FIGURE 4.4 shows two <div>s that are identical except that the second one is shorter and displays a scrollbar because of content overflow.

Here is the HTML for the two <div>s:

```
<div style="float:left; width:150px; background-color:#dde7e9;
   border-color:#999999; border-style:solid; border-width:1px;
   margin:2px; padding:10px; overflow:auto;">
     <p>Four score . . . created equal.</p>
```

```
</div>
<div style="float:left; width:150px; background-color:#dde7e9;
   border-color:#999999; border-style:solid; border-width:1px;
   margin:2px; padding:10px; overflow:auto; height:100px;">
      <p>Four score . . . created equal. </p>
</div>
```

The overflow:auto **property on both tags results in a scrollbar on just the second**
<div> **because it's the only** <div> **that is too small to display all of the content. The**
float:left; **attribute positions the second** <div> **to the right of the first** <div>
unless the browser window is too small to display both. In such a case, the second
one drops below the first one, as in FIGURE 4.5.

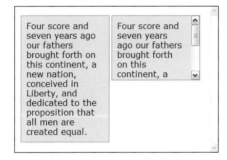

FIGURE 4.4 A <div> on a
Wider Window

FIGURE 4.5 A <div> on a
Narrower Window

FIGURE 4.6 shows both an absolutely positioned <div> (rendered at exactly the positions specified with left and top) and a relatively positioned <div> (offset from where it would have been located if positioning had not been used at all). The sidebar presents the code.

FIGURE 4.6 Absolutely and Relatively Positioned <div>s

POSITIONED <DIV>S

Here is the code for the <div>s in Figure 4.6:

```
<div name="relative" id="relative"
    style="position:relative; left:50px; top:0px;">
        <p>RELATIVE<br />Four score . . . created equal.</p>
</div>
<div name="absolute" id="absolute"
    style="position:absolute; left:25px; top:100px;">
        <p>ABSOLUTE<br />Four score . . . created equal. </p>
</div>
```

Tables versus <div>s

Page layout is on the verge of a major revolution. Although we must still use tables and table cells to set the width of columns on the page if we are at all worried about our visitors having older browsers, we are rapidly approaching the time when we can depend instead upon positionable <div>s. We can set the <div> size, background colors, background images, and selective borders, as well as position the <div> precisely on the page. The major obstacle right now to replacing tables with <div>s is that sometimes the various browsers render and position them slightly differently.

As powerful as `<div>`s are, however, we shouldn't ignore tables just because `<div>`s are a fun new tool. Tables are virtually bulletproof in all browsers, with only the most minor of rendering differences. Additionally, there are some problems that are easier to solve with tables than with `<div>`s. For instance, a sliced image is very easy to reassemble in a table, but not so easy with `<div>`s. The point is to use both tables and `<div>`s, as appropriate.

Adobe Flash

Adobe Flash can be used to render an entire site, not just for animation. A Flash site uses just enough HTML to embed the Flash files. Flash renders everything else, from images to text to navigation links to data pulled out of a server-side database. In a Flash-based site, "pages" are no longer discrete; instead, they are each just one location (or animation "cell") within the single Flash file that encompasses the entire site.

There are advantages to rendering an entire site in Flash:

- A Flash site can be graphically stunning while at the same time generally smaller than the equivalent full-screen JPEGs or GIFs.

- The latest Flash authoring platform includes Adobe Flex/ActionScript, an XML-based language that facilitates both client-side and server-side programming.

- Flash is component-based; that is, parts of a page can be reloaded without refreshing the entire page.

- Flash makes it easier to build web sites that resize well to display on multiple media, including mobile devices.

Of course, there are disadvantages to Flash-based sites as well:

- Although Flash files are inherently smaller than their equivalent JPEGs and GIFs, that advantage is often more than offset by the fact that every bit of content on the entire site is now graphical. Obviously, that can present download issues.

- The graphical nature of a Flash site also means that search within the site (by search engines and by site-specific search functions) is not as effortless as it is on an HTML-based site, because a word on the site is no longer a word; it's just independent pixels arranged into a *picture* of a word.

- The browser's Back and Forward buttons don't work as most users expect. They return to the very beginning or end of the entire animation, rather than to the previous or next action within the animation. Although a well-designed Flash site always provides its own Back and Forward buttons, most users are so habituated to relying on the browser's Back button that they use it anyway, thereby losing their places in the sites.

● ● ●

SLICED IMAGES

A sliced image is one that is cut into pieces that can be manipulated independently, perhaps for rollover effects. See Chapter 3 for more on sliced images.

- Bookmarking "pages" within a Flash site bookmarks entry to the site, not the lower-level areas, as visitors intend.

Although it's likely that Flash-based sites will become more popular in the future, it's unlikely that Flash will replace HTML entirely. Instead, it's a question of using the right technology for the right purpose. For instance, an "experience" site such as a movie or fan site would be a fine candidate for a Flash-based layout.

This book will not delve into Flash technology any further, because the depth that would require is beyond the scope of this book.

Aesthetic Issues

The "information overload" of a disorganized, chaotic, overfilled page repels visitors so quickly and thoroughly that they may very well shut down; they decide it's not worth bothering with the mental gymnastics of sorting out the jumble. As Steve Krug of *Don't Make Me Think* fame says so succinctly, "If something requires a large investment of time—or looks like it will—it's less likely to be used."

In contrast, well-organized pages with adequate empty space give visitors an impression of simplicity, even if the page is chock-full of stuff. The point is that the way you choose to structure your pages has a strong bearing on your visitors' comfort level.

Filling the Display Window

We already know that we design for the lowest (within reason) common denominator of screen resolution. But then what happens when a page is viewed on a display system that is either larger or smaller? There are two ways we can accommodate this situation, dubbed *solid layout* and *liquid layout*.

Solid Layout

With solid layout (sometimes referred to as *ice layout*), we design the page to fit the smallest window size we expect the visitors to have, filling the background of larger windows with a color or image. **FIGURE 4.7** shows an example of solid layout, centered on the page, as it looks in both a wide window and one that is too narrow to display the content without horizontal scrolling. The sidebar shows the HTML for this particular example. The properties that create the solid design are highlighted.

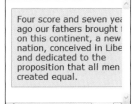

FIGURE 4.7 Solid Layout in Two Different Window Widths

Solid Design Displayed in a Wide Window   Solid Design in a Narrow Window

▨▨▨ HTML REVIEW: SOLID LAYOUT

Here is the code for the centered, solid layout shown in Figure 4.7:

```
<body style="text-align:center;">
<div style="width:200px; background-color:#dde7e9; text-align:left;">
   <p>Four score . . . created equal.</p>
</div>
</body>
```

The width property ensures that the <div> is always precisely 200 pixels wide, regardless of the visitor's window size. The text-align:center property on the <body> tag centers the <div> if it's smaller than the window, as on the left in Figure 4.7. If the content is too large for the window, the browser inserts scroll bars (horizontal and/or vertical) on the <div>, as on the right in Figure 4.7.

We could instead use a table to create a similar layout, especially when we want to treat multiple rows and columns as a whole. In the HTML below, the first column of the table is always fixed at a width of 100 pixels. The second column fills the remaining 100 pixels of the 200 pixels specified for total table width. Here's the HTML:

```
<body style="text-align:center;">
<table style="width:200px;">
   <tr>
     <td style="width:100px;">Gettysburg Address</td>
     <td>Four score . . . created equal.</td>
   </tr>
</table>
</body>
```

Some designers prefer that content in a solid layout be left-justified (the default) on the page, with all excess background filling only the right side of the screen. Others prefer to center the content on the screen, by specifying center alignment as illustrated in our examples. Of the ten major web sites that use solid design (from our informal poll of twelve sites), six are centered, while three sites and one home page are left-justified, as **TABLE 4.3** shows.

TABLE 4.3 PAGE ALIGNMENT OF THE TWELVE REPRESENTATIVE SITES

| | Fixed Width Pages | | Not Applicable: |
	Centered	Left-Justified	Page Resizes to Fit Window
adobe.com	X		
amazon.com			X
cnn.com		X	
ebay.com		X	
imdb.com			X
mapquest.com		home page	lower-level pages
microsoft.com	X		
msn.com	X		
msnbc.com		X	
randmcnally.com	X		
ticketmaster.com	X		
yahoo.com	X		

Liquid Layout

Liquid layout means the page automatically expands or contracts to fill all available screen area, using expandable `<div>`s or `<table>`s. **FIGURE 4.8** shows how the liquid HTML in the sidebar displays in both a wide window and a narrow one.

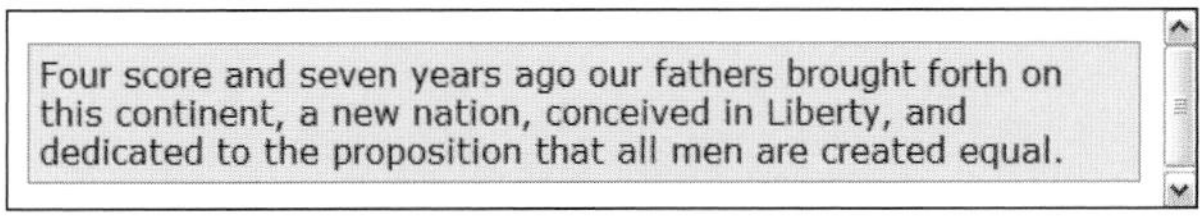

Four score and seven years ago our fathers brought forth on
this continent, a new nation, conceived in Liberty, and
dedicated to the proposition that all men are created equal.

Liquid Design in a Wide Window

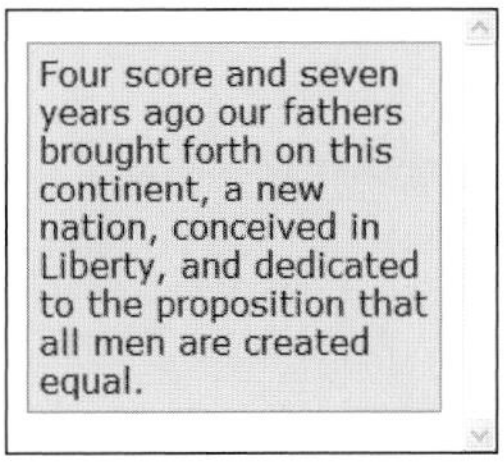

FIGURE 4.8 Liquid Layout
in Two Different Window
Widths

Four score and seven
years ago our fathers
brought forth on this
continent, a new
nation, conceived in
Liberty, and dedicated
to the proposition that
all men are created
equal.

Liquid Design in a Narrow Window

HTML REVIEW: LIQUID LAYOUT

Simply omitting a width on the <body> and the <div>/<table> that contains the
content means that the page expands and contracts to fill the available width.
The liquid layout HTML for the <div> in Figure 4.8 is shown below:

```
<body>
<div style="background-color:#dde7e9; text-align:left;">
    <p>Four score . . . created equal. </p>
</div>
</body>
</html>
```

Similarly, tables can expand and contract as long as:

- The table width is either omitted or specified as a percent.

- There is at least one column that doesn't have a fixed, pixel-based width.

For the example below, the first column is always 100 pixels wide, while the sec-
ond column expands and contracts to fill the remaining width of the window.

```
<body>
<table>
    <tr>
        <td style="width:100px;">Gettysburg Address</td>
        <td>Four . . . created equal.</td>
    </tr>
</table>
</body>
```

• • •

MAX-WIDTH **AND**
MIN-WIDTH

CSS *max-width* and
min-width properties
would seem to solve the
problem of content areas
that are either too wide
or too narrow. Unfortu-
nately, as of this writing,
they are not recognized
by Internet Explorer, the
browser with the largest
market share.

If lines of text end up expanding to more than 500–600 pixels wide, they can be hard to read because the visitor's eyes cannot easily maintain tracking when moving from the end of one very long line to the beginning of the next line. Since there's no cross-browser solution to setting a maximum width, we must rely on visitors having the good sense to downsize the window if the lines of text are too long to read easily.

Comparison of Solid versus Liquid Layout

There are advantages to both solid and liquid layout.

With solid layout, you can be fairly confident of what the page will look like when the visitor sees it, regardless of screen size and resolution. In contrast, liquid layout fully embraces the medium of the web but is also much less predictable and much harder to create and test. Of the twelve popular web sites we have been consulting throughout this chapter, only two, Amazon and IMDb, use liquid layout. See **TABLE 4.4** for a summary of advantages and disadvantages of both layout styles.

TABLE 4.4 LIQUID VERSUS SOLID LAYOUT

	Solid Layout	Liquid Layout
Description	• Page fits within a set number of pixels horizontally.	• Page expands and contracts to fit the visitor's horizontal window dimension.
Advantages	• Tight control over how the page displays on a visitor's screen.	• Uses the entire window. • Can eliminate horizontal scrolling at most window sizes. • Works (in theory) for all screen sizes.
Disadvantages	• Wasted background on larger windows. • Fewer elements can be placed on the page.	• Impossible to control exactly how the page looks on a visitor's screen. • Lines of text can be hard to read if they become too wide. • Almost impossible to make the page look good at all window sizes.

Building Blocks of Page Layout

Before we can examine how to create unified yet interesting page layouts, we must first look at the various interacting elements that we can manipulate when creating those layouts. Those elements are line, shape, and color.

Line

Lines can be thick or thin, uniform or varied thickness, solid or interrupted, fuzzy or hard-edged, graceful or nervous or sharp. The line you choose can help to create a mood.

Line can divide, connect, decorate, organize, and contain. For instance, horizontal and vertical *rules* (lines) can divide a page or connect two parts of a page together. Borders are often decorative, although borders around just a portion of a page can be used as organizers and containers, too. Lines can distinguish and delineate an object, whether the lines are visible (a different color from the object) or implied (same color as the object). Invisible lines are also the main component of grids, which can be used as an organizing principle for the page. Grids are discussed in greater depth later in this chapter.

FIGURE 4.9 is an example of invisible, organizing lines crafted into a three-column grid, with the header images at the top covering both the left and center columns.

• • •

QUIPS AND QUOTES

"Who can't appreciate the beauty of soft rounded hills in a pastoral landscape? Contrast that with the hard angular feel of mountains jutting from the ground. Line is responsible for the mood of these two contrasting natural settings." – From *Using Design Basics to Get Creative Results*, by Bryan L. Peterson.

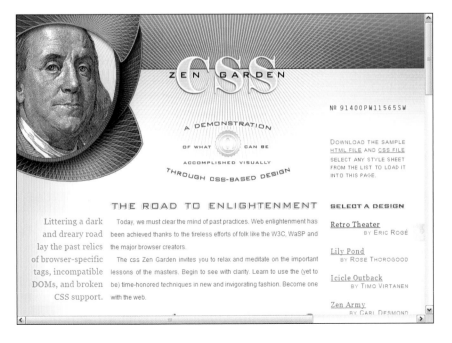

FIGURE 4.9 Underlying Grid ("C-Note," www.csszengarden.com/?cssfile=126/126.css, by Brian Williams)

FIGURE 4.10 uses line in a more obvious way, with the white outlines delineating the grid.

FIGURE 4.10 Connecting Lines and Outlines ("Pleasant Day," www.csszengarden.com/?cssfile=119/119.css, by Kyle Jones, www.justkyle.com)

• • •

CSS ZENGARDEN

Throughout the book, we will look at pages from www.csszengarden.com, a site dedicated to illustrating the power of CSS. All pages on the site use exactly the same HTML content file; the radically different visual designs are produced solely by linking the HTML to different CSS files created by some of the finest designers on the web.

Shape

Lines, either visible or invisible, contain shapes, which in turn can enliven a page that might otherwise be just unrelieved text. Geometric shapes are formed on a page by images, block elements in HTML (tables, table cells, and <div>s, with and without borders), and even background images for the entire page. Even the implied outline of body copy (a block of text) forms shapes—a paragraph takes on a shape, as does a group of paragraphs. Blocks of text (set, presumably, in black type) tend to "read" as dark gray shapes if set with close spacing, or lighter gray if set with wider spacing.

The page in **FIGURE 4.11** is dominated by shape.

FIGURE 4.11 The cityscapes, both horizontal and vertical, plus the clouds near the top, provide interest on the page. ("Zen City Morning," www.csszengarden.com/ ?cssfile=177/177.css, by Ray Henry, www.reh3.com)

The best way to evaluate the shapes on a page is either to hold a printout of the page upside down (because it's difficult at best to hold a monitor upside down), or to stand back from the display and squint. Either way, words and tiny details fade away, leaving an overall impression of the dominant shapes and the directions in which they seem to move.

Color

Color is our most powerful tool for conveying ambiance and attitude. Think of the different moods portrayed by a black background with fiery red graphics, versus a site built from earth tones like brown, clay, and subdued gold, versus a site of white with pastel pink and yellow. Undeniably, color schemes evoke distinct moods, so skillful use of color is vital. In fact, the next chapter is all about the manipulation of color. In the meantime, however, our primary concern is how color can be used to delineate and organize divisions of a page. For example, blocks (or shapes) of different background colors can group similar elements on the page, section off parts of a page, or focus attention on more important areas. **FIGURE 4.12** shows color used as an organizer.

FIGURE 4.12 Color as an Organizer ("Simple," www.csszengarden. com/?cssfile=174/174. css, by Shawn Chin, www. shawnchin.com)

Visual Harmony

An effective design walks a fine line between being just serene enough to lull the viewer into thinking the page is easy to use and just stimulating enough that the viewer actually *wants* to use it. Too much serenity, and the site is boring. Too much stimulation, and the site is visually chaotic.

Using architecture as an example, let's consider the "stick figure" home of **FIGURE 4.13A**, in which tension and chaos reign. Contrast that with the house of **FIGURE 4.13B**, with its overall impression of serenity and calm. Most people would agree that the house of Figure 4.13B is more visually pleasing.

What factors influence our impression that the first house is chaotic, while the second one feels elegant and organized? The second house *reiterates the same basic shape*, a rectangle, for most design elements, including the shape of the house itself, the windows, the shutters, and the door. It also repeats the same dimensions for most of those rectangles. Even though the attic window is shorter than the other windows, it has the same width as the windows below. If the design for some reason necessitated making the attic window narrower than the other windows, it could still be kept in harmony by retaining the same relative height-to-width ratio of the other windows rather than by retaining the horizontal dimension.

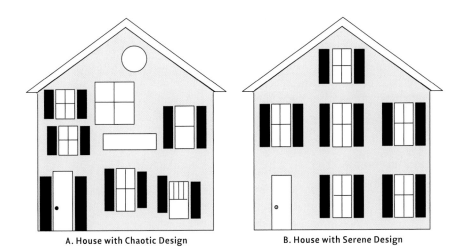

FIGURE 4.13 Chaos versus Repetition and Alignment

A. House with Chaotic Design   B. House with Serene Design

Another factor influencing the serene look of the second house is that *the edges of the various rectangle elements align with each other* whenever possible. Second-story and attic windows align precisely with the windows or door beneath them, and the tops and bottoms of the windows align as well.

Finally, there is plenty of empty space on the second house, while the first house has almost no unfilled space—there are too many decorative elements on the façade.

In summary, the first house makes no attempt to provide continuity of shape, to align those shapes with each other, or to leave some spaces unembellished. As a result, it looks haphazard and makes us uncomfortable; few folks would be willing to shell out a down payment on a house with such obvious design flaws.

How does all of this relate to web page layout? Just as an architect tries to organize a building façade to be visually pleasing, so too should you strive to make sure a page looks simple, uncluttered, coherent, and organized. If visitors feel it will take too much mental effort to sort out all of the visual *noise* (clutter), they might very well bail out of the site. At the same time, we need to know how to stimulate visitors by piquing their interest with new, contrasting, and surprising elements. The right balance between such serenity and stimulation provides a pleasing visual harmony.

Techniques for Providing Visual Harmony

Let's look at the techniques for manipulating the visual characteristics of a page to strike the perfect harmony between serenity and stimulation.

Limit the number of elements on the page.

Eliminate text and graphics that don't really contribute to the site's purpose. Most of the time you shouldn't try to cram too much information on a page. There are exceptions to this rule. For instance, portals like Yahoo! or MSN, by their very nature, need to present a lot of information on the home page. Still, both Yahoo! and MSN are well-organized to reduce visual chaos, so the visitor feels comfortable and able to come to grips with the myriad choices.

Repeat elements.

Within a given page, repeat elements: shape, size, proportion, color, or layout. Such repetition adds to the serenity of a web page in the same way that repeating the same size and shape of windows adds serenity to a building.

For the site as a whole, repetition of color schemes, layouts, logos, navigation schemes, and graphic styles from page to page promotes *visual continuity* (also called *visual consistency*), creating a feeling of order, organization, and rhythm. For instance, continuity is in evidence when you repeat curvilinear, organic shapes, or only sharp-edged, nervous graphics, for the entire site. In *Layout Index*, Jim Krause calls such repetition *visual echoes.*

Repeat a standard page layout throughout the site.

To facilitate continuity, create a general-purpose blank page template that proscribes repeating items (logo, navigation, and content areas) and use the template as the underlayment for most pages on the site. Visitors can then create a mental picture of the page layout, never having to search for the main navigation, or logos, or titles, or the content area, or anything else, for that matter. In this case, repetition isn't boring; it's consistent, which is indeed comforting and efficient, and grounds the viewer.

Still, not every page must be absolutely identical. There might be a different decorative graphic on each page, or a different background color keyed to the subject matter of that page. Often the layout of the home page breaks away from the layout of lower-level content pages. And at times, a lower-level content page needs to use a different layout because its content is radically different. Let's say the majority of a site uses a two-column layout, with a menu bar down the left column and a content area in the right column. A single page on the site might require the entire width of the window for a large data graph, in which case you might justifiably move the links to a horizontal bar across the top of the screen. Even so, those links should be so similar to the links on the other pages that they are instantly recognizable as navigation.

In short, vary the consistent structure of the pages only when you have good reason to do so. In pages that break from the norm, though, you must be even more careful that all of the other page elements are consistent.

Align elements.

As much as possible, line up the outside edges of the various page elements. For instance, **FIGURE 4.14** shows three versions of an HTML form. The elements on Figure 4.14A don't line up at all; as a result, the form is visually confusing and amateurish. Figure 4.14B aligns the left sides of both columns of elements, and it looks much more serene. Figure 4.14C is controversial; many experts state that you shouldn't combine both *right justification* (on the labels) and *left justification* (on the form fields) on the same page. Nonetheless, it does look much calmer than the first example, and arguably even calmer than the second example. Moreover, the proximity of the labels to the input areas makes it easier to see how the each label relates to a form element. In any case, the more you can align elements on the layout, following the invisible lines we examined earlier, the more cohesive the page looks.

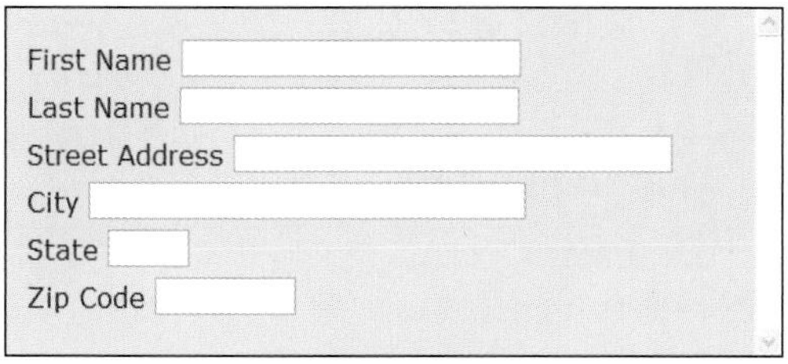

A. No Alignment

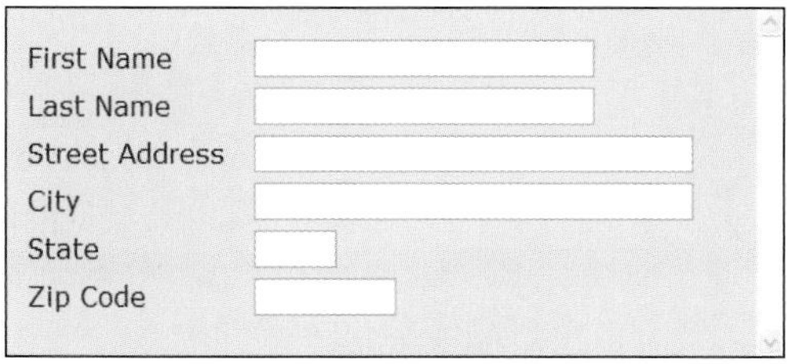

B. Left Alignment

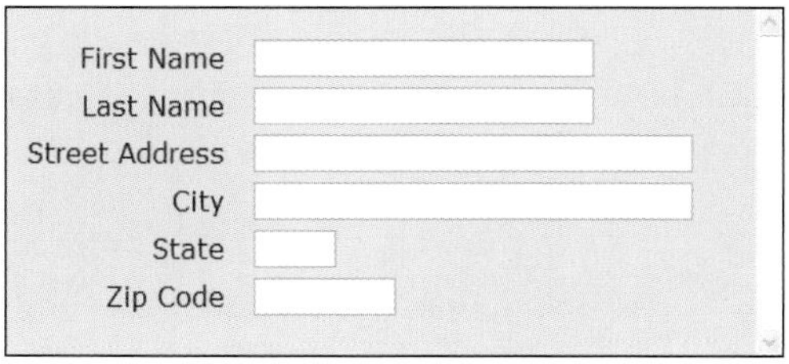

C. Left and Right Alignment

FIGURE 4.14 Form Alignment

The form we just looked at illustrates the use of an underlying *grid*, the framework upon which most layouts are built. A grid is nothing more than an invisible structure of rows and columns—a structure that has been used in newspapers and magazines for decades. A grid helps to unify the page, because there is a clear structure that the viewer perceives, even if only subconsciously.

Tables and `<div>`s establish the grid. **FIGURE 4.15** turns on the table borders from Figure 4.14C so that we can see the "spacer" columns that ensure "breathing room" between elements on the page. CSS margins and padding could be used instead to provide the same breathing room.

FIGURE 4.15 Underlying Grid from Figure 4.14C

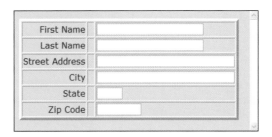

Chunk related information.

Organizing the various page elements into *chunks* (clusters of related elements) also helps to make the page appear to be simpler. A news portal like www.msn.com uses several obvious chunks, including headers like "MSNBC News," "FOX Sports," "Also on MSN," and "Money," all so that users can zero in on the topics that interest them without being forced to read through the links that don't.

The tools used to chunk content are examples of Krause's *visual adhesive*: a graphic element that forms what he describes in *Layout Index* as "a connection between the scattered elements while adding aesthetic interest at the same time." Visual adhesive holds the page together aesthetically as well as conceptually, so that the various elements don't seem to be plunked randomly on the page.

Consider using some type of visual adhesive if your page seems to lack interest or appear disjointed. Visual adhesive tools include the following:

- Prominent headings and subheadings. Don't overdo headings, however. For instance, if you have the label "Search" next to a search input field, you don't need a "Search" heading as well.

- Bulleted or numbered lists.

- Indentation. Elements that are indented to the right seem to be subordinate to any non-indented item above.

- Single spacing (or other close spacing) *within* groups or chunks, and double spacing (or other looser spacing) *between* groups or chunks.

- Similarity of style—fonts, colors, graphic styles, and so on—to group elements together.

- Horizontal and vertical rules (using `<hr>`, graphics, one-sided borders, or background colors on skinny table columns) to both separate and join.

- Table, cell, and `<div>` borders. Much of the time, table borders are invisible, particularly when a table or `<div>` is used only as a positioning aid. Still, borders have gotten much more attractive, diverse, and versatile over the years. Graceful CSS borders can be specified differently for each side of the element and can sport various colors, styles, and widths.

- Varied background colors or images on tables, cells, and `<div>`s.

- Sidebars (such as those used in this book) and links to pop-up windows. Both serve the same purpose as footnotes in a book; they pull peripheral information out of the main flow of the page. A definition for a term, for instance, might appear in a pop-up window if the user clicks on the term, conserving visual space in the main window while at the same time allowing visitors who need the information easy access to it, and visitors who aren't interested to ignore the link entirely.

- The `<fieldset>` tag, shown in **FIGURE 4.16**, which has the advantage of being recognized by screen readers as a grouping tool. See the sidebar for the `<fieldset>` HTML.

FIGURE 4.16 Fieldset Tag as Visual Adhesive

THE `<FIELDSET>` TAG

Figure 4.16 shows a chunk of related elements wrapped in a `<fieldset>` tag. An optional `<legend>` tag specifies the header for the chunk.

Here is the HTML:

```
<form>
<fieldset>
   <legend>Hobbies</legend>
```

```
    <p>Please check all topics of interest: <br />
    <input name="hobby" type="checkbox" value="fishing"
       checked="checked" /> Fishing<br />
    <input name="hobby" type="checkbox" value="golf" /> Golf<br />
    <input name="hobby" type="checkbox" value="tennis" /> Tennis</p>
</fieldset>
</form>
```

The `<fieldset>` tag and associated CSS may behave inconsistently in different browsers. For instance, colors may work for the border but not for the legend text, and adding CSS styling at all can result in squaring off the rounded corners. Be sure to test thoroughly.

The more complex the page, the more important it is that you use organizational tools like these to chunk the elements. Notice that the MSN portal we discussed earlier uses many of these tricks to great advantage.

Manipulate contrast to create a visual hierarchy.

Contrast is the difference in the characteristics of various elements such as line or shape or color. Simply stated, any item that is *different* stands out. For instance, a curvy shape contrasts with a page full of sharply angular shapes, and fire-engine red contrasts with a page of mainly pastel colors like soft pink and pale blue. Contrast is the primary tool for creating visual stimulation and emphasis, imbuing the page with impact.

Varying the contrast between elements leads not only to an interesting page, but also creates a *visual hierarchy* such that the most important elements are the ones that stand out on *first read*—the first impression users get of a page. Web guru extraordinaire Lynda Weinman calls this the "strategic prioritization of information." We don't want every element on the page to have equal weight, all clamoring for attention. We should make the elements that we want the users to notice the most prominent. Navigation? Announcement of a sale? A news flash? We emphasize those "most worthy" elements by using one or more visual characteristics that contrast with—that stand out from—the other elements on the page. In doing so, we manipulate our visitors' focus.

For example, **FIGURE 4.17A** has no visual hierarchy. Not only would people be disinclined to read the entire announcement, it would also be difficult for them to pick out the most important information, such as the date and time. Readers would be puzzled and confused by such a lack of visual hierarchy. **FIGURE 4.17B**, on the other hand, uses type size, density, spacing, and alignment to provide a clear visual hierarchy that makes the information easier to comprehend.

Presenting Yourself to Advantage in a Second Interview bySusan Smith of Career Services. Do you want to esure that job offer? Come to this presentation and we'll tell you everything you need to know in order to impress recruiters, from your attire to your attitude to how to answer that sticky question, "What level of compensation do you expect?" We'll even provide free pizza and sodas! When: Tuesday, February 28, 3:30 p.m. Where: Computer Science Building, PM 253. Registration required. Sign up at the Department of Computer Science, Computer Science Building, PM 460. Presented by the Department of Computer Science and Career Services, Northern Illinois University.

A. No Visual Hierarchy

FIGURE 4.17 Contrast Used to Create a Visual Hierarchy

Presenting Yourself to Advantage in a Second Interview
by
Susan Smith of Career Services

Do you want to esure that job offer? Come to this presentation and we'll tell you everything you need to know in order to impress recruiters, from your attire to your attitude to how to answer that sticky question, "What level of compensation do you expect?"

We'll even provide **free pizza and sodas**!

When: Tuesday, February 28, 3:30 p.m.

Where: Computer Science Building, PM 253.

Registration required. Sign up at the Department of Computer Science, Computer Science Building, PM 460.

Presented by the Department of Computer Science and Career Services, Northern Illinois University

B. Strong Visual Hierarchy

The web page in **FIGURE 4.18** has a distinct visual hierarchy. Our eyes are drawn first to the "Creative Suite 3" box because of the bright colors, distinctive background image, and large size. This element has more *visual weight* than the other elements on the page. Obviously, this site is serious about promoting its Creative Suite 3 resources.

FIGURE 4.18 Web Page with a Strong Visual Hierarchy ("Adobe Create Suite 3 Resource Center," www.peachpit.com/ promotions/promotion. aspx?promo=135771 as it appeared on September 6, 2007. ©Pearson Education, Peachpit Press. All rights reserved.)

In any given case, contrast can be subtle or extreme, depending upon how much impact we want it to have. **FIGURE 4.19** illustrates the characteristics that we can manipulate to create contrast, including:

- Line: thick versus thin versus implied (invisible), smooth versus nervous, solid versus interrupted.

- Shape: circular versus rectangular, angular versus curvy, simple versus complex.

Line Contrast

Shape Contrast

Size Contrast

FIGURE 4.19 Contrast

Color Contrast

Texture Contrast

Typography

This shows typographical contrast, such as FONT, **bold**, and *italic*.

Typography Contrast

This shows focus contrast.

Focus Contrast

Space Contrast

Direction Contrast

Style Contrast

- Size: large versus small, tall versus short. All other things being equal, large is more attention-attracting than small, so the most important elements on the page should usually be the largest. Even otherwise nondescript content text can take center stage if placed in the largest block on the page.

- Color: one color versus its *complementary* (opposite) color (think red versus green), bright versus dull, light versus dark, sophisticated versus crayon colors. Generally, the brighter, more intense colors attract attention over duller, less intense colors. Another way to use color is to reverse the colors of foreground and background in selected areas. For instance, if the majority of the page is black text on a white background, the reverse of white text on a black background stands out.

- Texture: smooth versus textured, solid color versus pattern.

- Typography: bold or italic versus normal, elaborate typeface versus a simple one. Big, bold, and elaborate are the most likely to attract focus.

- Focus: sharp versus blurred. Sharp focus usually draws attention the most successfully.

- Space: congested versus open, *positive* (filled) versus *negative* (unfilled), near versus far (an optical illusion in two-dimensional space), two-dimensional versus a three-dimensional illusion (using perspective, shadowing, or change in size, color, or texture).

- Direction: horizontal versus vertical versus diagonal, direct versus meandering.

- Style: representational versus abstract, cartoony versus photo-realistic, simple versus elaborate.

Exercise restraint when using contrast. Each time we add another contrasting element to a page, we are diluting the contrast of any other *focal points* (areas that draw our attention). Take care not to provide so much contrast on the page that none of the elements has focus. In short, when visual chaos reigns, visual hierarchy vanishes.

Provide white space.

Include plenty of *white space* (unused space, also called *negative space*), even if the "white space" is actually red or blue or chartreuse. White space provides the eyes with respite, imparting a feeling of "breathing room." In the web page in **FIGURE 4.20**, we see a hefty amount of white space (in this case, actually black space) that contributes to the clean, elegant, and dramatic look of the site.

FIGURE 4.20   The more white (or black) space that surrounds a page element, the more that element is emphasized. ("Night Drive," www.csszengarden.com/?cssfile=064/064.css, by Dave Shea)

Manipulate visual balance.

Visual balance refers to the placement of items on the page. *Symmetrical balance*, in which similar elements are placed equally on both sides of a center line, provides balance by default, as in **FIGURE 4.21**. Symmetrical balance can be mind-numbingly boring: centered heading, centered photo, centered text block. However, it doesn't have to be that way; you can instill "excitement" into this rigid structure. For example, in the case of Figure 4.21, symmetrical balance works well because the page uses texture, and graphics, and other variations to provide visual "relief."

We can often achieve a more exciting and dynamic visual balance with *asymmetrical balance*, as shown in **FIGURE 4.22**. For instance, a large, heavy graphic on one side of the page might be balanced by several smaller graphics on the other side. The design in Figure 4.22 balances the large block of text in the lower left with the smaller but more dramatic vertical skyline on the right.

To create a feeling of tension and unrest, you might purposely make a page obviously unbalanced, as in **FIGURE 4.23**. The page is heavily weighted to the left and bottom. In this case, unbalanced works well because it gives the page a very modern, edgy feel.

FIGURE 4.21 Symmetrical
Balance ("Hoops—
Tournament Edition,"
www.csszengarden.
com/?cssfile=167/167.
css, by David Marshall, Jr.,
Art Director, http://www.
pixelflexmedia.com/)

FIGURE 4.22 Asymmetrical
Balance. ("Zen City Morning,"
www.csszengarden.com/
?cssfile=177/177.css, by Ray
Henry, www.reh3.com)

FIGURE 4.23 Unbalanced
(www.pixelflexmedia.com/,
by David Marshall, Jr.,
Art Director)

Choose a composition center.

Just as symmetrical balance can be boring, so can be a *composition center* (area of focus) that is dead-center in the middle of a page. Think of professional landscape photos; only rarely does the horizon line up across the exact horizontal center, because a centered horizon is often unexciting. Instead, photographers normally position the horizon either one third or two thirds of the way down on the photo. That is, follow the *rule of thirds* by dividing the page into thirds horizontally and vertically, and use one or more of the intersection points as the focus of interest. **FIGURE 4.24** shows image-division using the rule of thirds, with *sweet spots* (intersecting points) indicated by superimposed dots.

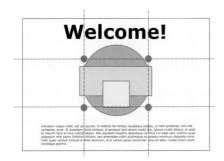

A fairly lackluster composition.

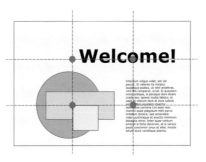

Because the major areas of emphasis are near the sweet spots, this compostion seems both more dynamic and more professional.

FIGURE 4.24 Composition Center (Diagrams courtesy of Jeff Cernauske. "A SimpleSunrise," www.csszengarden.com/ ?cssfile=158/158.css, by Rob Soule)

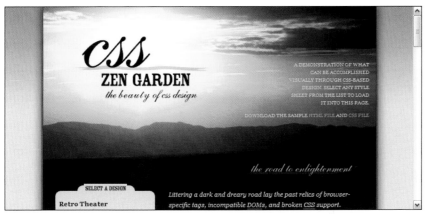

The off-center CSS Zen Garden area superimposed on the sunset draws our eye first.

Employ the golden-mean rectangle.

When creating rectangular shapes, keep in mind that the *golden-mean rectangle* is the most visually pleasing. A golden-mean rectangle has an approximate width-to-height ratio of 1 to 1.6, as illustrated in **FIGURE 4.25**. For example, a rectangle that is three inches tall and five inches wide is a golden-mean rectangle, as is one that is five inches tall and eight inches wide. It's no accident that these particular dimensions are used for many common objects, such as flags and photographs.

FIGURE 4.25 Dimensions of a Golden-Mean Rectangle

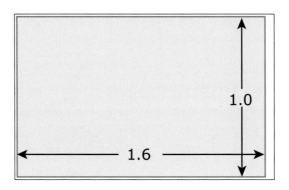

Round out a "rectangles only" layout.

MORE ON THE GMR

For more on the fascinating mathematics behind the golden-mean rectangle, see Kimberly Elam's *Geometry of Design*.

Golden-mean rectangles notwithstanding, pages filled with nothing but rectangles—visible table cells, rectangular photos, horizontal rules, blocks of text—can become boring. For variety, you might try to include some rounded or irregular shapes:

- Use rounded corner "borders" on tables, cells, or `<div>`s (as in Figure 4.12, with the rounded-corner images), or irregular borders.

- Use an image editor to round or blur the edges of an image, or cut out the background entirely, replacing it with transparency, as for the Chanel watch photograph in Figure 4.22.

- Use graphics that cross over the implied background grid, as with the butterfly that crosses over into another column in **FIGURE 4.26**.

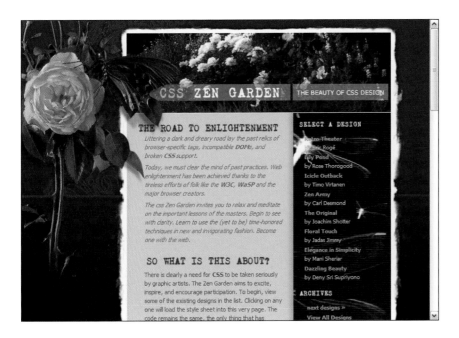

FIGURE 4.26 Breaking the Grid ("Butterfly Effect", www.csszengarden.com/ ?cssfile=154/154.css, by Kevin Linkous, www.sitemaker.us/)

Rectangles of uninterrupted text can be boring, too. To add pizzazz, you can employ the following techniques, some of which are illustrated in **FIGURE 4.27**:

- Snake text blocks around images.

- Vary *leading* (spacing between lines).

- Interrupt long blocks of text with larger headlines or *pull quotes* (quotations or text excerpts in larger type and set apart in a box).

- Employ *decorative caps* (an initial capital letter that is enlarged and some-how embellished) and *drop caps* (an initial capital letter that is enlarged and descends below the line of text).

Four score and seven years ago our fathers brought forth on this continent, a new nation, conceived in Liberty, and dedicated to the proposition that all men are created equal.

Now we are engaged in a great civil war, testing whether that nation, or any nation so conceived and so dedicated, can long endure.

Snaking Text around a Graphic and Varied Leading

The Gettysburg Address

Four score and seven years ago our fathers brought forth on this continent, a new nation, conceived in Liberty, and dedicated to the proposition that all men are created equal.

"CONCEIVED IN LIBERTY"

Headline and Pull Quote

Four score and seven years ago our fathers brought forth on this conti-nent, a new nation, conceived in Liberty, and dedicated to the proposition that all men are created equal.

Now we are engaged in a great civil war, testing whether that nation, or any nation so conceived and so dedicated, can long endure.

Decorative Drop Cap

FIGURE 4.27 Breaking Up Text

Striking a Balance

Too much serenity is monotonous. Too much contrast and stimulation are visually chaotic. To avoid either of those design problems, there must be a certain amount of serenity, but not too much, and a certain amount of contrast, but not too much. If resolved skillfully, the tension between serenity and stimulation can offer a visual harmony that balances the page. Generally, it's most effective to make all of the elements on the page uniform first, and then choose only a few things to tweak in order to add contrast.

Positioning Page Elements

Web surfers have become accustomed to certain layout conventions, in particular, the arrangement with main navigation horizontally across the top of the page and/or vertically down the left side. This inverted "L" page layout has been popular throughout the history of the web, for good reason:

- The top and left areas display on every user's screen, regardless of the user's window size and resolution. As a result, this area is the screen's most valuable real estate and is the most consistently visible place for such critical page components as the logo and site navigation. If those same elements were at the bottom right side of the window, they might very well disappear in a downsized window or on a lower-resolution display.

- The Western world reads left to right, top to bottom, so our eyes are trained to land on that upper-left corner first.

Visitors are so comfortable with this inverted "L" for navigation that they don't need to think about it at all. That's not to say that you can never put links anywhere else. Nonetheless, if you are going to violate traditional expectations, you must overcompensate by making the new conventions crystal clear; "road less traveled" navigational elements must be even more prominent and even more consistent in order to make up for their unconventional location.

● ● ●

ONE GOVERNMENT SITE RECOMMENDS RIGHT-SIDE NAVIGATION!

A U.S. Government usability site actually recommends right-side navigation because there is less mouse movement needed between the navigation and the scrollbar. See www.usability.gov/guidelines/navigation.html#four.

The most important information on the page should be "above the fold;" that is, it should be visible when the user first opens the page, without scrolling vertically. The term "above the fold" comes from the newspaper industry, in which the most important or intriguing articles are deliberately put on the top half of the first page so that they are visible when the folded newspapers are stacked in sales racks. It's the same idea for a web page; only if you can capture a visitor's attention with that first view will he or she bother to scroll down the page. Therefore, use the area "above the fold" to capture your visitors. All of the commercial web sites that we have seen in this chapter have done that.

Where will the "fold" be when a visitor opens a page? We never know for sure, because of all of the resolution and window size inconsistencies discussed earlier. A rule of thumb is to assume the fold is at about 390 pixels, which is approximately the size of a window opened at full-screen in an 800 x 600 display.

Required Page Elements

The page layout is a visual framework from which we hang the content and graphics. That visual framework should include the following elements on every page:

- Logo and company identification. Keep in mind that a visitor doesn't always come in the "front door," that is, the home page. Therefore, we must be sure to let her know where she has landed if she is dropped into the middle of our site by virtue of a bookmark or a *deep link* (a link that bypasses the home page).

- Page identification or title. Without that, a visitor doesn't know the purpose of the page she is currently viewing.

- Main navigation, including a link to the home page. After all, we hope that the visitor will continue to browse the site further after viewing the current page.

- Local navigation (if needed) for getting to sub-pages.

- A standard footer, if appropriate. A footer might provide copyright information, date of last update, or links to privacy and legal notices. Additionally, there might be a repeat of the main navigation that appears at the top of the page. Such bottom navigation eliminates the need for visitors to scroll back to the top in order to move forward. It's often presented in the form of small text links, even if the navigation at the top of the page is graphical.

The Home Page

The home page has some unique requirements of its own. Since it's the site's entrance point and its most valuable real estate, it should serve as table of contents for the site as a whole, as well as indicate how to access the content. The more important areas of content should, of course, have more prominent focus. It's always good to try to reveal at least a bit of real content on the page, too, not just navigation, so that visitors come away with a better feel for what the rest of the site contains.

Still, the home page shouldn't contain elements that don't have relevance to the site as a whole. For instance, it would be a waste of valuable home page space if Amazon were to report the results of the company's softball team there. Customers, the primary audience of the site, simply wouldn't care. Keep in mind that choosing content for the home page is often a political war between entities and departments in an organization, all of whom think that their own content deserves to be featured.

Storyboarding: Sketching the Layout

At some point, we need to put the preliminary layout for the individual pages down on paper or into digital format—a process called *storyboarding*. The first stage of this process is a *grayscale* sketch (shades of gray), with no color, no real content (use "greeked," or nonsense, text) and no graphics (although placeholders for future graphics should be indicated). This grayscale version is sometimes called a *wireframe* as well as a storyboard. **FIGURE 4.28** shows an initial, hand-drawn storyboard sketch for a simple page layout.

FIGURE 4.28 Storyboard: Layout Sketch

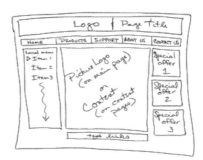

The purpose of a grayscale storyboard is to show the layout and underlying grid of the page: where the logo, navigation, page title, content, and main images will be located. We deliberately omit graphics and color at this stage because we want everyone to focus on critiquing just the layout.

Only after the grayscale sketch has been approved should we progress to a story-board that includes color and graphics, sometimes called a color *comp* (screen mock-up or prototype). To create the comp, some designers use an image-editing program such as Adobe Photoshop or Fireworks, while others prefer creating the comp as a fully-coded HTML page. Let's look at each method.

Using an Image Editor to Create a Comp

In general, designers who are artists first, web developers second, often prefer sketching the comp in an image-editing program, rather than creating a skeletal HTML page. Sketching this way is often faster than writing HTML, and it provides more freedom. That very freedom is also the primary danger: Any number of won-derful graphic designs simply cannot be translated into efficient and effective HTML code without making compromises in either the design or the HTML. As a result, sketching in an image editor is a viable method only if the designer keeps in mind the limitations of HTML and is willing to compromise the design when he runs up against those limitations.

If you build your comp in an image editor, many of your graphic elements are already completed, or at least close to being completed, when the comp is finished. For instance, if you are happy with the logo that you designed for the comp, you can export just that small section of the overall comp image to a file that is then inserted into the HTML with an `<img>` tag.

Using HTML to Create a Comp

Building a comp in HTML is often preferred by designers who are techies first, designers second. Although somewhat more time-consuming than sketching in a image-editing program, this method keeps the designer grounded in the reality of what HTML can and cannot do well, thereby circumventing the need for a site rede-sign after someone figures out that the design simply won't work in HTML. As a final benefit, creating the comp in HTML results in a skeleton HTML file that can evolve into the production web pages.

Page Templates

Either way, after the layout sketches have been tweaked and approved, you are ready to create layout templates for the site. These templates, which show layout and other design characteristics, are content-free HTML files that are the basis for each new page as the site is constructed—the consistent foundation on which you "pour" the content during that construction phase.

BONUS TOPIC:
Reusable Code

See the book's web site for more on using page templates, server-side includes, and other techniques for reusable code.

There are two ways to build a template:

- Create and save a standard HTML page that contains the layout elements but no content, and manually copy that empty page into the HTML editor each time you add a new page to the site.

- Use the template-creation features built in to many development environments, such as Dreamweaver. The template starts out like a normal web page, but you designate some areas of the template page as being protected (modifiable only from within the template) and others as unprotected (modifiable within individual pages, for the variable content). Each new page is simply linked to the template, thereby loading the entire standard page layout. That standard layout can be altered only within the template, not within the page itself, but it then becomes available to all of the pages that link to it. Thus, changing page layout for hundreds of pages might well involve changing only a single template.

Page Layout and Accessibility

Building page layout so that pages are accessible is challenging, to say the least. Tables are particularly problematic for the visually impaired. Screen readers read tables from left to right across each row, and then drop down to do the same on the next row. Automatically reading a table in this order causes two problems:

- Many tables aren't designed to be linearized; that is, read left to right, top to bottom.

- By the time a screen reader reads a cell entry in a data table, it's no longer clear which headers apply for that cell data.

Remedies for such problems in data tables (as opposed to layout tables) include:

- Use `title`, `caption`, and/or `summary` attributes to describe the purpose and overall layout of the table.

- Use the structural markup tags `thead`, `tfoot`, `tbody`, `th`, `colgroup`, and `col`. Screen readers emphasize content within these tags in such a way that the structure is clearer.

- Assign each column or row header a unique `id` attribute, and then use the `headers="headerID1 headerID2... "` attribute to associate the appropriate data cells with their headers. The latest screen readers are able to read the appropriate header information for each data cell.

- Use the `abbr` attribute to provide a shorter description of repetitive elements in appropriate header or data cells.

For both data tables and layout tables:

- Avoid nested tables. They are tricky for screen readers to interpret correctly.

- Try to structure tables (both data tables and layout tables) so that they make sense when read left to right, top to bottom. Read them aloud as a test to see if they make sense when linearized. Provide an alternative but equivalent page if it's impossible to structure a single page so that it makes sense for all audiences.

But of course we're not designing with just tables, and we need to remember that accessibility standards apply to other layout tags as well:

- Convey page structure with structural markup tags (header tags, blockquote, lists, etc.), because screen readers read such structural markup in a different tone of voice. Don't use structural markup tags just for visual formatting, such as header tags to provide boldface or `<blockquote>` to specify indentation.

- Structural markup tags may be *augmented with* but should not be *replaced by* visual cues, since the visually impaired don't have access to such cues.

- `<h2>` elements should follow `<h1>` elements, `<h3>` elements should follow `<h2>` elements, and so on. Don't skip levels (for example, `<h1>` directly to `<h3>`) in order to get the formatting you need. Instead, keep the levels in numeric progression and use CSS to alter formatting.

- For ordered lists, use a numbering scheme that independently conveys the level of each list item. For instance, compound numbers such as the following are more informative about context than simple numbers:

  1. top-level item

     1.1 subordinate item

        1.1.1 sub-sub item

An alternative to compound numbers would be a list that changes the numbering scheme for different levels, such as:

  I. top-level item

     A. subordinate item

        1. sub-sub item

- Use the `<ul>` and `<li>` elements for bulleted lists. If you aren't happy with the default bullet styles, use CSS to change them.

- Although accessibility guidelines encourage the use of style sheets, you should still design documents so that they make sense without them (that is, the document should be written in a "logical" order). For example, when an HTML document is rendered without associated style sheets, it must still be possible to read the document. Then, apply style sheets to achieve visual effects using properties such as float and position.

Summary

Although variety and contrast can be a good thing, too much visual noise will make the page visually confusing and overwhelming. A page should look clean and well-organized even if there are many elements on it. You must walk the line between providing enough contrast to keep the viewer on target and stimulated, yet not so much stimulation that he or she becomes overwhelmed. At the same time, you must provide enough continuity from page to page that the users are always aware that they are still on your site.

Design Checklist

The following checklist serves two functions: to summarize the major points and "rules" presented in this chapter, and to help you ensure you've done all you should before finalizing any web site you are creating.

File Size and Resolution—*Did you:*

- Limit file sizes appropriately?

- Take into consideration browser inconsistencies?

- Pull most of the CSS and JavaScript out into external files that are reused throughout the site?

- Reuse graphics, audio, and video from page to page?

- Avoid gratuitous graphics, animation, and sound?

- Use smaller images rather than larger ones whenever possible?

- Minimize the number of unique navigation buttons?

- Determine an appropriate page size, in pixels?

- Avoid horizontal scrolling?

- Provide a "print page" option, when appropriate?

Building Blocks of Page Layout—*Did you:*

- Choose between frames, Flash, tables, and `<div>`s appropriately, when laying out the page?

- Choose appropriately between solid and liquid layout, and then control them properly?

- Make use of line (rules, borders, outlines, invisible grids) to organize your space, separating or connecting portions of your page?

- Select an appropriate type of line for the mood you want to convey?

- Choose appropriate shapes to add interest, movement, division, and connection to your page?

- Employ shapes (graphics, multiple column layouts, etc.) to break up overwhelming blocks of text?

- Squint at the page to see if the arrangement of shapes is pleasing?

- Apply color as an organizer for the page?

Visual Harmony—*Did you:*

- Provide continuity of mood, color scheme, layout, navigation, and graphics throughout all of the pages in the site in order to promote visual harmony, the balance between serenity and stimulation?

- Limit the number of elements on the page?

- Repeat elements for visual consistency?

- Align elements within an underlying grid?

- Employ visual adhesive (headings, bulleted and numbered lists, indentation, spacing, proximity, similarity and difference in style, horizontal and vertical rules, background colors, borders, sidebars, and `<fieldset>`) to chunk related information?

- Use line, shape, size, color, texture, typography, style, focus, space, and direction to manipulate contrast, thereby creating a visual hierarchy?

- Avoid creating so much contrast that you lose track of focal points?

- Provide enough white space to give respite from a sense of visual clutter?

- Choose an appropriate balance for the mood you want to portray, such as symmetrical balance for a calming mood, asymmetrical for interest, or unbalanced for tension?

- Avoid using the center of the page as the composition center?

- When creating rectangular shapes, consider following the proportions of the golden-mean rectangle (1 to 1.6)?
- Break up a "rectangles only" layout with rounded or blurred edges, graphics that cross the implied grid, masked backgrounds on photographs, graphics with irregular shapes, text snaked around graphics, varied leading, headlines, pull quotes, decorative caps, drop caps, and pop-up windows?

Positioning Page Elements—*Did you:*

- Provide obvious navigation on every page, usually on the top or left side?
- Position the most important information above the fold?
- Include the logo and company identification, page identification or title, main navigation (including a link to the home page), local navigation (if used) and a standard footer (if used) on every page?
- Make sure that the home page serves as an appealing "table of contents" for the entire site?
- Include only important elements on the home page?

Storyboarding—*Did you:*

- First create a grayscale wireframe of the page, in order to evaluate the layout without the distractions of content, color, and images?
- Create a color comp of the page, using either an image-editing program or HTML?
- Use a template to create an appropriate, standardized layout for the site?

Accessibility—*Did you:*

- Use style sheets but also design the document so that it also makes sense without them?
- For data tables, use `title`, `caption`, `summary`, `headers`, `id`, and `abbr` attributes as well as structural markup?
- Avoid nested tables?
- Try to structure both data and layout tables so that they make sense when read left to right, top to bottom? If that is impossible, provide an alternative but equivalent page?
- Convey page structure with structural markup tags?
- For ordered lists, use a numbering scheme that conveys the level of each list item?
- Use style sheets to change a list's bullet style or bullet image, if needed?

CHAPTER FIVE

Color

FROM *COLOR HARMONY FOR THE WEB*, BY CAILIN BOYLE:

"The relation of color to mood is so ingrained that it is like a trigger response."

FROM *COLOR: THE BEST WORK FROM THE WEB*, BY JEFF CARLSON, TOBY MALINA, AND GLENN FLEISHMAN.

"The challenge for all designers is to make each color count, whether you're drawing from a deep pool or a paint-by-numbers scheme."

No one can deny that color "colors" how we react to what we see. Color schemes evoke moods; they can be playful or sophisticated, cold or warm, chic or dingy, energetic or calm, gloomy or sparkling, elegant or childish, earthy or romantic, professional or campy, fiery or ominous. Color choices define a web site at a glance. Consequently, color can be a web designer's most persuasive and powerful tool.

Color has been used as a communication tool for centuries. In the print world, color has been, of course, an inestimable and abundant benefit, but also, unfortunately, expensive and (once printed) inflexible. Thus, web color has a distinct advantage over printed color, because web color is completely free. Additionally, web designers can modify complete color schemes easily and on a whim, without concern for costs.

Still, using web color effectively can be challenging. The mood evoked by a color scheme is influenced by:

- Commonly accepted psychological effects. For example, yellow is usually viewed as a happy color, while red is considered to be energizing.

- Individual tastes, based on complex emotional responses, not logic. For instance, some people feel black is depressing, while others view it as dramatic.

- Age. Children and teenagers often have very different color tastes than their elders.

- Gender. As a whole, men and women often prefer very different colors.

- Culture: Different cultures from around the world often have very different color aesthetics and societal customs and mores associated with particular colors.

Another problem is that web color, though free, can be somewhat limited in scope. If as a child you were quite content with a box of ten Crayola crayons, you won't have a problem with those constraints. If you felt severely restricted with a gigantic box of 512 crayons, you might find that the colors you crave may not be easily available, especially if you are restricted by the colors available on older computer systems. Creating a color scheme with a limited palette can be intimidating or frustrating, even for experienced designers (more about this limited palette later in the chapter).

Note: Computer screens and the print media present colors in completely different ways, so the examples in this book will not look exactly as they would on a computer screen.

Color Theory

We must first understand centuries of traditional color theory before we can understand how to translate that knowledge to color manipulation on that newfangled device, the computer screen.

The Color Wheel

A color wheel graphically represents the relationships between colors. The three major spokes of the traditional color wheel are the *primary colors*: red, yellow, and blue, as shown in **FIGURE 5.1**. Any color of the rainbow can be created by mixing some combination of the three primary colors plus black and white.

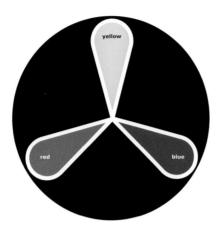

FIGURE 5.1 Primary Colors

Mixing adjacent primary colors generates *secondary colors,* so that yellow mixed with red produces orange, blue mixed with yellow produces green, and red mixed with blue produces purple (**FIGURE 5.2**).

FIGURE 5.2 Secondary Colors

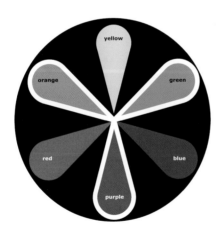

Moving right along, **FIGURE 5.3** illustrates how mixing adjacent secondary and primary colors yields *tertiary colors*; yellow mixed with orange produces yellow-orange, orange mixed with red produces red-orange, and so on.

FIGURE 5.3 Tertiary Colors

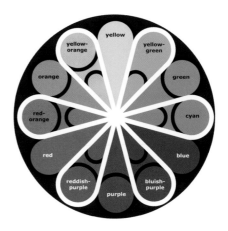

Blending all of the primary, all of the secondary, or all of the tertiary colors produces a very dark brownish-black color, as shown in **FIGURE 5.4**.

True neutral colors are black, white, and various shades of gray. Black and white cannot be obtained by mixing other colors, but you can obtain gray by mixing black with white. You can also obtain gray by mixing opposing colors on the color wheel, called *complementary colors*, as shown in Figure 5.4.

FIGURE 5.4 Complementary Colors

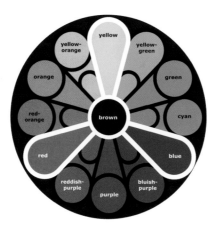

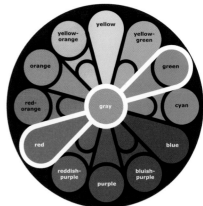

Mixing Three or More Evenly Spaced Colors to Obtain a Blackish-brown

Mixing Complementary Colors to Obtain Gray

TABLE 5.1 THE TRADITIONAL COLOR WHEEL

Traditional Color Wheel	Color Names	Derivation
Primary Colors	Yellow Blue Red	Not applicable
Secondary Colors	Green Purple Orange	Mixing two adjacent primary colors
Tertiary Colors	Yellow-green Cyan Bluish-purple Reddish-purple Red-orange Yellow-orange	Mixing one primary color and an adjacent secondary color
Neutrals	Black White Gray Blackish-brown	Not applicable Not applicable Mixing white with black or mixing two *complementary colors* (colors opposite one another on the color wheel) Mixing three evenly-spaced colors around the color wheel

Color Attributes

Color has four specific attributes: hue, saturation, value, and temperature.

Hue

Hue (or *chroma*) is the technical term for a specific color, like blue, green, or blue-green. Each of the separate wedges in the color wheel is a distinct hue. Hues can be mixed together to obtain other hues, just as red and yellow can be mixed to obtain orange.

Value

Value refers to the lightness or darkness of a color. Mixing white with a hue produces a *tint*, while mixing black with a hue produces a *shade*. **FIGURE 5.5** shows mixing pure red with white to form a pink tint, and mixing red with black to form a burgundy shade. Keep in mind that a *shade* of one relatively light hue, such as yellow, could well have a lighter value than a *tint* of another relatively dark color, such as purple. Tints like the pink in Figure 5.5 are said to be *high-key*, which is merely another way of saying they are light in value. Shades like the burgundy in the figure are *low-key*, or dark in value.

FIGURE 5.5 Tints (left) and Shades (right)

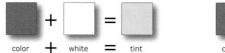
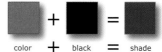

Saturation

Saturation refers to the level of purity or intensity of a hue. A *fully-saturated hue* is one that has not been mixed with black, white, gray, or the hue's complementary color, because any of those additions desaturates the color. Fire-engine red, Kelly green, and cobalt blue are fully-saturated hues, as shown in **FIGURE 5.6**.

FIGURE 5.6
Highly-Saturated Hues (left)
versus Desaturated Hues
(right)

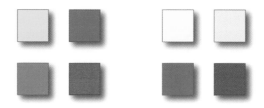

Another way to decrease a hue's saturation is to mix it with gray or with a small amount of the hue's complementary color. The result is called a *tone*, from which we get the term "toned down." See **FIGURE 5.7** for examples of similar tones of red being created in two separate ways.

FIGURE 5.7 Tones.
Red Tone Created by Mixing
with Gray (left). Red Tone
Created by Mixing with
Red's Complementary Color,
Green (right)

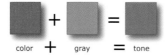
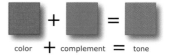

Less saturated colors, like tones and shades, are by definition less intense, which is beneficial when you are looking for sophisticated, earthy, or rich colors. On the other hand, they can also appear drab, dull, or grungy. That's not to say that grungy is a bad thing; it all depends on the mood you want to evoke.

Temperature

Color temperature refers to whether the color "feels" warm or cool. *Warm colors* are based on yellow, orange, and red, while *cool colors* are based on purple, blue, and green. **FIGURE 5.8** identifies warm and cool colors.

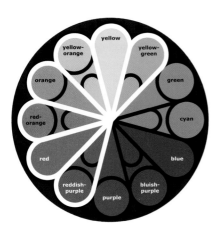
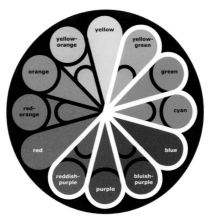

Warm Colors   Cool Colors

FIGURE 5.8 Color Temperature

TABLE 5.2 COLOR ATTRIBUTES

Color Attributes	Attribute Values	Explanation
Hue	Any hue on the color wheel	The base hue, unadulterated by white, black, gray, or the hue's complementary color.
Value	Light value	• *Tint:* a hue mixed with white to produce a lighter value. • *Light-valued tone:* a hue mixed with a light gray or a tint of the hue's complementary color.
	Dark value	• *Shade:* a hue mixed with black to produce a darker value. • *Dark-valued tone:* a hue mixed with a dark gray or a shade of the hue's complementary color.
Saturation	High saturation (high intensity)	A pure, unadulterated hue, of high intensity.
	Low saturation (low intensity)	• *Tint:* a hue mixed with white. • *Shade:* a hue mixed with black. • *Tone:* a hue mixed with gray or the hue's complementary color.
Temperature	Cool Warm	Greens, blues, purples Yellows, oranges, reds

Subtractive Color Mode: Reflected Light

• • •

MEASURING LIGHT

Light can be measured as either waves or particles. A full description goes beyond the scope of this book, and the resulting knowledge is of little practical use for manipulating colors on the web.

Color is produced by light waves. A beam of white light is actually composed of all of the colors of the visible spectrum. If such a beam of light shines through a prism, it splits into its individual waves, so that we see the entire rainbow of colors.

On the other hand, when a beam of white light strikes an object, the object *absorbs* some of the color waves while *reflecting* others. The color that we see is the color that the surface *reflects*. For instance, when we look at a yellow sunflower, all colors of the light spectrum are absorbed by the sunflower except for the color yellow, which is reflected and thus perceived by our eyes. This color system is termed the *subtractive color mode*, because colors that are *absorbed* by the object are *subtracted* from the colors that we can see. Subtractive color mode is what's going on when we look at any object that does not project its own light, and it is the base upon which traditional color theory (and traditional art) rests.

Additive Color Mode: Projected Light

Web color works quite differently. Instead of using *reflected* light, a computer monitor uses *projected* light, much as the sun, a light bulb, and a television screen use (or just *are*) projected light. Here, we see a beam of light, so we perceive light waves combined rather than separated. For instance, a pixel of white on the screen is actually the combination all of the available color waves. (Remember the prism?) This color system, then, is called the *additive color mode*, because all of the colors are added together to produce the color we see.

Since additive (web-based) colors are produced by projected light from computer display phosphors, light waves are mixed together without concern about what a surface might absorb—there is no surface to do the absorbing. The web designer is blending light rather than pigments. As we will soon see, much of what we know about traditional color theory is turned upside down with additive color mixing for computer displays.

A pixel is, of course, a single dot of color on the screen, composed of a varying mix of red, blue, and green phosphors, which is why this color system is referred to as RGB. Even the color wheel changes for RGB color, because now the primary colors are red, green, and blue.

FIGURES 5.9, **5.10**, and **5.11** present the RGB primary, secondary, and tertiary colors, respectively. Similar colors to the traditional color wheel are represented, but they are derived in different ways. For instance, the secondary colors are now yellow, magenta, and cyan. The mind-boggler here is that yellow is mixed by combining equal amounts of green and red, a concept that is simply not intuitive to most of us.

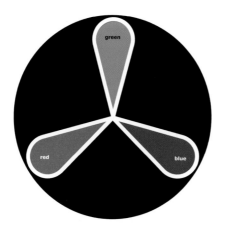

FIGURE 5.9 RGB Primary Colors

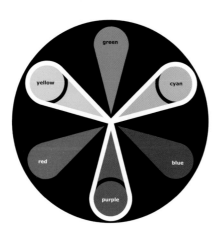

FIGURE 5.10 RGB Secondary Colors

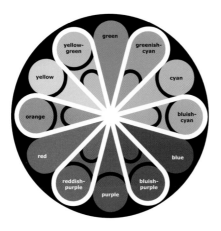

FIGURE 5.11 RGB Tertiary Colors

• • •

GETTING COOLER...

2/3 of the colors here are cool colors (the traditional color wheel is 50/50). Because of this, it can be more challenging to find good warm colors in the RGB color space.

TABLE 5.3 ADDITIVE VERSUS SUBTRACTIVE COLOR MODES
(DIFFERENCES ARE HIGHLIGHTED)

	Subtractive Color Wheel (Traditional non-web color based on reflected light)	Additive Color Wheel (RGB web color based on projected light)
Primary Colors	Red Yellow Blue	Red Green Blue
Secondary Colors	Purple Green Orange	Purple Cyan Yellow
Tertiary Colors	Bluish-purple Reddish-purple Yellow-green Cyan Red-orange Yellow-orange	Bluish-purple Reddish-purple Yellow-green Greenish-cyan Bluish-cyan Orange
Neutrals	Black White Gray	Black #000000 (the absence of color) White #FFFFFF (maximum value of all colors) Gray (equal proportions of all three primary colors)

RGB Color Codes

RGB colors are represented by a six-digit *hexadecimal* (base 16, "hex" for short) code. (The sidebars review both hexadecimal numbers and HTML color codes.) Each of the three pairs of hex digits can have a maximum value of FF. The higher the number, the more of that particular hue is in the color, and therefore the higher the saturation of that color. Thus, #FF0000 is a red of maximum saturation and #870000 is a less saturated red. #FFFFFF is pure white (because white is the combination of all colors) and #000000 is black (because, on a computer monitor, black is the absence of color). **FIGURE 5.12** presents a few sample colors and their RGB codes. Note that the hex pair with the highest value is the dominant hue of the displayed color. For example, red is the dominant color of #F23846 (red="F2," green="38," and blue="46") because "F2" is a higher number than "38" or "46."

• • •

RGB COLOR CODES: UPPERCASE OR LOWERCASE?

RGB codes, like HTML itself, will work just fine when written either in uppercase or lowercase. Throughout other chapters, they are shown in lowercase, to match the lowercase requirements of the newer XTHML standards. In this chapter, however, we'll show them in uppercase because uppercase is easier to read both in the text and on the figures.

FIGURE 5.12 Sample RGB Colors

HTML REVIEW: RGB COLOR CODES

Some of you may be familiar with the decimal color codes used in image-editing software for the print industry, which normally uses the code "255, 255, 255" to represent the maximum values of red, green, and blue, respectively. The equivalent HTML color code would be "#FFFFFF." The numbers are now represented in hexadecimal (see an upcoming sidebar for more about hexadecimal numbers). The hexadecimal code consists of the pound sign ("#") followed by six hexadecimal digits. The first pair of hex digits specifies the amount of red in the color, the second pair specifies green, and the third pair specifies blue (that is, #rrggbb). "FF" is the maximum value for a given color in HTML, just as 255 is the maximum value for a color using the print codes.

A 6-digit hexadecimal code can store 16.8 million (16^8) different color codes, which in turn supports 16.8 million unique colors, termed *true color* in geek-speak. Older computer systems may not be powerful enough to display in true color.

Color codes can be used in HTML and CSS for most visible elements. For example:

```
<body style="color:#ffff00;"> . . . </body>
<td style="background-color:#001234;"> . . . </td>
```

FYI: HEXADECIMAL NUMBERS

Human beings normally work with *decimal* (base 10) numbers, which probably relates to the fact that the system was developed as primitive man carefully counted on ten fingers. As a refresher, let's look at how the base ten system works.

Take the number 1,234 in base 10, written 1234_{10}. Here's how this number breaks down:

$$1\ 2\ 3\ 4_{10} =$$

4×10^0	=	4×1	=	4
3×10^1	=	3×10	=	30
2×10^2	=	2×100	=	200
1×10^3	=	1×1000	=	1000

$$1234_{10}$$

All numbers work in this way, whether base ten, or base two, or base 31; the position of a digit dictates the value it actually represents.

Computers don't have ten fingers, but instead have two "fingers," or states, for their electrical gates: on and off. As a result, binary (base 2) is really the native number system for computers. However, binary is difficult for humans to use. Contrast our 1234_{10} with its binary equivalent, 10011010010_2. You see the problem—binary numbers need more digit positions to represent any given value, because only two digits, 0 and 1, can be used.

It turns out that binary numbers convert easily to hexadecimal (base 16) numbers, because hexadecimal numbers are also powers of two—(16_{10} being nothing more than 2^4). Hexadecimal numbers are represented using the digits 0–9 (which mean exactly what you would expect them to mean) as well as the alphabetic characters A–F, using the following conversion table:

A = 10

B = 11

C = 12

D = 13

E = 14

F = 15

Thus, the number 1234_{10} converts to $4D2_{16}$, a much more compact way to reference what is essentially a binary number. Here's the proof:

$4D2_{16} =$

2×16^0	$=$	2×1	$=$	2
$D \times 16^1$	$=$	13×16	$=$	208
4×16^2	$=$	4×256	$=$	1024

				1234_{16}

Note again that the same number is represented by 10011010010_2 in binary, 1234_{10} in decimal, and $4D2_{16}$ in hex. It's easy to see that the larger the base number, the fewer the digits needed to represent the number. Hex numbers are certainly more compact than decimal numbers. Such compactness turns out to have benefits. For instance, a six-digit hex color code system can identify more than 16 million discrete colors. A six-digit color code in decimal could identify at most one million colors. An extra 15 million colors is indeed a very good thing.

The Web-safe Palette

There is a *palette* (a collection of available colors) of 216 colors that is at least somewhat predictable across the various hardware and software platforms. Called the *web-safe palette* (or, previously, the *safety palette*), these colors are recognized universally by all browsers and systems (well, except the really ancient systems, anyway). Although the colors don't *appear* exactly the same on all systems because of the vagaries of different monitors, they are at least *recognized* unambiguously by all systems.

The web-safe colors were chosen mathematically, not because they are necessarily the colors you would elect to use most often. RGB codes for web-safe colors are made up of the digit zero plus the other hex digits that are multiples of three: 3, 6, 9, C (12), and F (15). (Please don't ask why they are in multiples of three. Ours is not always to reason why…) Additionally, the digits are always used in equal pairs. For instance:

- #3366FF is web-safe, because it consists of pairs of identical digits, all multiples of three.

- #2255AA is not web-safe because the digits are not multiples of three.

- #3693CF is not web-safe because the digits, though multiples of three, are not paired identically.

Each step up in the allowed number pairs, such as from 33 to 66, represents a 20% increase in the saturation for that hue. **FIGURE 5.13** presents a few examples of web-safe colors. We will look at the entire web-safe palette, in several incarnations, in the next section.

FIGURE 5.13 Sample Web-safe Colors and Codes

Many colors possess names as well as hex codes. For instance, you could say "color: red" in your CSS. The hitch is that only ten of these color names translate to precisely the same color code in all browsers. You'd think that something as straightforward as "red" should always translate to #FF0000, but unfortunately, that isn't necessarily true. For instance, the color name "brown" translates to #A52A2A in Navigator 7.2 and to #993333 in Internet Explorer 6. Although newer versions of Internet Explorer and Firefox are more consistent with each other, it's still safer to use hex codes, not names.

Virtually all graphics programs and web development environments provide their own versions of the web-safe palette. Unfortunately, the web-safe palette is severely restrictive, especially when it comes to providing the subtler, more sophisticated colors that many designers crave. So what happens if you choose to use a color that is not web-safe? If a visitor has a system powerful enough to see that particular color, the color displays properly. If not, the browser does one of two things: either it uses its best judgment to shift the color to the nearest color that it does recognize, or it dithers the color.

Dithering is alternating pixels of two different colors with the intent of fooling our eyes into perceiving a third, intermediary color—that is, essentially, by faking it. **FIGURE 5.14** gives you a visual comparison of dithered and non-dithered color. Dithering on a computer screen works in much the same way that our eyes blend individual frames of a flip-book to simulate what we perceive as smooth "movement."

Even though our eyes perform this blending function automatically, the grainy look of dithering can still be noticeable and distracting, particularly in large areas of what should be solid color. Although dithering is not always bad (sometimes we might even do it on purpose for special effects), most of the time solid color is preferable to dithered color.

FIGURE 5.14 Dithering

Solid, non-dithered color, 6x6 pixels, zoomed in.

The same non-dithered color, not zoomed in.

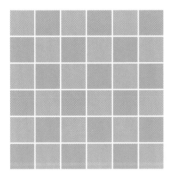

Ready for my close-up: the optical illusion of the original color.

When you don't look too closely, it looks pretty realistic, doesn't it?

Because of this problem, some experts still advise limiting ourselves to the non-dithering, web-safe palette. The web-safe palette is indeed limiting, however; 216 colors are not many colors for a 512+-crayon designer. Inevitably, the exact color that we envision is simply not available in the web-safe palette.

That leaves us with a dilemma: do we restrict ourselves to that limited palette of just 216 colors to make sure that our colors don't shift or dither, all because of the few remaining users who cannot recognize more colors? Or, do we recklessly and joyfully pick from the marvelous, gorgeous, and expressive 16.8 million colors that most, though perhaps not all, of our users are capable of seeing?

In fact, there are so few of the older 256-color computer systems remaining now that most experts are already proclaiming the demise of the web-safe palette. Still, the answer to the web-safe palette question is, "It depends." It depends on whether a significant portion of your audience is likely to have older computers that support only 256 colors. It depends on whether you expect your site to be viewed on PDAs

• • •

WHY ONLY 216 WEB-SAFE COLORS ON 256-COLOR SYSTEMS?

Of the 256 officially available colors, 40 are reserved for the browser's use, leaving only 216 for the web-safe palette.

• • •

UN-"SAFE" PHOTOS

Never worry about whether photographs (continuous-tone images) are web-safe. They won't be, because you cannot control those colors, and they will dither, and that's okay. It's simply not noticeable in all the "noise" of a typical photo.

• • •

PNG COLOR CORRECTION

PNG, a newer graphics format, has built-in color correction so that colors in graphics will be more consistent across various systems. However, none of the major browsers currently support this feature.

or cell phones, which may support only 256 colors. Even for those users, web-safe colors are most critical in large blocks of solid color in graphics and in HTML background colors, where dithering or color shifting is most apparent. If neither of these circumstances seems to affect a large number of your users, then feel free to use any colors that strike your fancy.

Color Rendering on Different Systems

Different systems can't be counted on to display a color all in the same way. The combination of a particular system's operating system (Mac or Windows), browser, monitor, and video card all have an effect on the color output. It's much like viewing a row of different models of TVs in an appliance store; each one renders color a bit differently.

Because of this, the color that ends up displaying on a visitor's system may vary greatly from the color that displays on your system, even if the two colors use the same RGB color code. For example, #999966 looks barn red on some systems and raspberry on others, a variance that most designers would consider to be, well, significant.

In particular, *LCD* (flat Liquid Crystal Display) screens typically have a much brighter and more saturated palette than CRT monitors. Additionally, the viewing angle of an LCD screen alters the way the colors appear. If you are designing on an LCD screen, it's absolutely critical that you check the colors on a CRT monitor early in the design process.

Another factor that affects colors on the screen is the system's *gamma*, the measure of the lightness or darkness of a system's display. The lower the gamma measurement, the lighter and brighter the colors look. Macintosh computers have a default gamma of 1.8, while Windows systems have gammas around 2.2 (assuming that the visitor hasn't tweaked any settings on the display, something we regrettably can't control). The upshot is that if you design on a Mac, the colors will look darker and murkier when displayed on a Windows machine. Of course, the reverse is also true; a page created on a Windows PC looks much lighter and brighter on a Mac.

Although there are utilities to tune the gamma of your system, they are of limited help, because you cannot tune your visitor's gamma to match your own. For now, the best you can do is to be aware of gamma differences and test your pages to make sure they are acceptable at different gamma settings. In fact, many image-editing packages allow you to check your images at a gamma different from that of the native gamma of your development computer. Alternately, you can simply make sure your page looks good on a Windows PC, because it's usually a safe assumption that it will almost invariably look better and brighter on a Mac.

To further complicate matters, as was mentioned earlier, a color you choose might not be recognized at all by users' systems. **FIGURE 5.15** shows how this can cause problems with a continuous-tone gradient.

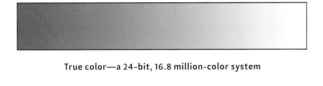

True color—a 24-bit, 16.8 million-color system

Not as smooth—an 8-bit, 256-color system

Banding—a 4-bit, 16-color system

FIGURE 5.15 A Gradient Viewed at Varying Color Depths

True color can display all 16.8 million colors and is the standard in newer computer systems (see the sidebar for an explanation of bits and their meaning in this context). Under these circumstances, all of the subtle color changes are recognized. With 8-bit color, there is some degradation; some of the colors in the gradient are not recognized, so the blend between colors is not as quite as smooth. With only 4 bits, the degradation is now obvious, with distinct lines (called *banding* or *posterizing*) between the 16 colors remaining in the image.

BITS AND COLOR DEPTH

A *bit* is a binary (base two) digit that can hold only two unique numbers: either a zero or a one. A 4-bit number can hold 16 unique digit combinations:

0000	0001	0010	0011
0100	0101	0110	0111
1000	1001	1010	1011
1100	1101	1110	1111

Since a 4-bit color system can hold only 16 numbers, it can keep track of only 16 colors. An 8-bit number can hold 2^8 (256) unique combinations, so it can keep track of 256 different colors. Finally, a 24-bit number holds an astounding 2^{24} (16.8 million) unique combinations, so it has the potential to recognize 16.8 million colors. We refer to the number of colors a system recognizes as its *color depth*.

These days, only the few users with very old computers have 4-bit systems, so we have pretty much stopped worrying about those systems. Therefore, our goal is to make sure that our pages look stunning on the 24-bit true color systems and at least presentable on 8-bit (256 color) systems.

Defining Colors for the Web

• • •

COLOR IN IMAGES

Specifics of using color and transparency in images will be covered in Chapter 6.

Most print-media artists working with subtractive colors find mixing colors to be intuitive; they don't need to research how to mix orange paint, because, for example, orange really looks like it should be (and actually is) a combination of red and yellow. Conversely, web color mixing is often not intuitive; yellow certainly does not appear to be a combination of green and red. Web artists therefore rely heavily on selecting from predefined palettes built into the software. We'll examine those next; however, as we will see later in this section, we don't need to be limited by the available palettes if we know how to sample or mix colors on the screen.

Choosing from Predefined Color Palettes

Most palettes provided in graphics and web development software are limited to a small number of hues, because it would be impossible to show all 16.8 million possible hues on the screen at the same time, even if the palette used only a single pixel per hue. Often, we use web-safe palettes as a jumping-off point, tweaking the colors from there, simply because they are a manageable and representative set of colors. Let's look at the palettes in Adobe Creative Suite to see what is available.

The web-safe Color Cubes Palette in **FIGURE 5.16** can be awkward to use because it physically separates related colors. For instance, colors appearing to be versions of yellow are in three different cube areas of the palette, which makes it tricky to pick two or three harmonious variations of a hue.

FIGURE 5.16 Adobe's Color Cubes Palette

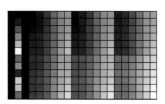

FIGURE 5.17 shows the Continuous Tone Palette used in Adobe Creative Suite. The colors are identical to the web-safe colors in the previous figure, just organized in a different way. You can think of this palette as a long tube that has been split horizontally to lie flat on the page. This palette is more helpful than the Color Cubes Palette, because now most related colors are in the same vicinity, and only those that are on the top and bottom are separated from their immediate relatives.

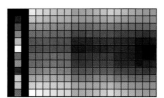

FIGURE 5.17 Adobe's
Continuous Tone Palette

The Continuous Tone Palette is not a true continuous tone palette, regardless of its name, because the colors are still discrete. A true continuous tone palette is a gradient with infinite choices, as is presented by the Adobe System Color Picker palette shown in **FIGURE 5.18** (accessed by clicking on the globe icon when presented with color choices). You have a better shot at getting closer to your desired color with this palette, because there are more colors available. Even so, it's tough to pick the perfect color by clicking on just a single pixel. When that single pixel of color is used on a larger area, it inevitably looks quite different, just as a 1" x 1" paint sample in the paint store looks very different when slapped up on the walls of an entire room.

BONUS TOPIC

For instructions to install the Visibone web-safe palette in Fireworks, see the book's web site, www. VisualDesignModernWeb. com.

FIGURE 5.18 Adobe's
System Color Picker

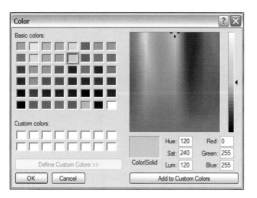

A better-organized palette, again web-safe, is offered by VisiBone, as shown in **FIGURE 5.19**. It's shipped with newer versions of Adobe Photoshop, but you must download and install it for Adobe Fireworks.

FIGURE 5.19 The VisiBone
Palette

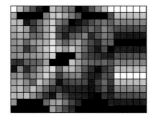

Another, perhaps more intuitive, way to display web-safe colors is by using a hexagon palette, as shown in **FIGURE 5.20**.

FIGURE 5.20 Hexagon
Palette: A More Intuitive Way
to Show Web-safe Colors

    HEXAGON PALETTE

In the hexagon, or hexagonal, palette color codes are abbreviated with only a single
digit representing each pair of digits. An axis for each of the three primary and
three secondary RGB colors radiates out from the pure white in the center to one of
the points of the hexagon on the outside edge. Each axis is terminated on the outside border with an extra color chip showing the color that "governs" that axis, so
it's easy to find the appropriate axis. For instance, locate the blue chip at the very
bottom, and follow it upward. First, you cross the *shades* of blue on the outside, then
primary blue around the middle, then *tints* of blue toward the center, and, finally,
white in the dead center. *Tones* are in the outside diamonds that span each axis.

The hexagon palette image is available for download from the book's web site.

The black-outlined larger hexagon of chips halfway out on the palette displays the hues of full saturation. Inside that hexagon are the tints/pastels, and outside are the more sophisticated tones and shades, with blacks and grays showing up in a repeated pattern on the outside border. Colors evolve as we rotate around the wheel, such that red blends into orange, and orange into yellow, and yellow into green, and so forth. It now becomes effortless to pick several colors that are related in some fashion to each other, such as a red, a dark red, and a pink.

The hexagon palette is more artistically intuitive than most available palettes, and it's mathematically correct as well. Each color code transforms into the code of the adjacent colors by following a mathematical progression.

The primary problem with this palette is that it won't fit into the tiny palette areas provided by the development environments. Instead, you must open the palette as a normal graphics file within the application, and then use the eyedropper tool/ color picker tool (see next section) to sample colors from it.

Regardless of the palette we choose, there will be only a limited number of colors shown, usually only the 216 web-safe colors; because of space limitations there simply isn't room to show all 18.8 million colors. How do we get to the remaining millions of colors? One alternative is to pick the web-safe color closest to what we have in mind, and then tweak the color using the color mixing techniques that we'll discuss in a bit.

Sampling Colors

Many development environments and image-editing packages offer eyedropper/ color picker tools. If the tool is selected and moved over a color on the computer screen, it "samples" the color and provides the HTML color code. Often, the eye-dropper tool works even if it's moved off of its native window, that is, onto the computer's desktop or the window of another open application. For instance, the eyedropper tool in Fireworks can be moved off of the Fireworks window over to an independent window, such as a browser window, allowing you to determine and copy the color codes of any web site.

Taking the process a step further, you can reveal the color codes of virtually any object that will fit on your scanner bed, be it fabric, a magazine ad, or autumn leaves. The process is the same; you first scan the object, and then you can sample it.

Mixing Colors Manually

As we've seen, palettes are a convenience, but they don't come close to tapping the power of the 16.8 million colors available to us. For that, we need to mix colors manually. For each of the color types we're about to discuss, we'll look at three mixing techniques:

- Manipulating the RGB color code mathematically (a whole new spin on "paint-by-number").

- Using a color *gradient* (a gradual blend from one color into another).

- Using a semi-transparent color overlay.

As we manipulate the color codes, remember that #FFFFFF is white and #000000 is black. It makes sense, then, that to make a color lighter in value, we "add" white; that is, the digits in the code get larger, approaching #FFFFFF. Looking at #CAF0E6, we might guess that it is a fairly light tint.

To make a color darker, we "add" black; the numbers get smaller until they approach #000000 (again, the code for black). Thus, #30421A is a fairly dark color. The fastest way to use the mathematical technique is to use a standard palette first to get a baseline color that is close to what you ultimately want, and then go on to tweak the color mathematically to end up with precisely the one you need.

Mixing Neutrals

True neutrals are white, black, and variations of gray, and have RGB color codes that are composed of three equal hex pairs, as shown in **FIGURE 5.21**. Any color code that consists of three equal pairs, such as #D3D3D3 or #999999, produces some version of gray on the screen.

FIGURE 5.21 Mixing Grays Mathematically

The higher the numbers in the code, the lighter the gray, because, as we have seen, the code is approaching the code for white. Conversely, the lower the numbers, the darker the gray. Thus, a color code of #CACACA is a much lighter gray than #4F4F4F.

We can also use a graphics package to create a shape and fill it with a gradient that shades from white on one side to black on the other, resulting in an infinite spectrum of grays along the gradient. **FIGURE 5.22** shows such a gradient. Use the eyedropper/color picker tool of an image-editing package to select a color from along the gradient. If you need web-safe colors, alter the resulting hex code to "snap" it to the nearest web-safe gray.

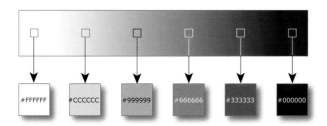

FIGURE 5.22 Mixing Grays with a Gradient

Mixing Tints

To create tints of a color using a mathematical technique, pick a base hue like #00FFFF (maximum saturation cyan) and alter the code mathematically so that it approaches white. To do that, add progressively larger but equal amounts of the other hex pair(s): #00FFFF > #33FFFF > #66FFFF > #99FFFF > #CCFFFF, as illustrated in **FIGURE 5.23**.

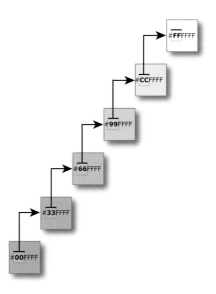

FIGURE 5.23 Mixing Tints Mathematically

● ● ●

SAFE CYAN

Cyan is the base hue for most of the following examples. We are using only web-safe results here, but you can of course use a wider variety of colors if you are not limited to web-safe colors.

Another way to mix a tint is to use a graphics package to create a shape and fill it with a gradient that shades from the original color on one side to white on the other. **FIGURE 5.24** shows just such a gradient. Use the eyedropper tool to select a color from along the gradient. If you need web-safe colors, alter the resulting hex code to "snap" it to the nearest one.

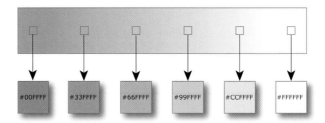

A final way to mix a tint is to layer a semi-transparent white shape over the original base color. To do this with the color cyan:

1. Create a shape filled with cyan.

2. Overlay the original shape with a copy that has a white fill and an intermediate transparency value, such as 50%. Tweak the transparency percentage of the overlay until you get the exact color you need. (A transparency example isn't illustrated because transparency is impossible to portray in print.)

Mixing Shades

To generate shades of a color by altering the hex code mathematically, progressively reduce the hex pair(s) for the base hue until the color approaches black, as shown in **FIGURE 5.25**. Here, the cyan pairs were first reduced to CCCC, then 9999, and so forth, with black as the ultimate result.

FIGURE 5.25 Mixing Shades Mathematically

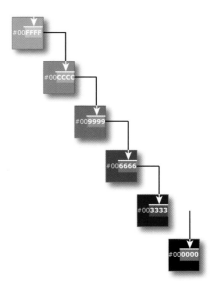

Mixing shades with a gradient is identical to mixing tints with a gradient, but uses black at the opposite end of the spectrum instead of white, as shown in **FIGURE 5.26**. To mix a shade using an overlay, repeat the directions for mixing a tint, but use a semi-transparent black overlay.

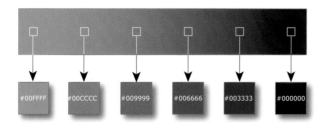

FIGURE 5.26 Mixing Shades with a Gradient

Mixing Tones

Mixing tones mathematically is a bit more complicated than mixing tints or shades. Now, we change the color code to approach gray (all three RGB pairs are closer to being equal) by simultaneously reducing the hex pairs for the base hue—cyan—while increasing the other pair. **FIGURE 5.27** illustrates a few of the tones that could result.

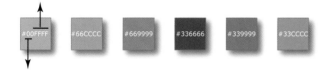

FIGURE 5.27 Mixing Tones Mathematically

Essentially, you create a tone by adding gray to a color. That is, you add both components of gray: black and white. You add the black by reducing the hex pair for the original color (as you would do to create a shade) and you add white by increasing the other hex pairs (as you would do to create a tint). In doing so, you are decreasing the numeric difference between the base hue pair and the other hues, thus approaching a pure gray (equal values of all three pairs).

As you reduce the pair for the base hue and increase the other pairs, you must remember that the base hue must always remain as the largest pair(s) in the RGB code. After all, being the largest is what makes it the base hue in the first place. For instance, if we attempted to mix a tone of cyan and ended up with #996666, we would have lost the cyan dominance and replaced it with a version of red.

Yet another way to produce a tone is to start with a gray of the correct value, and then tweak it mathematically toward the dominant color you have in mind, as in

FIGURE **5.28**. The original grays are in the center row, while the tweaked, near-gray colors are above and below.

FIGURE 5.28 Mixing Tones by Starting with Gray

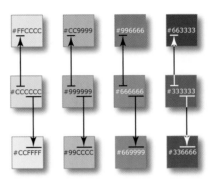

As you have probably already guessed, you can also use a gradient, this time blending from the original hue to an appropriate value of gray or to the hue's RGB complementary (opposite) color. The top of **FIGURE 5.29** shows blending from cyan to gray, while the bottom shows blending to cyan's RGB complement, red. Keep in mind that the value of the resulting tone can be controlled by changing the values of both the original hue and the complementary hue. For instance, to end up with a lighter tone of cyan, choose lighter values of cyan and/or the blending colors of gray or red.

FIGURE 5.29 Mixing Tones with a Gradient

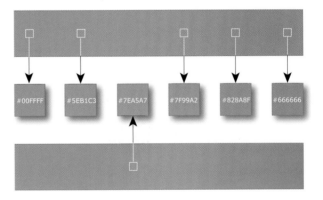

Once again, you could also mix a tone by overlaying the hue with a semi-transparent gray or the hue's complement.

One of the more sophisticated trends in web design these days uses light-valued tones, grayed down from the more common pastels. Think of them as a hybrid between tones and tints. To produce them, use one of the techniques just described, but start with a very pale gray, like the gray furthest to the left in Figure 5.28.

Mixing Other Colors

You can also skew a hue toward one of its neighboring colors. For instance, you might want a yellow to have a greenish tint, or a red to have purple undertones. To accomplish this mathematically, increase the code for the pair or pairs that best reflects the direction you want the hue to go. Alternately, construct a gradient between the two colors, as in **FIGURE 5.30**.

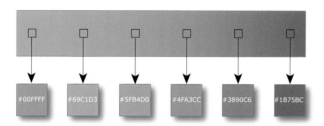

FIGURE 5.30 Altering the Hue

You can skew an entire group of colors all at once in a certain color direction as a way to create a unified palette, as shown using Adobe's continuous palette as the "model" in **FIGURE 5.31**. For instance, all of the colors could be lightened in a single step by overlaying a 50% transparent white over the top. Alternatively, the same palette could be given an overall yellowish cast by superimposing a transparent yellow over the top, which renders the colors on the palette more harmonious because they all have the color yellow in common. In any case, you can then use the color picker to choose the colors you need from this new, altered palette.

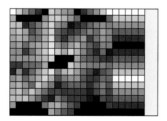

Standard Palette

FIGURE 5.31 Altering an Entire Palette

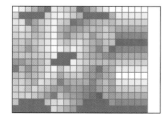

Same Palette with a 50%
Semi-transparent White Overlay

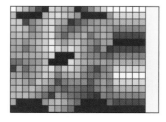

Same Palette with a
Semi-transparent Yellow Overlay

TABLE 5.4 COLOR MIXING

Color	Method	Explanation
Neutrals (black, white, and shades of gray)	Mathematical	All six digits must be equal, with lighter grays approaching white (#FFFFFF) and darker grays approaching black (#000000). Examples: #666666 (dark gray) and #CCCCCC (light gray).
	Gradient	Create a gradient between white and black, and then pick from the gradient.
Tints	Mathematical	Start with the code for the dominant hue and progressively add more of the other colors' hex digit pairs until they approach white. Example: #0000FF (blue) becomes #CCCCFF (light blue).
	Gradient	Create a gradient between the hue and white, and then pick from the gradient.
	Overlay	Overlay the hue with a semi-transparent white.
Shades	Mathematical	Start with the dominant hue's code and progressively decrease the hue's hex digit pair until the pair approaches black. Example: #0000FF (blue) becomes #000066, a dark blue.
	Gradient	Create a gradient between the hue and black, and then pick from the gradient.
	Overlay	Overlay the hue with a semi-transparent black.
Tones	Mathematical	• Start with the dominant hue's code, decreasing the dominant hue's hex digit pair toward black while simultaneously increasing the other colors' hex digits toward white. Example: #0000FF (blue) becomes #666699 (a dark tone of blue). • Start with a gray of the desired value, and increase dominant hue's hex digit pair. Example: #666666 (dark gray) becomes #666699 (a dark tone of blue).
	Gradient	Create a gradient between the hue and gray or between the hue and its RGB complement, and then pick from the gradient.
	Overlay	Overlay the hue with a semi-transparent gray or the complementary RGB color. Example: overlay blue with yellow, its RGB complementary color.
Altering the hue	Mathematical	Start with the dominant hue's code and increase the hex digit pair for the color you want to influence the original hue. Example: #0000FF (blue) becomes a purplish-blue by increasing the red hex digit pair, with #9900FF as the result.
	Gradient	Create a gradient between the dominant hue and the desired undertone hue, and then pick from the gradient. Example: create a gradient between blue and purple if you want a purplish-blue.
	Overlay	Overlay the dominant hue with a semi-transparent version of the desired undertone hue, and then pick from the gradient. Example: overlay a blue with a semi-transparent purple if you want a purplish-blue.

Choosing a Color Scheme

It's worth repeating that the single most important thing you can do to build appeal, mood, and ambiance for your site is to select an appropriate color scheme. There really are no awful colors—any color can look attractive when placed with appropriate color companions. Even though web colors are mixed differently than traditional media, that doesn't mean that you need to learn all new theories to make color work on the web; the old theories about pleasing color schemes still hold true. For instance, yellow always looks good with its related color of orange whether the yellow was created with paint (subtractive color) or pixels (additive color).

Sometimes the color scheme is a given: we can't imagine IBM allowing any color other than blue to dominate its web site, or the Chicago Bulls using any colors other than red and black, or Victoria's Secret using anything other than pink, or the Republic of Ireland using anything other than green…Well, you get the idea. Many organizations have long-established color schemes from which you simply cannot deviate. In this case, creating the color scheme for the site can be as straightforward as choosing colors from the logo, followed by choosing a few additional tints or shades of those colors for variety.

When you are allowed to choose your own colors, you first need to consider the audience and purpose of the site. A site for children might employ primary colors or some other design of fully-saturated brights. A rock group site might use a funky combination of neon colors, or a dark and murky scheme, depending upon the mood the band wants to project. A more staid and stable color scheme, like monochromatic blue, is appropriate for a corporate site (again, think "Big Blue," IBM).

Colors evoke particular associations and emotions in our minds. Here is a summary of some of those associations for the Western world:

- Yellow: cheerful, sunny, upbeat, happy, luminous, intense. Popular example: The high-energy label of the Absolut Citron logo.

- Orange: energetic, cheerful, glowing, vital, upbeat, playful, happy, comedic, festive, loud, popular with children. It carries many of the same qualities of its components of yellow and red. Orange lost popularity for many years because of its association with the period of the late 1960s and early 1970s but is now making a comeback. When lightened to peach or coral: soft, upscale, nurturing, healthy. When darkened to deep rust: sensual, earthy, spicy, warm, ethnic. Popular example: The vibrant orange of Sunkist Orange soft drink cans.

- Red: Attention-demanding, energetic, exciting, courageous, hot, aggressive, dynamic, fiery, intense, passionate, sexy, bloody, warning, angry, prideful. The most attention-gathering color. When deepened to shades and tones: rich, lush, elegant, refined. When lightened to hot pink: shocking, energetic, youthful, trendy, vibrant, faddish. When lightened to paler pink: romantic, tender, feminine, sweet, sentimental, soft, delicate. Popular examples: the energy of the red Coke logo and the feminine mood of Victoria's Secret.

- Purple: rich, elegant, creative, spiritual, confident, eccentric, sensual, daring, futuristic. When deepened to a darker purple: regal, majestic. When lightened to lavender: soft, sweet, genteel, nostalgic, delicate. When grayed to a tone: sophisticated, subtle. Popular examples: the magnificent feel of the traditional purple robes of royalty.

- Blue: tranquil, calm, peaceful, meditative, restful, reliable, traditional, clean, fresh, cool, icy, alluding to sky and water, divine, cold, sad. When deepened to darker blues: powerful, authoritarian, credible. When lightened to pale blues: soft, serene. When tinged with green (like teal): rich, unique, upscale, appealing to both genders. When tinged with purple (periwinkle): warm, trendy, energetic. Popular example: the reliability implied by IBM's "Big Blue" color scheme.

- Green: natural, fresh, clean, healthy, hopeful, youthful, abundant, rebirth, spring, soothing, cool, clean, woodsy. When deepened to darker greens: richness, security, safety, prestige, safe, secure, stately. When lightened to paler greens: calm, soothing. Popular example: The Kelly green that represents the Republic of Ireland or the healthy green packaging of Green Giant foods.

- Brown: durable, earthy, rustic, organic, healthy, ethnic, substantial, solid, timeless, reliable, stable, antiquity, permanent, drab, dirty. When lightened to tans and beige: rock, sand, natural, classic. Popular example: UPS's drab but eminently reliable brown color scheme.

- White: pure, clean, chaste, pristine, innocent, bright, clarity, hygienic, healthy, stark, minimalist, cold. When deepened to off-whites: warm, friendly, calm. Popular examples: white is the color of wedding dresses and "the hero on the white horse" in Western culture.

- Black: sophistication, elegance, chic, dramatic, mysterious, powerful, stylized, somber, ominous, foreboding, death, depression, despair, fear. Popular example: The elegant black of the Chanel logo or a man's tuxedo.

Fully-saturated hues portray a mood that is vivid, intense, or childlike. Tones and shades usually look sophisticated, while tints are associated with babies or femininity. Colors that can be described by a single, commonly-accepted word are considered less complex and less sophisticated than colors that require uncommon or

multiple words for description. Contrast the level of sophistication of easily identified colors like "red" or "orange" or "green" with colors like "mauve," "salmon,"
"celadon," or "grayish-green with a blue undertone."

Different cultures have different symbolism and associations for colors, and sometimes it's important for those of us who tend to be occidentocentric to be reminded
of that. The classic example is that while white portrays purity and the celebration
of a wedding in Western culture, it's symbolic of death in some Eastern cultures.
Green and yellow have particular connotations in both Islamic and Buddhist cultures. People from Eastern cultures seem to prefer brighter colors in very different
schemes than in traditional Western art. And many Russian citizens today might
well have negative associations with the color red, symbolic of Communism. Entire
books are devoted to color symbolism around the world; if you are designing a web
site for a culture outside of your own, your best bet is to research that particular
culture thoroughly. Even then, test the site with people native to the culture before
releasing the site to the general public.

After deciding upon the ambiance you want to portray, you need to consider the
actual colors that best portray it. Simple schemes are the easiest color combinations for beginning designers to use, so, most of the time, you should limit your color
scheme to variations of one, two, or at most three colors. Although we have all seen
gorgeous web sites employing many more colors that that, it takes a master's hand
to pull off unifying a large number of colors. More often, pages with myriad colors
look disjointed, amateurish, and chaotic.

Remember the two houses we looked at in back in Chapter 4, one with bad layout,
one with a classic layout? **FIGURE 5.32** revisits the classic house, this time showing
every element in a different color. Again, this is not a house most people would be
willing to buy because it looks chaotic. In the same vein, a web page on which every
element is a different color also looks chaotic.

FIGURE 5.32 House of
Many Colors

The point is that you shouldn't fall into the trap that every element on the page needs to be a different color. In fact, the opposite is true; every color you use on the page should usually appear in more than one place on the page. You might use one color extracted from the logo for text links and navigational graphics, another color from the logo for backgrounds, and a third color from the logo for headers, subheads, table backgrounds, and dividing rules. Repetition of color is the surest way to unify a page.

For visual consistency, most sites should also repeat the same colors throughout the entire site. You might think such repetition would be considered boring, but it is really a reassurance to visitors that they are still in the same site as the home page.

That said, sometimes colors might vary from page to page because of a color-coding scheme. For instance, perhaps Amazon could use a blue header and a blue navigation tab for all book pages, green for all movie pages, and purple for all music pages. Even so, the different colors should be of approximately the same value and saturation, express the same mood, and still appear to be part of a unified, site-wide color scheme. The blue Amazon book pages could have small touches of green and purple, and the green movie pages could have touches of blue and purple. Finally, if the color scheme changes for different pages, it's even more critical that other characteristics of the site are consistent, such as layout, navigation, and graphics.

Color Proportions

When repeating colors throughout the site, you shouldn't use equal amounts of each color. In a three-color scheme, for instance, using 33% of each color on a page would lead to a boring page without a focal point. Instead, you might use one color for the page background (perhaps 60% of the color on the page), another color for elements like headers or graphics that need a certain amount of emphasis (perhaps 30% of the page), and reserve the third color—usually the most striking—for items that you want to give the most emphasis, like a "Sale Today!" announcement. Think of the color choices as being proportionate to the colors in a man's business outfit: 60% of the color, usually fairly subtle, is in the suit itself. 30% of the color, usually a bit brighter, is in the shirt, and 10%, usually the most vivid color, is in the tie. In short, the bright tie accents, but doesn't overwhelm, the remainder of the overall image.

Color Schemes

Certain predictable color combinations are usually successful. We will look at the most common: monochromatic, complementary, triad, analogous, warm, and cool. All of these are based on the traditional color wheel discussed earlier in the chapter. It's our job as designers to translate these traditional color schemes to the RGB color wheel.

Monochromatic Color Scheme

A *monochromatic color scheme*, which employs tints and shades of a single hue, is one of the easiest for beginning designers to employ effectively. In **FIGURE 5.33**, the color wheel shows the tints and shades of green that are used to great effect in the site design shown below it. Monochromatic color schemes tend to be unified, harmonious, and professional. On the other hand, they can be mind-numbingly dull when poorly used.

Monochromatic Scheme on the Color Wheel

FIGURE 5.33
Monochromatic Color Scheme

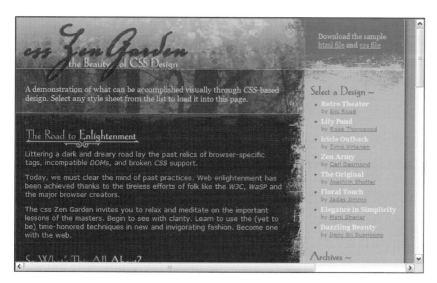

Monochromatic Web Site: "Moss," www.csszengarden.com/?cssfile=153/153.css, by Mani Sheriar, Sheriar Designs, www.manisheriar.com

Complementary Color Scheme

A *complementary color scheme* uses two colors opposing each other on the traditional color wheel. **FIGURE 5.34** shows several complementary color schemes extracted from the color wheel as well as a real-world web site that effectively uses the complementary colors of blue and orange. Fully-saturated complementary colors create the most vibrant, jarring, and attention-getting of color schemes, creating tension and the illusion of movement, which is why a complementary scheme is often used for team colors. For that, it works well, but using one color for text and its complement for the background is a very bad idea; the resulting optical illusion can make the text appear to "jitter" on the screen.

FIGURE 5.34
Complementary Color
Scheme

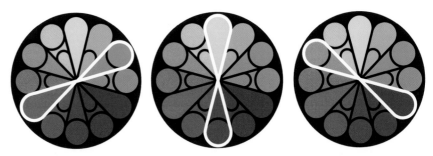

Complementary Color Scheme:
Red and Green

Complementary Color Scheme:
Yellow and Purple

Complementary Color Scheme:
Orange and Blue

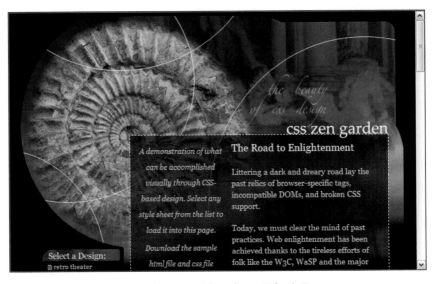

Complementary Color Scheme: "Atlantis,"
www.csszengarden.com/?cssfile=028/028.css,
by Kevin Davis, http://alazanto.org

Complementary color schemes can be tamed, however, if you convert the fully-saturated hues to tints, shades, or tones. For instance, the web site shown in Figure 5.34 tones down the colors just a bit and further curbs the color scheme's innate exuberance by using a black background. Also think of the soothing look of pale lettuce green and baby pink, which are nothing more than tints of the complementary colors red and green. Similarly, burgundy and dark forest green, shades of red and green, can look rich and dramatic without being jarring.

Triad Color Scheme

A triad color scheme, as shown in **FIGURE 5.35**, uses three evenly spaced colors around the traditional color wheel. Triad schemes can be bold and vibrant, but at the same time jarring, though not quite to the same degree as a complementary color scheme. The most widely-employed triad scheme, the three traditional primary colors of red, blue, and yellow, is used in the web site shown in Figure 5.35.

FIGURE 5.35 Triad Color Schemes

Triad Color Scheme:
Orange, Green, and Purple

Triad Color Scheme:
Red-Orange, Yellow-Green,
and Purplish-Blue

Triad Color Scheme:
Yellow, Blue, and Red

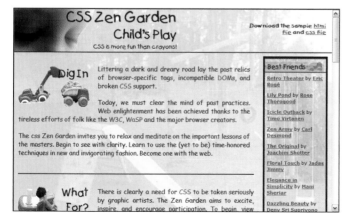

Triad Color Scheme: "Child's Play,"
www.csszengarden.com/?cssfile=http://www.syrensongdesigns.com/child's-play,
by Michelle Bennet, Syren Song Designs, http://www.syrensongdesigns.com

Analogous Color Scheme

An analogous color scheme, as shown in **FIGURE 5.36**, relies upon several colors adjacent to each other on the color wheel. Think of the citrus hues of yellow, orange, and green; or the warm hues of yellow, orange, and red; or the various hues of blue and green. Usually harmonious, stylish, and pleasing, an analogous color scheme is among the easiest of schemes to pull off successfully.

FIGURE 5.36 Analogous Color Schemes

Analogous Color Scheme: Yellow-orange through Green

Analogous Color Scheme: Blue through Reddish-Purple

Analogous Color Scheme: Red through Yellow

Analogous Color Scheme: "A SimpleSunrise,"
www.csszengarden.com/?cssfile=158/158.css, by Rob Soulé, www.couchfort.net

Warm Color Scheme

A warm color scheme is an analogous variant based on yellows, oranges, and reds, as shown in the color wheel in **FIGURE 5.37**. It's warm, cozy, and inviting. Warm colors appear to advance; they seem closer to the viewer. The web site in Figure 5.36 used a warm color scheme.

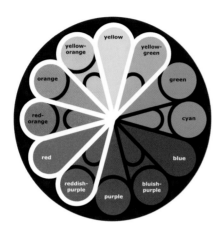

FIGURE 5.37 Warm Color Scheme

Cool Color Scheme

A cool color scheme is another analogous variant, based on purples, blues, and greens, as illustrated in **FIGURE 5.38**. Cool colors seem to recede from the viewer, appearing further away. The perception of distance is the result of our unconscious experience in viewing far-away objects, such as distant mountains, through the bluish haze of the atmosphere. Cool colors are usually perceived as slick, sophisticated, and professional. It therefore makes good business sense that so many corporations use variations on blue for their branding.

Note that the borderline colors of yellow-green and reddish-purple can be either warm or cool, because they blend well with both schemes.

FIGURE 5.38 Cool Color
Schemes

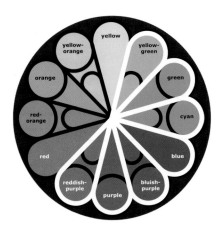

Cool Color Scheme: Reddish-Purple
through Yellow-green

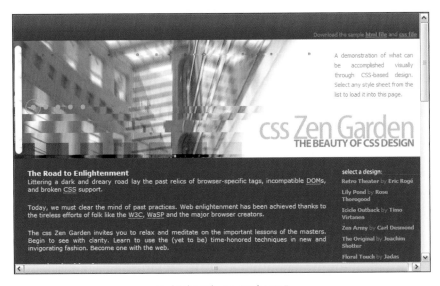

Cool Color Scheme: "arch4.20,"
www.csszengarden.com/?cssfile=/004/004.css, by Dave Shea

TABLE 5.5 COLOR SCHEMES

	Description	Ambiance	Example
Monochromatic	Tints and shades of a single hue	Unified, harmonious, and professional	White, light blue, medium blue, dark blue, and black
Complementary	Two colors opposing each other on the traditional color wheel	Vibrant, jarring, and attention-getting	Orange and blue
Triad	Three evenly spaced colors around the traditional color wheel	Bold, vibrant, potentially jarring	Yellow, blue, and red
Analogous	Several colors adjacent to each other on the color wheel	Harmonious, stylish, and pleasing	Yellow, orange, and green
Warm	Variations of yellow, orange, and red	Warm, cozy, and inviting	Yellow, orange, and red
Cool	Variations of greens, blues, and purples	Slick, sophisticated, and professional	Green, blue, and purple

Inspiration for Color Schemes

Pay attention to color trends in fashion and home décor, because colors that are hot in those areas today will be hot on web sites tomorrow. As of this writing, earthy tones like browns and oranges have returned after decades of being ridiculed as a passé holdover from the 1970s. In fact, a recent home decorating magazine quoted several interior designers as saying that "brown is the new black." Shades of gray also seem to be replacing black as the neutral of choice on the web, particularly in high-end market web sites, like Chanel and Mercedes. These sites are often rendered primarily in grayscale, with only a few well-placed shots of color.

For ideas for appealing color schemes, simply look around. Inspiration can come from unlikely locations:

- A favorite sweater or coffee mug.
- Ads on TV.
- Opening credits of movies.
- Catalogs, advertisements, and fashion and decorating magazines.
- Displays in gift, home, and fashion stores. Walk into any Crate & Barrel in the United States to see the trendiest colors in design today.

• • •

CRAYOLA CRAYONS

A box of crayons can be an excellent color reference. Buy the biggest box you can find for everyone on the development team.

- Paint samples and palette brochures from paint and decorating stores.

- Fabrics in decorating stores.

- Reference books for artists.

- A box of Crayola Crayons.

Rip the pages out of magazines and save them in a "tickler" file for future reference. If you see a fabric that inspires you, purchase a tiny sample and stick it in your file, too. Carry a small digital camera with you to capture real-world inspirations (say, the exterior of a building, the lobby of a beautiful hotel, or a gorgeous fall landscape) that won't fit in a file folder. In other words, pilfer! Unlike graphics and content, color schemes are not copyright-protected. If you find a scheme you like and can tweak it to make it yours, then by all means, do so.

Another way to choose colors is to pick them out of a photo or graphic that you have already chosen for the site. A photo of a woman wearing a red sweater might lead to a color scheme of red (from the sweater) and tan (from skin tones).

Color Contrast

Contrast is the degree of difference between the various color attributes. As examined in Chapter 4, contrast is used to emphasize some items while de-emphasizing others. We can use the four color attributes discussed earlier in the chapter to create contrast:

- **Hue:** complementary colors, such as blue and orange, have the greatest contrast.

- **Value:** lighter colors contrast with darker colors, like pale lavender versus dark purple.

- **Saturation:** Highly saturated colors contrast with colors of low saturation, like a bright Kelly green versus a dark forest green.

- **Temperature:** Warm colors (yellow, orange, red) contrast with cool colors (purple, blue, green).

Both extremely high contrast and extremely low contrast pages can be challenging to read. Think of the high contrast of red on green, or the low contrast of yellow on white, and you can envision the difficulty.

For maximum legibility, foreground elements like text and graphics should always contrast in *value* with the background elements. For instance, black text on a white background offers excellent readability. Swapping the white for a pale yellow background would still work. However, placing that black text on a navy blue background would be almost illegible because there is only negligible contrast in value between black and navy blue. The rule is that we should be able to remove all color from a design, thereby converting it to the equivalent grayscale image, and the design should still be legible. Temporarily converting a page to grayscale is a great way to assess the underlying quality of a design without the distraction of color. Many graphics packages as well as browser plug-ins allow you to convert an image or web page to grayscale temporarily to check value contrast.

● ● ●

VIEWING A PAGE IN GRAYSCALE

The AIS Toolbar, an Internet Explorer plug-in, includes a button that temporarily converts the page display to grayscale. See www.visionaustralia.org.au/ais/toolbar for a free download.

Contrast is a nifty tool for accentuating some elements while de-emphasizing others. For example, employing dark tones for most of a page, while using a vivid orange for a title, emphasizes the title. Used shrewdly, contrast can be a very effective means of playing up the areas we choose to emphasize. Used unwisely, contrast serves only to call attention to the wrong elements.

Colors "read" differently depending upon their contrast with adjacent or background colors. Look carefully at each individual red ball in **FIGURE 5.39**. Some of the balls look like a brighter or a softer red than others. In truth, all of the red balls are the same color; they just appear to be different colors because of their backgrounds.

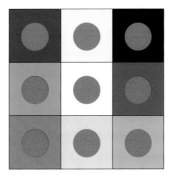

FIGURE 5.39 Adjacent Colors Affect Color Appearance

Placing high-contrast colors next to one another magnifies the perception of contrast. Conversely, placing an intense color next to a softer color, like the red ball on the yellow background, makes the strong color seem stronger and the soft color appear softer. Situating a highly saturated color like this fire-engine red next to a muted tone like the gray makes the red seem so vivid that it almost shimmers. Placing the red on white doesn't seem to affect the red much, but the white takes on a pinkish cast. Red and green, complementary colors, create a tension that makes the red seem somehow redder. Red on black also seems to make the red look redder, but without the same level of tension. High contrast schemes such as these have sharp "edges" between the colors, which creates tension, excitement, and drama.

On the other hand, the red looks the most subdued when placed on similar colors like the pink or orange. Low contrast combinations such as these have softer edges and appear to be calm, soothing, and even elegant.

In any case, the degree of contrast between colors certainly affects the overall mood of a site. See **FIGURE 5.40** for a color scheme in which the colors are of similar value and saturation, thus imparting a tranquil, more elegant mood.

FIGURE 5.40 Low Contrast Color Scheme

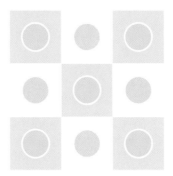

Background Colors

As we just saw, we need to have sufficient value contrast between foreground and background. Designers for the print media have always insisted that it's easier to read dark text on a light background, which (not coincidentally?) is the least expensive way to print. In any case, many designers bring that dark-on-light prejudice to the web, and believe that dark backgrounds should be avoided. Anecdotal evidence suggests that older viewers in particular are more inclined to dislike dark backgrounds.

Actually, there seems to be a prejudice against black backgrounds in particular. Yes, black backgrounds have been overused, often in amateurish web sites. But should that alone be enough to give black backgrounds a bad rep? Black (or the trendier update, dark gray) can make the other colors on the page look more intense in a way that white can't, and the effect can be stunning.

In fact, many designers feel that the web is a completely different media from print, and light-colored text glowing from within a dark background can be dramatic as well as easy on the eye. With any dark background, though, the text must be of a sufficient weight, size, and value that it shows up effectively on a dark background. Also, the default colors for links *must* be changed, because they are intended for a light background, not a dark one.

We have already seen how contrasting adjacent colors affect the way a color "reads." Now let's look at how neutral backgrounds and separators make a difference. Notice how very different the color scheme in **FIGURE 5.41** looks, depending on whether there are neutrals present, or when white or black separators and/or backgrounds are used. Generally, the use of neutral separators or other neutral elements in an image tends to make the colors "pop." Omitting the neutrals makes the image look more edgy and modern. Most people seem to prefer the calmer look of separation between colors, with neutrals serving as foils for the dominant colors. Black, in particular, makes an excellent foil for all but the darkest of colors.

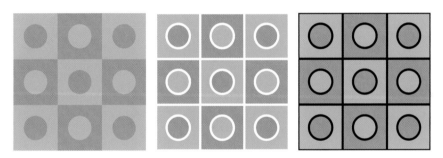

FIGURE 5.41 Neutral Backgrounds and Separators

No Neutrals, No Separator   White Separators   Black Separators

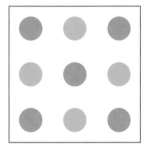
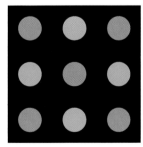

White Background   Black Background

Link Colors

Default link colors are set by the viewer's browser, usually blue for unvisited links, red for active links, and purple for visited links. These colors obviously clash with many color schemes we might want to use. For instance, they would look annoyingly garish on a page of subtle browns and gold earth tones. We can, of course, use CSS to change our default link colors. But should we do that?

There is indeed controversy on the issue. Usability experts often claim that we are interfering with the visual cues that users have come to expect when we change the colors of navigational elements; after all, making our pages user-friendly is more important than making them color-coordinated. Still, web surfers are far more sophisticated than they were just a few years ago. They know to look for other link affordances—color emphasis, underline, font change, or a mouseover effect—to lead them to the navigation. As long as we provide at least one (perhaps all) of these other cues, it can be quite acceptable to change navigational colors.

Printed Materials

What if a viewer wants to print your page? If he or she has a color printer, fine. If not, some of your carefully-chosen colors might disappear on a grayscale printed page. Red and green might be easy to differentiate on a color monitor but could very well translate to the same shade of medium gray on a laser printer. You must test your page by printing it in grayscale from within the browser, just as your user would. If it doesn't print legibly, you have several choices:

- Tweak the colors until it does. If the foreground and background values provide enough contrast (as they should under any circumstances), the page should usually translate well to grayscale.

- Provide a link to a separate, "printer-friendly" version of the page, usually black content on a white page background, with minimal graphics.

- Link to a separate, external CSS file with the `media` attribute set to `print`. Again, use black content on a white page background.

MEDIA ATTRIBUTE

See Chapter 4 for more on the *media* attribute.

Perhaps the colors and graphics you design for the web site are also being used (or *repurposed*, as the marketing folks say) on collateral printed materials like brochures and business cards. Keep in mind that color is expensive in print, so the company might want graphics such as logos to translate well to black and white for cheaper printing costs. In the same vein, a web design with a dark background and light foreground might be better reversed to dark ink on a light background when printed as a brochure.

The standard color space for printing presses is CMYK, for Cyan (bluish), Magenta (reddish), Yellow, and blacK (don't even ask why "K"). The CMYK color scheme is skewed a bit from the blue, red, and yellow color wheel typically referenced for the traditional subtractive color mode; the transparent pigments used by printing presses require somewhat different mixing formulas. Different medium, slightly different color wheel, yet again.

Translation between RGB and CMYK is built into many graphics programs. The translation is far from perfect; printed colors and screen colors will never, *ever*, be identical because the two media are not identical. Screen displays excel at portraying the brightest colors but show subtler hues less effectively. Print media have exactly the opposite attributes. And even then, there are intra-media differences; for example, printing on glossy paper is more likely to come close to reproducing the colors of a web page than printing on non-glossy paper.

Color and Accessibility

10% of the male population is color-blind. There are various forms of color-blindness: red-green, green-brown, and so on. We cannot possibly avoid all of the colors that could be misinterpreted by all visitors with color vision impairment.

Nonetheless, it's easy enough to make sure our pages are legible to anyone with color vision impairment. As already stated (repeatedly), there must be sufficient value contrast between the foreground and background colors such that the hue itself is irrelevant for legibility, as demonstrated in **FIGURE 5.42**. For instance, Figures 5.42 C and E would be legible to the same viewer, because the former uses different values (light versus dark), while the latter places both colors on a neutral background. Again, viewing your page in grayscale mode can show whether or not there is sufficient value contrast when the color information is removed. The AIS toolbar mentioned earlier allows viewing a color page in grayscale mode, as someone with color impaired vision might see it.

In addition to paying attention to value differences, we should also make sure that color alone is never the only clue to meaning. For instance, traffic signals are still discernible to the color-impaired because the red and green lights are always in the same position. One area that we need to be particularly careful of is navigational links. If color is the only cue for distinguishing links from normal text, then color-blind visitors might not be able to distinguish links from normal text. Therefore, we need to make sure to use other affordances on the links as well, such as underline, boldface, or italics.

See www.w3.org/TR/WAI-WEBCONTENT-TECHS/, www.usablenet.com, and www.Adobe.com/Adobe/accessibility for further information on color accessibility.

FIGURE 5.42 Red-Green
Color Impairment

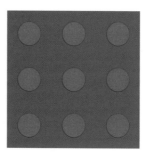

A. Green on Red with Similar
Value: Illegible to Someone with
Red-Green Color Blindness

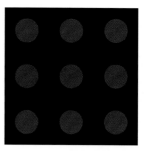

B. Green on Red with Similar
Value, as Seen by Someone with
Red-Green Color Impairment

C. Green on Red with Sufficient
Value Contrast

D. Green on Red with Sufficient
Value Contrast, as Seen by
Someone with Red-Green Color
Impairment

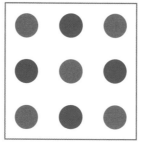

E. Red and Green on Neutral
Background

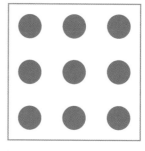

F. Red and Green on Neutral
Background, as Seen by
Someone with Red-Green Color
Impairment

Summary

Color is powerful, evoking mood and ambiance instantly. Color on the web is cheaper to use than printed color, although there are myriad technical difficulties we must cope with if our web pages are to display as intended. Nonetheless, working with color can be one of the more creative and satisfying aspects of designing a user interface.

Don't be afraid to play with color. After all, colors on digital media can be changed on a whim if you don't like them. Use color in unexpected ways and you might just get unexpected results. We leave this chapter with "thinking outside of the box" inspiration in the form of a Xerox ad, **FIGURE 5.43**.

FIGURE 5.43 Creative Use of Color (©2007 Xerox Corporation. All rights reserved. Xerox®, Phaser® Work Centre®, and Xerox Color, It Makes Business Sense are trademarks of Xerox Corporation in the United States and/or other countries.)

Design Checklist

The following checklist serves two functions: to summarize the major points and "rules" presented in the chapter, and to help ensure you've done all you should before finalizing any web site you are creating.

Did you:

- Choose an appropriate and appealing color scheme for your identified audience, providing the mood and ambiance that you intended? Be sure to consider factors such as age, gender, and culture.

- Provide sufficient contrast in color and value between foreground and background such that text and all links (static, on mouseover, visited, and active) are clear and easy to read?

- Choose background color and separator neutrals (or lack thereof) that interact appealingly, to show off colors to best effect?

- Choose prominent colors for the elements on the page that you want visitors to notice first, while using more subdued colors for the elements of lesser importance?

- Test the page at different gammas and at both 24-bit and 256-bit color depths?

- Test the page on different systems just to make sure the colors are still legible, even if they look very different?

- Limit yourself to the web-safe palette, particularly in large areas of solid color, if a sufficient number of your viewers have older computers?

- Specify hex codes for colors, rather than ambiguous color names?

- Create an appropriate color scheme with a limited number of colors, re-use each of the colors in several places, and use the colors consistently throughout the site?

- Test the page for printing on a black and white printer or provide a printer-friendly version of the page?

- Design your page so that it is appropriate for repurposing, if that's necessary?

- Test your site for accessibility by viewing in a grayscale format?

CHAPTER SIX

Graphics

MARK BAKALOR, WWW.EFUSE.COM/DESIGN/
WEB _ GRAPHICS _ BASICS.HTML:

"Years ago, the Web was little more than black text on a gray background. The infrequent graphic took about three weeks to load, it cost three cents to buy a loaf of bread, and I had to sludge through seven feet of snow just to get to school. Times have changed, the snow has melted, and the Web has become a place where visitors expect slick, professional graphics."

Graphics are great fun and very seductive. They can convey information quickly and memorably, and their embellishing, enriching presence can add greatly to the appeal of a site. In fact, we have come to expect graphics on all professional sites, so much so that we view sites without engaging graphics as amateurish. Always, though, we need to remember that graphics should draw the visitor's attention to the real message and content, whatever they are, not distract from them.

Graphics increase the time it takes to download pages on the site. They are, by their very nature, large files—only audio and video files are larger. Large graphics files and their resulting long download times are acceptable when our target audience is known to have fast internet connections. They are also appropriate for sites in which the graphics themselves are the main attraction, such as an art gallery, a photography site, a gaming site, or a fan site. But because many consumers still have slow telephone dial-up lines, most public-access web pages should minimize total file sizes, including graphics files.

Consequently, we must be judicious in choosing graphics; each image should be *optimized* (compressed) and should have truly wondrous impact if it is to justify the bandwidth price the visitor pays.

Principles and Terminology

Before we delve into the important and sometimes addictive world of working with graphics, as usual, we'll review some basic guidelines and terminology to set the stage.

Principles of Employing Graphics

Let's look first at the general principles for cashing in on the benefits and beauties of graphics while at the same time avoiding slow downloads for our visitors.

Avoid gratuitous graphics.

Use graphics only when they have a purpose that merits the download hit. It's fine even if that purpose is nothing more than to embellish the page, as long as the graphics truly do support the ambiance of the site. On the other hand, using an image for a simple horizontal rule might increase download time without providing any real "bang for the buck." Perhaps a standard <hr /> tag could perform the desired task equally well.

By the same token, we might want to avoid using navigational images (as opposed to text links) for the majority of the site's navigation. Think about it: If each of perhaps 50 major navigational links on a site requires a button with unique text on it, and each button has a rollover version as well, the result is 100 different images to download for the site, just for navigation, and 100 different images to maintain.

Because of such image inflation, many sites are abandoning the "text on button" look that was so popular just a few years ago.

Save images in the appropriate format.

If we use the wrong file format for a particular image, the file will be unnecessarily large. By choosing the appropriate file format with appropriate optimization settings, we can greatly reduce file sizes. We will look at this topic in depth later in the chapter when we examine specific image formats.

Reuse graphics.

The first time an image is referenced, it's downloaded into the browser's cache on the visitor's computer. From then on, it's retrieved not from our server, but from the visitor's hard drive, which means fast display. As a result, a logo or a navigation bar that is a rather large file might be acceptable if reused on multiple pages. Remember, though, that the browser reuses an image only if the URLs are identical; two copies of a single image, each retrieved from a different directory on the server, are completely different images to the browser.

Reduce image size.

Use images that are just large enough to serve their purpose, no larger. A smaller image is, as you might expect, a smaller file that loads faster. One way to reduce image size is to *crop* out (cut away) extraneous background that adds little to the image's impact. We can also reduce the overall size of the image; a 500 x 500 pixel image contains four times as many pixels as the same image sized at 250 x 250 pixels. If you must use a large image, consider providing a *thumbnail image* (smaller version) that links to the larger version, thereby giving visitors a choice of whether or not to wait for the larger image.

Use height and width attributes appropriately.

Although the browser is capable of figuring out image dimensions if `height` and `width` are omitted on the `<img />` tag, explicitly including those attributes makes a page display more quickly because the browser doesn't have to do any calculations. Also, since the browser loads text before it loads images, it can allocate the appropriate amount of space for the images before they actually appear. As a result, the text displays in its proper position right off the bat, rather than being repeatedly rearranged on the fly to fit around the images as they are rendered on the page, one by one.

Don't use `height` and `width` attributes to *change* an image's size on the page, however, because:

- Decreasing image size with `height` and `width` does not reduce download time, since the browser must still download the original large file anyway.

- Increasing image size with `height` and `width` seriously degrades the quality of the image.

If an image needs to be resized, do it yourself in an image-editing program, not in the browser.

Include the alt parameter on all images.

alt text has multiple benefits:

- It displays in screen readers, so that visually impaired visitors know the purpose of the image.

- It displays when an image link is broken or when images are turned off in the browser.

- In newer browsers, it displays on rollover, providing elaboration to all viewers.

- It's indexed by search engines and can elevate a site's rankings for search words, whereas any text embedded in the image itself is invisible to search engines.

If an image contains text, then the *alt* attribute should usually repeat that same text. Otherwise, the *alt* text should describe the purpose of the image. If the image is purely decorative, with no informational content at all, include an empty *alt* attribute:

```
<img alt="" ... />
```

That way, screen readers don't have to waste time reading meaningless text.

Terminology

Now we're a big step closer to getting to "play," but before going further, we need to agree on common graphics terminology.

Graphic Types

Content graphics are graphics used to represent data of some sort. This category includes data graphs and charts, maps, pictures of products, and screen prints. Many content graphics are straightforward, but some, particularly those presenting complex data in visual ways, are not. Finding ways to present data in a visual way is a problem not just for web site design, but for any type of communication.

Thematic (also termed *decorative*) *graphics* are purely for embellishment, controlling focus, and support of branding. Examples include logos, decorative photos, borders, dingbats, and custom bullets.

Navigational graphics are unique to the web and include clickable buttons, standalone icons, or icons adjacent to text links. Refer to Chapter 3 for guidelines specific to navigational graphics.

● ● ●

DISPLAYING INFORMATION EFFECTIVELY

The classic treatment on displaying information graphically is *The Visual Display of Quantitative Information* by Edward R. Tufte.

Anti-aliasing

In the commercial print world, which boasts 3200 dots per inch or even higher resolution, ink dots are so tiny that they blend together to provide perfectly smooth curves and diagonal lines. On the web, with its 72–100 pixels-per-inch resolution, pixels are large enough to be seen by the naked eye. Curved or diagonal lines are particularly problematic, because pixels can present an obviously jagged, stair-step appearance (termed "aliased"), as shown in **FIGURE 6.1**.

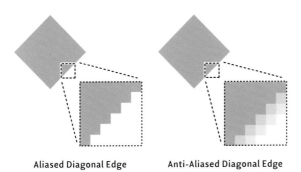

Aliased Diagonal Edge   Anti-Aliased Diagonal Edge

FIGURE 6.1 Aliasing versus Anti-aliasing

The remedy for the "jaggies" is *anti-aliasing*, which refers to a technique for smoothing the jagged, pixelated appearance of a diagonal or curved line on a screen display. Anti-aliasing adds tiny bits of transitional colors between the object and its background, thereby blending the pixelated edges gradually into the background color. As a result, the edge appears smoother. Figure 6.1 on the right shows an enlarged example of anti-aliasing for a diagonal edge. Even though the "anti" part of "anti-aliasing" sounds like a negative thing, it's really something we try to employ whenever possible.

In Fireworks, we set anti-aliasing in the *stroke* (outline) window for objects with a visible outside stroke, and in the *fill* (solid color inside the outline) window for objects without an outside stroke. Use "soft" or "anti-alias" to turn on anti-aliasing, and "hard" to turn it off.

• • •

ANTI-ALIASED TEXT EMBEDDED IN GRAPHICS

See the discussion about text anti-aliasing in Chapter 7.

Transparency

Although all web images are required to have rectangular shapes, we sometimes want an image to appear to be an irregular shape, like the color wheel in **FIGURE 6.2**. One way to impart such a non-rectangular illusion is to color the background of the rectangular image to match the HTML page background color, just as our rectangular color wheel image appears to have a white background to match the book's white page background.

Unfortunately, a color specified in an image-editing program sometimes doesn't match the *same* color generated by a web browser even if the color codes are identical, because they were created and rendered in different programs. Therefore, a faint outline of the rectangular image might show, particularly on older computer displays. Patterned backgrounds are even more problematic, because chances are slim that a background pattern on an image would line up precisely with a background pattern on a web page.

Consequently, one of the most useful attributes of some graphic formats is *transparency*, in which the web page background shows through areas of the image designated as transparent. When loaded into the browser, a transparent image "floats" on whatever background is in effect. See **FIGURE 6.3** for an example of the color wheel image (with a transparent background) now floating on top of patterned background.

To use transparency, we initially create our image on a *canvas* (background) temporarily set to the same color as the intended web page background, just so that we can see how the image looks on that color as we are creating it. Then, just before *exporting* (converting and saving) the image to a web-friendly format, we change the canvas color to *transparent*. The Optimize panel in Fireworks, shown in **FIGURE 6.4**, specifies the characteristics of the file when saved for the web, including turning on transparency.

FOLLOWING WITH FIREWORKS

Although Adobe Fireworks is used for the examples in this chapter, all web-friendly image editing software packages have similar features.

FIGURE 6.3 Image with Transparent Background, Floated over a Patterned Background

FIGURE 6.4 The Optimize Panel in Fireworks

But transparent backgrounds can cause anti-aliasing problems. After all, what edge-blending (anti-aliasing) colors should be used if there's no background color to blend to? Unless told otherwise, most image editors anti-alias to white. That's fine if we're putting the image on a white background, but if we're placing it on any other color, the result is a white "halo" that sets the image off from the background instead of blending it in. **FIGURE 6.5** shows a faint white halo around the teal diamond as the result of anti-aliasing to the default white but placing the diamond on a black background. To avoid the halo effect, we use the *matte* (background) color setting in the Optimize panel (again, see Figure 6.4) to tell the software that any image element adjacent to a transparent area should be anti-aliased to a specific color.

FIGURE 6.5 Anti-aliasing to an Improper Color

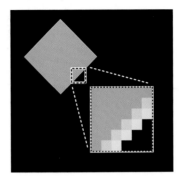

In the case of a patterned background as in Figure 6.3, our choices are not so straightforward, since the background consists of two or more colors. We have three matte options:

- Use the most prevalent color in the pattern for the matte.

- Choose an intermediate value between all of the colors of the pattern. The matte color for Figure 6.3 was an intermediate gray.

- Turn off anti-aliasing entirely.

When in doubt, try all three options before deciding which is the least obtrusive.

Index transparency, the transparency setting chosen in Figure 6.4, is fully supported by virtually all browsers but offers only two transparency options: fully transparent and fully opaque. On the other hand, *alpha channel transparency* supports multiple levels of transparency; for instance, some elements in an image could be at a 50% level of transparency, while other elements might be at a 25% level. An image employing alpha channel transparency doesn't require anti-aliasing to a specific matte color; the image can be floated upon any color background without worry about an unwanted color halo. Unfortunately, as of this writing, most web browsers don't completely support alpha transparency, so it's best to avoid it.

Interlacing

Normally, an image appears in the browser as a line-by-line download. That is, a few lines of the image appear on the screen, and then there may be a pause before a few more lines appear. The process continues, top to bottom, until the entire image is displayed. **FIGURE 6.6A** shows one intermediate step in the download process for a typical line-by-line image download.

Interlacing refers to an alternate way to load an image. Visitors first see a complete but low-resolution, very pixelated version of the image that is incrementally replaced by higher-resolution versions until the final version appears. **FIGURE 6.6B** shows a partial download for the same image as Figure 6.6A, but now interlacing is in effect, and visitors see a low-quality but recognizable image faster than with a typical line-by-line image download.

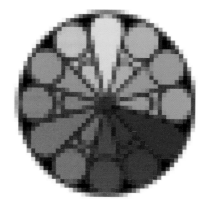

FIGURE 6.6 Interlacing

A. Download in Progress
for a Non-interlaced Image

B. Download in Progress
for an Interlaced Image

Although interlacing may actually increase the download time a bit, visitors may *perceive* it as being shorter. Obviously, interlacing is more important for large graphics files than for smaller ones. There seems to be no strong consensus either way as to whether or not interlacing should be employed, but, in fact, few sites today seem to use it. Interlacing is specified on the Optimize panel, as previously shown in Figure 6.4.

Graphics File Compression

Web-friendly file formats can compress images into smaller file sizes. Some compression techniques retain every single bit of image data, without degradation, no matter how many times the image is saved. Other graphics formats are said to be *lossy*, which means the compression algorithm discards some image data each and every time the image is saved, all as a tradeoff for better compression.

Although the easiest way to avoid such negative effects might be to avoid lossy formats entirely, the web doesn't currently allow that option (as we'll soon discuss). For now, though, realize that the first defense is to avoid saving over (that is, overwriting) the original image. Always preserve a pristine, original copy, saving all modified versions under new names. In that way, multiple saves don't compound the negative effects of a lossy format.

Vector Images

Vector images don't specify individual pixels but instead store an image as a series of mathematical equations. For instance, the vector specifications for a 100 x 100-pixel rectangle would be the vertical and horizontal dimensions, the thickness and color code for the *stroke* (outline), and the color code for the *fill* (solid area) inside the rectangle. Since the underlying equation remains the same, regardless of the values of those equation elements, the image's file size remains the same whether it displays at 10 x 10 pixels or 1000 x 1000 pixels.

Vector graphics scale beautifully; we can change the display size without compromising quality in the least, because, again, the basic equation remains the same. Common vector-based formats include native files created in Fireworks (file extension .png), Corel Draw (.dwg), and Flash (.fla). Unfortunately, vector graphics are not appropriate for non-mathematical images such as photographs, and Flash files are the only vector graphics that are currently completely reliable on the web.

Bitmapped/Raster Images

Bitmapped (also called *raster* or just *bitmap*) *images* are made up of individual pixels mapped to two-dimensional grids. A 30 x 30-pixel bitmap image must keep track of each of its 900 pixels individually, including the color code for each, while a 300 x 300-pixel graphic must keep track of 90,000 pixels. Obviously, bitmaps are a much less efficient way to store image data than the mathematical formulas used by vector images, with file sizes increasing dramatically as image size increases. Nonetheless, bitmapped formats are the only practical way to store pixel-based, continuous-tone images such as photographs.

Bitmap images degrade when scaled: after all, how can we scale discrete, indivisible pixels to, say, 135%? Not well. The loss of quality is particularly evident when a bitmap is enlarged, because pixels that don't exist in the original have to be invented for the new, larger version. Although image-editing programs can make some fairly intelligent decisions about how to invent those pixels, the result is never as good as it might have been had the pixels existed in the original image.

● ● ●

RESAMPLING BITMAPPED IMAGES

Besides bicubic interpolation, other available resampling methods include bilinear interpolation and soft interpolation, which add some blur to images, and nearest neighbor interpolation, which gives a pixelated, jagged effect. See www.dpreview.com/learn/?/Glossary/Digital_Imaging/Interpolation_01.htm.

The process of adding or subtracting pixels to resize or rotate a bitmapped image is called *resampling* or *interpolation* (translation: "educated guess"). Image-editing programs often provide a choice of resampling methods. Luckily, the only one we really need to remember is *bicubic interpolation* (usually the default), the most sophisticated and accurate method for web imaging.

After reducing the size of a bitmapped image with bicubic interpolation, try applying a sharpening filter like "Unsharp Mask" (available in most image editing programs) to restore any sharpness lost in the resampling process.

● ● ●

UNSHARP MASK: A STRANGE NAME FOR A SHARPENING FILTER

"Unsharp Mask" is a traditional darkroom technique that involves merging a blurred image (hence the "unsharp") with a normal image. See www.earthboundlight.com/phototips/unsharp-mask.html for a more involved explanation.

Bitmapped file formats include BMP, TIFF, PSD (Adobe Photoshop), JPG, GIF, and compressed-for-the-web PNG files. Of these formats, only JPG, GIF, and compressed PNG are intended for display on the web.

CONVERTING A BITMAPPED IMAGE TO A VECTOR IMAGE

If we can convert a bitmapped image to a vector image, we may be able to resize and manipulate it more effectively. Such conversion is not usually successful with photographs but can be appropriate for flat color images like cartoons and diagrams. A few image-editing programs have vector conversion algorithms built in, such as:

- The "Modify > Bitmap > Trace Bitmap" command in Flash. Once you've converted the image, you can always export it to another file format like PNG for further editing.

- The "Live Trace" command in Illustrator, followed by Object > Expand.

- The Filter > Stylize > Trace Contour command *or* Find Edges in Photoshop (though the latter method is not at all intuitive and the result requires further tweaking).

Master Images

It's best to create and maintain your original master images in either a vector file format or a high-resolution bitmap format, even if the images will eventually end up as low-resolutions bitmaps on the web. Why? Because:

- If stored in vector format, images can be scaled, rotated, and manipulated end-lessly without loss of quality.

- If stored as a high-resolution bitmap, we have more pixels available when edit-ing and manipulating the images. High-resolution bitmapped images always scale better than low-resolution images.

- High-resolution bitmapped images can be used for print as well as for the web. The reverse is often unsuccessful.

For the most part, we will create, manipulate, and maintain our original images in a format like BMP, TIFF, PSD, or non-compressed PNG, and then *export* (convert and save) copies of the originals to a web-friendly, bitmapped format before embedding them in a web page. Notice that even graphics that are best as vector images must be exported to a bitmapped format (JPG, GIF, or compressed PNG) for display on the web, with Flash being the only exception. **TABLE 6.1** recaps the basics of graph-ics formats.

We will look at the three bitmapped web formats next. We'll defer discussion of the vector-based Flash format until a later section that examines animation.

TABLE 6.1 GRAPHICS FORMATS

	Vector Graphics	Bitmap Graphics
Storage method	Mathematical equations	2-D pixel mapping
Types of images	Best for geometric shape-based (rather than pixel-based) images. Examples: cartoons, diagrams, line drawings.	Best for pixel-based images. Examples: photographs, gradients, some patterns.
Resizing quality	Resizes without loss of quality	Degrades (best results with a bicubic interpolation method)
File size related to image size	File size is stable regardless of image size	File size can increase exponentially with image size
Common non-web image formats	Native Fireworks PNG, Adobe Illustrator, Corel Draw	BMP, TIFF, Photoshop's PSD, Corel Paint
Web formats	Only Flash	JPG, GIF, compressed PNG (some features not supported)

Image Formats for the Web

Next, we'll examine the three image formats currently appropriate for non-animated web display: JPG, GIF, and PNG.

JPG Format Graphics

JPG (pronounced "jay-peg" and also written JPEG) stands for Joint Photographic Experts Group. It uses either a .jpg or .jpeg file extension. As you might guess from the name, JPG is intended for photographs and similar images that incorporate lots of colors, tiny bits of colors (often as small as individual pixels), and smooth color changes like gradients, realistic 3-D shading, and shadows. **FIGURE 6.7** shows a photo that would be best stored in JPG format. JPG supports true color imaging, up to 16.8 million colors. It doesn't support transparency or animation. Although a form termed Progressive JPG does allow interlacing, Progressive JPG is not widely supported by current browsers.

TRUE COLOR

See Chapter 5 for further discussion of true color.

FIGURE 6.7 JPG Example

JPG File Compression

JPG compression is lossy. Specifically, saving a file to JPG:

- Blurs crisp edges between adjacent colors.

- Adds *artifacts*, also called *noise* (random pixels of a different color), to areas of solid color.

- Alters the colors of the original.

FIGURE 6.8, a JPG saved with fairly heavy compression, illustrates some of these problems. Keep in mind that this image is not really a good candidate for saving as a JPG, so the problems are exaggerated.

FIGURE 6.8 Lossy JPG Compression, 20% Quality Setting

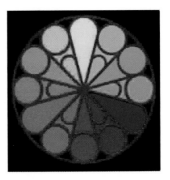

The degradation of this image reminds you to never save over an original image when lossy compression is in effect, or the original high-quality image will be lost forever. Instead, maintain the original as an unadulterated master copy (preferably in some format other than JPG) and make any and all alterations only to copies.

JPG compression is a variable type of compression, which means that we choose how much quality degradation we can tolerate as a tradeoff for smaller file sizes. From within image-editing software, we can view the effects of various compression rates and then decide which version is the best compromise between image quality and file size. Four possible compression previews from Fireworks, as shown in **FIGURE 6.9**, should convince you not to be afraid to try very heavy compression. As you can see, even the heavy compression in the 30% quality image on the lower left can deliver an image of acceptable quality. After all, a very high-quality image is wasted on an inherently low-resolution computer display anyway. **FIGURE 6.10** shows an Optimize panel for exporting a file to JPG.

Crisp focus and high contrast are the enemies of efficient file compression in the JPG format. Consequently, we can also minimize JPG file sizes by adding a small amount of blur in non-critical areas and by reducing the contrast between the lightest and darkest areas in a photo.

FIGURE 6.9 JPG Compression Previews from Fireworks

FIGURE 6.10 Optimize Panel for a JPG

As we have seen, JPG doesn't support transparency, animation, or cross-browser-supported interlacing. To use these features, we need to turn to GIF instead.

GIF Graphics

GIF, or *Graphics Interchange Format*, works best for line-based images with areas of solid color, such as cartoons, diagrams, line art, and graphic text. Figure 6.2 earlier showed an image that would be best stored as a GIF. GIF supports index transparency, interlacing, and animation.

A GIF image can store up to 256 colors. If we want an image to be web-safe, but we didn't create the original with a web-safe palette, we can specify a web-snap palette when we export the image to GIF. The image editor then converts every non-web-safe color to what it believes to be the closest web-safe color. Although it's probably safer for us to convert to web-safe colors ourselves, automatic conversion can be a time-saving first step when we are porting an existing image to the web.

What if we aren't restricted to a web-safe palette? Although GIF limits us to 256 colors, they can be *any* 256 colors out of the 16.8 million choices. In this case, we can choose a non-safe *adaptive palette* (colors chosen from within the image) to preserve our color choices accurately— as long as we don't exceed the GIF 256-color limit.

Unfortunately, images that include complex textures, *gradients* (gradual color blends from one color into another), or *drop shadows* (a three-dimensional effect that uses a gradient) can easily exceed that limit. In such cases, the image-editing program usually retains the 256 most frequently used colors and shifts the remaining colors to those 256 retained colors as best as it can. If we don't like the choices the program makes, we can choose to "lock" some of the more critical colors on the palette, so that they remain true.

We can also "fake" lost colors by turning on *dithering,* which alternates two similar colors to fool the eye into thinking a third color is present. Dithering, unfortunately, increases the file size of a GIF.

GIF File Compression

GIF employs a lossless/non-destructive compression algorithm, so that colors and crisp edges remain true when saved, and no artifacts or noise are introduced. The types of GIF images that compress most efficiently are those with few colors, horizontal bands of solid color, no noise or texture, no anti-aliasing, and no dithering. Let's look at how each of these characteristics affects GIF compression.

GIF images make use of a *color lookup table* (*CLUT*) to keep track of the colors in an image, so that every 6-digit color code (e.g., #FF0000) is stored only once, and its number (01 through 256) in the table is used as the cross-reference for each pixel that uses that color. The short explanation is that using the smaller positional code for each pixel results in a smaller file than if using the full 6-digit color code.

If fewer than 256 colors are used, the color code may be able to shrink even further. In summary, a lower *color depth* (the total number of colors) has the potential

• • •

PRONUNCIATION OF "GIF"

Is GIF pronounced "jiff" or "giff"? Although both pronunciations are accepted in the industry, Steve Wilhite, the creator of the GIF format, says he pronounces it "jiff." No particular reason, he says; that's just how he has always pronounced it. (Per Lynda Weinman in <creative html design.2>)

• • •

THE WEB-SAFE PALETTE AND OTHER COLOR CONCEPTS

See Chapter 5 for discussion of the 216-color web-safe palette, dithering, and other color concepts in use here.

to shrink the size of the file. **FIGURE 6.11** illustrates how increasing the number of colors in a 200 x 200-pixel image increases its file size.

3-Color Image, 3K   **212-Color Image, 11K**

FIGURE 6.11 GIF File Size Comparison: 3 Colors versus 212 Colors

The GIF compression algorithm starts at the upper left corner of an image, wends its way from left to right across the first row of pixels, and then works its way down the image row by row. When there are adjacent pixels in a row that are the same color, the algorithm stores the color code only once but keeps track of the number of pixels that repeat that color. As a result, a horizontal stripe compresses better than a vertical stripe, particularly a narrow one. **FIGURE 6.12** illustrates how horizontal stripes store more efficiently than vertical stripes.

 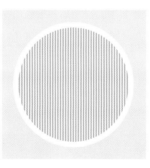

Horizontal Stripes, 3K   **Vertical Stripes, 4K**

FIGURE 6.12 GIF File Size Comparison: Horizontal versus Vertical Stripes

Anti-aliasing, gradients, dithering, pattern, and texture are double trouble when it comes to increasing file size; they interrupt horizontal bands of color and also increase the number of colors in an image. Notice in **FIGURE 6.13** that anti-aliasing enlarges the file size a bit from the original image in Figure 6.11A, while both a gradient and dithering increase it even more. Adding texture to the original image inflated the original file size by a whopping 1600%! The point is that the more we can minimize colors, vertical stripes, noise, pattern, texture, dithering, and anti-aliasing, the smaller the resulting GIF file.

FIGURE 6.13 File Size Comparison: Anti-aliasing, Gradients, Dithering, and Texture

Anti-aliasing, 4 K

Gradient, 22K
(25 K If Dithering Were
Turned On)

Texture, 54K

As we have seen, the JPG compression algorithm was designed for storing photos, while the GIF compression algorithm was designed for storing images composed of large areas of flat color in a limited color depth. In fact, photos (which are neither flat nor limited in color) are the very antithesis of everything that GIF depends upon for compression efficiency. Photos stored in the GIF format often result in very large files, and the images may well be degraded because of the 256-color maximum.

Even so, we sometimes need to export a photo to GIF because we require transparency or animation, neither of which can be accomplished with JPG. Under those circumstances, we can minimize degradation by specifying a non-safe adaptive palette in the Optimize panel, with dithering turned on. In **FIGURE 6.14** you see compared examples of a photo stored as GIF and JPG. Notice that although the GIF with dithering is acceptable, the JPG exhibits both the highest quality and the smallest file size.

FIGURE 6.14 200 x 300-Pixel Photo as GIF versus JPG

GIF Format, 256 Colors,
Adaptive Palette,
Dithering Off, 41K

GIF Format, 256 Colors,
Adaptive Palette,
Dithering On, 48K

JPG Format, 80% Quality, 20K

In a similar vein, any type of gradient (including 3-D beveling and drop shadows) or complex texture can be problematic when stored as a GIF. Once again, using a non-safe adaptive palette with dithering turned on can often produce acceptable results. **FIGURE 6.15** illustrates a gradient image stored at various color depths in GIF, as well as saved as a JPG. At lower color depths with dithering turned off, colors are altered and *banding* (striping instead of a smooth gradient) is apparent. The GIFs with the non-safe adaptive palette look smoother, but again, the JPG has the highest quality matched with a reasonable file size. If in doubt, save an image in multiple formats, and then check both the image quality and the file size before making a decision as to which one to use.

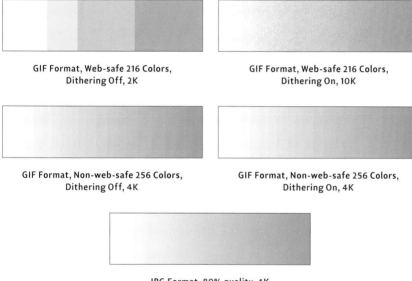

FIGURE 6.15 Gradient Saved in Various Formats

GIF Format, Web-safe 216 Colors, Dithering Off, 2K

GIF Format, Web-safe 216 Colors, Dithering On, 10K

GIF Format, Non-web-safe 256 Colors, Dithering Off, 4K

GIF Format, Non-web-safe 256 Colors, Dithering On, 4K

JPG Format, 80% quality, 4K

FIGURE 6.16 shows the Optimize panel in Fireworks for exporting an image as a GIF.

FIGURE 6.16 Optimize Panel for a GIF

PNG Format Graphics

PNG (Portable Network Graphics, pronounced "ping") is a newer graphics format intended eventually to replace GIF for everything but GIF animation (because PNG doesn't support animation). PNG won't replace the JPG format, because PNG is not ideal for continuous-tone images such as photos.

Although native PNG files as created in an image-editing program may contain vector information, they should be exported as bitmapped, compressed PNGs before being displayed on the web.

The advantages of PNG are myriad:

- A choice of three color depths:
  - 256 colors, which offers efficient storage of color-mapped images, much like GIF.
  - True color, which offers 16.8 million colors, a significant improvement over GIF. File sizes are increased by the additional color, however.
  - True grayscale storage, as opposed to GIF's less efficient storage of grayscale as nothing more than a version of an adaptive palette.
- Lossless compression, like GIF.
- Two-dimensional interlacing, an improved method of displaying images at progressively higher levels of detail. PNG interlacing is faster and of higher quality than GIF interlacing.
- Compression that is slightly more efficient than GIF compression, as long as the compression settings are chosen wisely.
- Gamma correction. The sRGB (Standard RGB color space) standard promises to define a consistent color display on any visitor's computer. It, too, is not currently supported well—not at all in Internet Explorer.
- Support for alpha channel transparency, which offers greater creative freedom than index transparency. Alpha transparency doesn't require anti-aliasing to a specific background color, which means an image looks good on whatever background color it's placed. It does come with a price: It can greatly increase file size, and, as of this writing, it is, at best, quirky. In fact, PNG alpha channel transparency is not supported at all in Internet Explorer. For now, it seems that alpha channel transparency will have to wait.

The Adobe Fireworks native file format is a modified version of the PNG format. Emphasis here on the word "modified"—the files as produced by Fireworks should not be used "as is" on the web, because they contain unnecessary information that

• • •

USING THE HTML <OBJECT> TAG TO INCLUDE PNG IMAGES

You may have heard that embedding a PNG <img /> tag in an HTML <object> tag is a hack that can provide a way to get around the lack of support in some browsers. Unfortunately, it also breaks the image in other browsers! Unless you have the luxury of developing a site for only a single version of a single browser, this fix alone doesn't seem to be reliable.

greatly increases file size. Note that other image-editing programs can export their native formats to compressed PNG as well.

PNG File Compression

Options for exporting PNG files are in the Optimize panel. To minimize compressed PNG file sizes, be sure to do the following:

- When exporting a PNG file, choose the lowest possible color setting that provides the required image quality: grayscale, 8-bit (256 colors), or true color (more colors than we can possibly cram into a single image).

- Use alpha transparency only when necessary (once it's actually widely supported), because it greatly increases file size. Export with index transparency if you need only two levels of transparency: fully transparent and fully opaque.

- Specify interlacing only on large images, because it provides little benefit for small images that already download quickly.

Combination Images

In general, we should avoid combining JPG-style art (continuous-tone art and photos) and GIF-style art (flat color illustrations and text) into a single image. If we export the resulting image as a JPG, the colors will be altered and noise will be introduced in the flat-color areas. If we export the image as a GIF, the continuous tone areas will be reduced to a maximum of 256 colors and the file could be quite large. Either way, some elements will be degraded because of the different compression algorithms.

Instead, consider creating two separate images: a background JPG and a foreground GIF or PNG. For instance:

```
<td style="background-image:url(jpgBackground.jpg)">
   <img src="gifImage.gif" ... />
</td>
```

The transparency of the GIF or PNG allows the background JPG to show through, and the result looks like a single image to visitors.

Yet another alternative is to *slice* (cut apart) the image into rectangular pieces that are reassembled into a table, with the whole thing appearing to be an unbroken image on the web page. Each slice can be optimized to suit its content, so that a slice of text on a simple background might be saved as a GIF, while a slice with a gradient is saved as a JPG. The downside is that colors might not match across the different image formats. **TABLE 6.2** recaps what we've learned about web file formats.

● ● ●

SLICED IMAGES

See Chapter 3 for more details on slicing images.

TABLE 6.2 WEB FILE FORMATS

	JPG (.jpg or .jpeg)	GIF (.gif)	PNG (.png)
Compression algorithm	Compression best suited for continuous-tone images such as photos.	Compression best suited to flat-color images such as line drawings and cartoons with horizontal lines and minimal patterns and gradients.	Compression best suited to flat-color images such as line drawings and cartoons with minimal patterns and gradients.
Variable compression	Yes	Yes, but only by limiting the number of colors in an image.	Yes, but only by limiting the number of colors in an image.
Lossless save	No: alters colors, blurs sharp edges, and introduces artifacts in flat-color areas.	Yes	Yes
Number of colors per image	True color (16.8 million colors)	256 color color-mapped "palette" images	• Grayscale • 256 color color-mapped "palette" images • True color (16.8 million colors)
Transparency	No	Index transparency (binary, either on or off)	• Index transparency (binary, either on or off) • Alpha transparency (256 levels), but it results in large file sizes and is not yet widely supported.
Animation	No	Yes	No
Interlacing	Yes, but JPG's progressive interlacing is not widely supported.	Yes	Yes

Acquiring Images

Often, we are responsible for obtaining images for a site, whether for decoration (like a logo) or for information delivery (like a picture of a product). Although we might create some images from scratch, many need to be *digitized* (somehow captured from the real world). A logo on paper or a standard photo might need to be scanned into a digital format, or we might take a photo with a digital camera as a way of bypassing the hassle of developing standard camera film. We will look at several image sources: commercially available stock photos and clip art, screen capture software, scanners, and digital cameras.

Stock Photos and Clip Art

Some web sites that offer stock photos and clip art are quite expensive, while others are either free or charge a very minimal fee, such as only a dollar or two per image.

All sites allow search by topic, such as "eagle" or "happy." Some sites permit filtering a search by color as well, so that a search for "happy" and "orange" would turn up only predominantly orange pictures that embody the concept of happy.

If we want to stay out of trouble with the U.S. Copyright Office, we simply cannot use images "borrowed" from other web sites. Unless a site specifically gives permission to use an image, assume that we cannot legally use it. Even if the site states that the images are copyright-free or royalty-free, be sure to read the licensing agreement for any fine print that might cause legal problems later.

BONUS TOPIC

See Resources on the book's web site for sources of stock photos, clip art, screen capture utilities, and more.

Screen Capture Utilities

Sometimes we need to capture a computer screen shot and embed it on a web page. Screen capture utilities are perfect for that task, providing the ability to capture pixels on an entire display, an entire window, or just a portion of a window. Some of these utilities are built into the operating system; others are easily obtainable.

Scanners

Scanners are the obvious tool for capturing images or text from printed pages, but they can also capture images from photographic negatives as well as images of relatively flat, real-life objects. For instance, autumn leaves arranged on a scanner bed can result in a stunning photographic effect. Don't be afraid to think outside of the box for creative ways to use a scanner.

Types of Scanners

In the last few years, *flatbed scanners* (for scanning flat materials such as photographs or printed pages) have improved dramatically in accuracy while decreasing dramatically in price. Some flatbed scanners sell for less than $100 today.

SCANNING AN IMAGE FROM A PRINTED PAGE

If an original image was scanned from a commercially printed page, a moiré pattern from the original printed dots can degrade the resulting scanned image. One method to reduce the impact of the moiré is as follows:

1. Blur the entire image slightly.

2. Reduce the size of the image slightly.

3. Use a "sharpen" command to restore some of the sharpness lost by the blur of the first step.

Some flatbed scanners have adapters for scanning negatives and transparencies, but the quality is a far cry from that of *dedicated transparency scanners*, which scan negatives and slides rather than printed materials. Since they scan original film, not pictures that were degraded somewhat in the printing process, they usually produce higher-quality images than flatbed scanners. Although some transparency scanners have a street price of $500 or so, the highly-rated ones seem to start around $1500.

Although transparency scanners do indeed deliver the most accurate images, once those images are degraded by being posted on the web at only 72–100 pixels per inch, complete with the inherent web color vagaries that we examined in Chapter 5... well, it seems that a transparency scanner, though terrific, is overkill unless we will also use the images for collateral printed materials.

Scanner Specifications

Even the less expensive scanners seem capable of extremely high resolution, scanning at 2400 dots per inch or higher. Color fidelity, then, not resolution, is really the mark of a high-quality scanner. How can you tell if a scanner has high color fidelity? Ideally, we would like to find a store that allows us to test several different scanners. Keep in mind that the only accurate comparison is to evaluate the resulting scanned images on the *same* computer, thereby eliminating any color variations resulting from different video adaptors and monitors.

Another way to tell if a scanner is capable of high color fidelity is to look at its technical specifications. At a minimum, a scanner should handle 24-bit color/true color (16.8 million colors) and have better than a 3.0 *luminosity rating* (also referred to as the *Dmax* rating). The luminosity rating shows how well the scanner can pick detail out of shadow areas on an image. Although our eyes are outstanding at perceiving such detail, scanners (as well as cameras, for that matter) are not so skillful. In any case, luminosity ratings today are in the following range:

- 3.0 luminosity rating or lower: low-end scanners, with less accurate shadow detail.

- 3.3–3.4 luminosity rating: mid-range scanners, with generally good shadow detail.

- 3.6 luminosity rating or higher: high-end professional-quality scanners, with very good shadow detail and very expensive price points.

Scanner Settings

When you scan an image, exactly what resolution settings should you use? Well, you could just automatically scan at the highest resolution. After all, higher settings should, in theory, provide higher quality, particularly if you want to use the image for high-resolution printed materials in addition to posting on the web. The problem is that higher resolutions produce much larger image files. Additionally, if you try scanning, say, an 8 x 10" original at the highest resolution and the highest color depth, there is a good chance you will hang your computer (well, if it's a Windows computer, anyway—at the very least, you can take a long lunch break while you wait for the results). Few computers can handle the pixel-crunching demands of an image file that large. Usually, it's safer to scan at a somewhat lower resolution, because, as we know, the web is a low-resolution medium.

But how do we know what resolution is correct for a given image? Let's review bit-mapped images a bit before we get to the mathematics of choosing a scanning resolution. Remember, bitmapped images don't resize well, because image-editing programs have a hard time inventing pixels out of thin air for enlargements and deciding which pixels to discard for reductions. As a result, it seems that scanning an image at precisely the number of pixels we need for display on the web will deliver the best results. For example, if we need a 200 x 300-pixel image, we want the scanner to deliver an image that is exactly 200 x 300 pixels.

Let's look at a sample calculation for an original image that measures 4 x 6 inches:

- The size on the web needs to be 200 pixels wide x 300 pixels tall.

- For width: 200 (target pixel width) divided by 4 (inch width of the original) = 50 *dpi* (dots per inch, the scanning resolution).

- For height: 300 (target pixel height) divided by 6 (inches of height of the original) = 50 dpi.

- Either way, the result is 50 dpi, so we can safely scan the image at that 50 dpi.

- Double-check the math:

  - 50 (dpi) times 4 (inches of width in the original) results in 200 pixels of width, exactly what we need.

  - 50 (dpi) times 6 (inches of height in the original) results in 300 pixels of height, again exactly what we need. (Note that some examples coming up won't be quite so cut and dried.)

Now that we see how this works, let's put the same calculation into a matrix that we can use for future calculations:

TABLE 6.3 CALCULATING SCANNING RESOLUTION, EXAMPLE 1

	Target of Number Pixels	Divided by	Original Image, in Inches	Equals	Scanning Resolution DPI
Width	200	÷	4	=	50
Height	300	÷	6	=	50

Let's try another example. This time, we need to display that same 4 x 6-inch photo at 600 x 900 pixels:

TABLE 6.4 CALCULATING SCANNING RESOLUTION, EXAMPLE 2

	Target of Number Pixels	Divided by	Original Image, in Inches	Equals	Scanning Resolution DPI
Width	600	÷	4	=	150
Height	900	÷	6	=	150

Now let's look at a trickier example, displaying the image at 400 x 500 pixels:

TABLE 6.5 CALCULATING SCANNING RESOLUTION, EXAMPLE 3A

	Target of Number Pixels	Divided by	Original Image, in Inches	Equals	Scanning Resolution DPI
Width	400	÷	4	=	100
Height	500	÷	6	=	83

Notice that now, the calculated scanning resolution is different for the height and the width. The differing results tell us that the *aspect ratio* (ratio of width to height) of the original image is different from the aspect ratio for our target web image. Unfortunately, we cannot scan height and width at different resolutions to suit the two different dpi results. Nor should we simply scan at one of the two calculated results, and then stretch or squash the image in one direction or the other so that it fits into the target dimensions. The result is obviously distorted and looks amateurish.

Instead, we scan at the higher of the two calculated resolutions (here, 100 dpi) and then *crop* (delete) the extra height on the dimension that is now too large. In this particular case, cropping an inch off of the height of the resulting image solves the problem:

TABLE 6.6 CALCULATING SCANNING RESOLUTION, EXAMPLE 3B

	Target of Number Pixels	Divided by	Original Image, in Inches	Equals	Scanning Resolution DPI
Width	400	÷	4	=	100
Height	500	÷	6	=	83 replaced by 100 (the scan results in 600 pixels vertically, but 100 pixels are cropped from the height after scanning)

Digital Cameras

Digital cameras are wonderful little devices for capturing images that can be displayed on a computer screen just moments after snapping the picture, without film and development costs. "Free" pictures might well encourage us to take more pictures, giving us a better chance of coming up with that one "killer" shot we need.

Of course, there are disadvantages to digital photography:

- The quality of photography may not be as high as that of traditional 35mm cameras, even when wielded by professionals; only the more expensive digital cameras are comparable. However, as we have seen, high-resolution photography is probably overkill for the web anyway.

- Only a limited number of images can be stored on a memory card. Larger or extra memory cards can compensate, but they can be expensive. An alternative is to download images to a laptop computer or portable storage device periodically.

- Only the more expensive digital SLR cameras (Single Lens Reflex, which practically speaking means that the camera accepts separate lenses) have a large selection of fun photography toys like filters and special lenses and such. Although filters can be applied on the image later, in image-editing programs like Photoshop and Fireworks, the results are often less natural looking than when applied from a camera lens.

Desired features of a digital camera, whether SLR or not, include:

- **A higher number of megapixels.** More megapixels means more pixels are captured, which in turn means the image is of higher quality and can be used at larger sizes without degradation. As of this writing, the cheaper digital cameras offer perhaps 4 megapixels, while more expensive cameras may exceed 10 megapixels.

- **Optical telephoto zoom.** This, of course, brings distant objects closer. The higher the number, the better. With digital SLR cameras, this measurement depends not on the camera itself but on the lens attached to it. In contrast, a *digital zoom* (as opposed to optical zoom) does only what Photoshop or Fireworks does when a bitmap is enlarged; that is, it invents pixels out of thin air. As a result, it's of little worth.

- **Wide angle zoom.** More of the image fits into the picture. For wide angle specifications, the smaller the number, the better. The better cameras have a 35mm camera equivalent of 28mm or less. With a digital SLR camera, this measurement depends not on the camera itself but on the lens attached to it.

● ● ●

THE NUMBER ONE HINT FOR TAKING GREAT PHOTOGRAPHS

Some professional photographers claim that the only difference between a professional and an amateur photographer is that the professional takes lots more pictures. A bit of an exaggeration, perhaps, but there is truth to the underlying concept that we have more chances at a great photo if we take lots of shots.

- **Fully automatic controls (focus, exposure time, and aperture), fully manual controls, or both.** There is no right answer here—it depends on whether or not you would ever want to override automatic settings. If you require manual settings, then chances are you know enough about photography to ignore this section entirely.

- **Built-in flash or externally-mounted flash.** The former is more convenient, but the latter is more powerful and adjustable.

- **Size of LCD viewfinder.** The larger the better.

- **Weight of camera and lenses.** The lighter the better, although this is of course a tradeoff with other features. SLR lenses equipped with large zoom lenses can be rather heavy.

Creating and Editing Images

After capturing a photo from a scan or from a digital camera, we may need to use image-editing software to correct flaws or enhance the image with artistic effects. We might remove blemishes, sharpen or blur the focus of selected areas, or make a gray sky blue.

We might also use image-editing software to create a graphic from scratch, such as to draw a 3-D button or to devise a new logo. Image-editing programs have become so powerful that even people who have no drawing skills are capable of producing some very professional effects.

The biggest player in image editing for the print industry has traditionally been Adobe, while the biggest player for the web industry was Macromedia. In 2005, Adobe acquired Macromedia. The synergy resulting from the merger of these two image-editing software giants has the potential to be a thing of wonder.

Adobe Photoshop is one of the most well-known, most powerful, and most expensive professional image-editing programs available. It gives outstanding results on most photo editing tasks and its advanced printing features make it the standard-bearer for the print industry. It's also highly "pluggable;" there are dozens of third-party plug-in programs that interact with Photoshop to do things that Photoshop is incapable of doing alone.

Adobe (previously Macromedia) Fireworks was developed specifically for creating web graphics, with the original files stored in a proprietary PNG format. Although Fireworks is quite capable of editing photos, it really excels at creating vector graphics, slicing images, and creating HTML for rollover effects. Fireworks is compatible with Photoshop special effects plug-ins.

Adobe's web site offers limited-time demos of Photoshop, Photoshop Elements (the "lite" consumer version), and Fireworks.

Despite the fact that Adobe software dominates the industry, design professionals use programs from other companies as well, such as JASC's Paint Shop Pro and Corel Photo-Paint/Corel Draw. A major advantage to Corel Draw is that it comes bundled with a library of hundreds of fonts, clip art images, stock photos, textures, and patterns.

Layered Images

When creating original graphics within an image-editing program, we generally work with *layers* in the master image. That is, each object (a shape, text element, or embedded bitmap) exists in its own layer so that we can manipulate it independently of the other objects.

FIGURE 6.17 shows two workspaces for a single Fireworks navigation button file: one workspace with only the at rest/"up" elements visible, the other with only the rollover/"down" state elements visible. Each workspace is accompanied by its Layers panel, with the "eye" icon next to each layer showing which layers are currently visible.

Workspace Showing "At Rest" Image

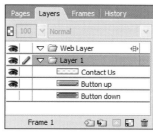

Layers Panel with "At Rest" Elements Visible

FIGURE 6.17 Master Button Image in Fireworks

Workspace Showing Rollover Image

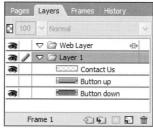

Layers Panel with Rollover Image Elements Visible

This particular file contains three layers:

- The "Contact Us" text, visible for both states.

- The at rest (i.e., "up") button shape, visible only when editing or exporting the at rest button.

- The rollover (i.e., "down") button shape, visible only when editing or exporting the rollover button.

By including both button images in the same file, we are assuring alignment and consistency between the two images after they are exported to a web-friendly format. The rollover button shape was easily created by copying the at rest shape but modifying the bevel to be "inset" (rather than "raised").

In the Layers panel, any layer closer to the top of the list is displayed in the workspace on top of any layers below it on the list. Thus, the "Contact Us" layer must be at the top of the list.

Exporting Images

We have already discussed some of the general principles of exporting original images to web-friendly formats like GIF, JPG, or PNG. Now we need to look a bit more closely at what is actually involved in exporting a file.

Exporting an image to a bitmapped format like GIF, JPG, or web-friendly PNG is called *flattening* the file, because the original layer-based objects no longer exist in the exported version. All that remains is a bitmapped, two-dimensional grid of independent pixels. The fact that the objects in the flattened image can no longer be resized or re-colored or manipulated independently is a good argument for always preserving a copy of the image in the original layered format so that we can, if need be, modify it later.

When exporting an image, we first turn on the elements we want visible in the image and turn off the ones we don't, by clicking on the "eye" icons next to the layers (refer back to Figure 6.17). We specify the overall file characteristics (file format, number of colors, compression rate, dithering options, interlacing, etc.) in the Optimize panel, as shown earlier in Figures 6.10 (JPG format) and 6.16 (GIF format). Finally, we either choose "Export" or "Save As" (depending upon the image editor) from the File menu.

Matching Colors across Software Packages

As already mentioned, colors chosen in different software packages do not necessarily look the same on a web page, even if they use the same color code. For instance, #FF0000 saved as a background in an image file may not necessarily match a web page background specified as #FF0000. And identical colors saved in two different JPG files are almost guaranteed not to match precisely, because JPG compression always alters the colors to some degree. Altered colors are less critical in smaller areas, such as matching text color to a color in a separate image, because the text strokes are generally small enough that small color differences are not readily apparent. Nonetheless, altered colors can be a serious issue if, for example, you want a large area of solid color in a graphic to be a perfect match for large area of solid color on a web page.

What remedies do we have when we need a "perfect" match?

- Use GIF or PNG transparency in the areas of an image that need to match an HTML background color. With that setup, the background of the web page shows through in the critical areas so that matching issues are irrelevant.

- Use GIF or PNG images when trying to match to an HTML code, because their colors aren't *deliberately* altered by optimization, as are JPG colors.

- Create a solid-color GIF background tile (say, 100 x 100 pixels) in the same graphics package as the image itself, and tile it as the background of the web page.

Dingbat Typefaces

Although typography in general is discussed in Chapter 7, one area of typography, *dingbat typefaces* (also called *symbol typefaces*), deserves mention here (**FIGURE 6.18**).

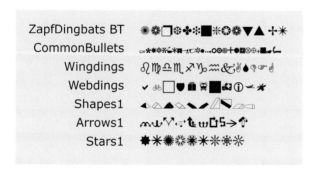

FIGURE 6.18 Dingbat typefaces include a wide variety of shapes, icons, and ornaments that are invaluable in creating images.

We should not use dingbat characters as traditional HTML content, because we can't count on our viewers having the same dingbat typefaces on their computers. We can, however, use dingbat typefaces within images, because the fonts are converted to nothing more than pixels when they're saved in a web-friendly GIF or JPG. Dingbat characters can be manipulated in the same way as more typical typefaces, so it's a snap to alter size and color or add a special effect.

The advantage to using a tiny shape from a dingbat typeface is that it is often less pixelated than if the same shape were drawn manually within an image-editing program. The circle on the upper left of **FIGURE 6.19** was drawn in Fireworks with the ellipse tool, while the circle on the lower right was created using the Shapes1 font, typing the uppercase "A" on the keyboard. The diagram was expanded so that we

BONUS TOPIC

See the book's web site, www.VisualDesignModern Web.com, for a chart of the keyboard equivalents for the most common dingbat typefaces.

can see how the pixels are less apparent and the lines smoother in the dingbat character on the right than in the shape on the left. The difference is most apparent at small sizes, when a tiny circle drawn manually in a graphics package might be rendered with only eight or so very rough pixels.

FIGURE 6.19 Using a Dingbat Character Instead of a Shape

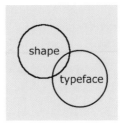

Dingbats saved as tiny images can serve as CSS replacements for traditional bullets, as in **FIGURE 6.20**.

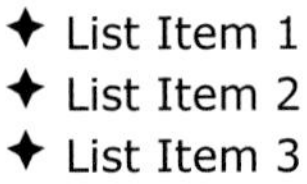

FIGURE 6.20 This bulleted list is the result of using the style `list-style-image: url(myStarBullet.gif)`.

✦ List Item 1
✦ List Item 2
✦ List Item 3

When repeated in a long row and saved as an image, dingbats can be used as a border or as a decorative replacement for an `<hr />`, as in **FIGURES 6.21 AND 6.22**:

FIGURE 6.21 One row of dingbats looks like a border.

✦✦✦✦✦✦✦✦✦✦✦✦✦✦✦✦✦✦✦✦✦✦✦✦✦✦✦✦✦✦

FIGURE 6.22 Several rows of dingbats together begin looking like a pattern.

FIGURE 6.23 shows a logo that uses a dingbat character to replace the dots on the "i"s.

FIGURE 6.23 Dingbat Character in a Logo

Effects, Filters, Textures, and Patterns

Most image-editing programs provide various effects, filters, textures, and patterns that can be applied to text and image objects (see **FIGURE 6.24** for a few samples). If an image-editing program doesn't provide enough variety, third-party plug-ins like Alien Skin's Eye Candy, Xenofex, or Splat can up the ante. A search on Google for "free Photoshop plug-ins" should come up with even more plug-ins for Photoshop and Fireworks.

FIGURE 6.24 Sample Filter Effects

No Effects

Glow

Outline with No Fill

Embossed

Outline with Solid Fill

Drop Shadow

Texture Fill

Blur

Twist and Face

Linear Gradient Fill

Raised Bevel

Eye Candy's Chrome Filter

Inset Bevel

Eye Candy's Fur Filter

Although effects can be great fun, they can be overused or applied with a heavy hand, and often too many effects end up on a single image. Always use effects and filters with restraint; the trend these days seems to be toward simpler, more graceful effects. For instance, the heavy, 10-pixel, 3-D bevels that were ubiquitous on navigation buttons just a few years ago (as in **FIGURE 6.25A**) look dated these days. Now, most sites use more subtle, 2–3-pixel bevels, if using bevels at all (as in **FIGURE 6.25B**).

FIGURE 6.25 Bevel Effects

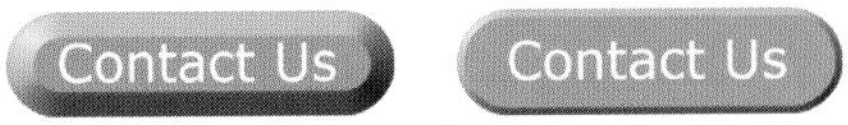

A. Outdated Heavy Beveling

B. Updated Light Beveling

FIREWORKS PLUG-INS

Supposedly, any plug-in advertised for Photoshop should work in Fireworks as well, although you will have to install it separately for each program.

In classical painting, light typically shines down from the top left, which is, not coincidentally, also the default lighting angle in most image-editing programs. Although we can alter the angle if we choose, we should make sure the light source shines at the same angle for every item on the page. Also keep in mind that a drop-shadow effect won't show up against a very dark background, but a glow effect in a light color does.

Whatever effect we choose, it's best if we can check what it looks like on an older, less powerful computer system. Some gradient effects, like drop shadow and glow, can look awful on older systems because there just aren't enough colors available for a smooth transition. The effect ends up looking *posterized* (showing distinct bands of color rather than smooth gradients).

Despite that, deliberately posterized effects (accomplished by lowering the color depth of the image), as in **FIGURE 6.26**, seem to be hot trend these days. The key to successful posterization seems to be that the image must be strongly, obviously posterized; subtle posterization could be mistaken for nothing more than a poor-quality image.

FIGURE 6.26 Posterized Photo, Using Only Four Colors

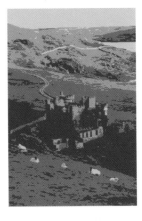

There are ways to "edge" a photo, other than just slapping the standard rectangular image on the page. Here are three ways (illustrated in **FIGURE 6.27**) to disguise the "rectangleness" of an image, all using transparency:

- Feather the edges out gradually to the background. Use a selection marquee with a "soft" stroke or "feather" option, depending upon the image editor. Reverse the selection, vary the width of the feathering (depending upon how far you want the blended effect to extend), and then delete the reversed selection.

- Round the corners of a photo, or cut it out to an irregular shape, often following the outline of the main subject of the photo. To do so, replace the deleted areas with either a transparent background or the color that matches the background of the web page.

- Use a third-party "edge" filter to curl, tear, or burn the edges of the photo. The example in Figure 6.27 shows the "torn paper" edge from Alien Skin's Splat software (see www.alienskin.com for further examples of such edges).

FIGURE 6.27 Edges for Images

Feathered Edge   Rounded Outline   Torn Paper Edge

Logo Design

A *logo* (also called a *trademark* or just a *mark*) is a particularly tricky graphic to design. Since a logo is typically used to identify an organization on all sorts of media, from signage to letterhead to business cards to, of course, the web, it must be:

- Simple and distinctive enough to have strong, identifiable visual impact. The Nike "swoosh" is a perfect example.

- Timeless, avoiding any trendiness that would date it rapidly.

- Compact and versatile, so that it adapts well to multiple media. For instance, a full-color logo must often translate well to black and white, for circumstances when color printing is too expensive or otherwise impractical.

- Unique, such that it doesn't violate any other organization's trademarks.

- Universal, using appropriate cultural associations while avoiding inappropriate or offensive connotations.

- Descriptive of the product or company (see **FIGURE 6.28**):

  - Descriptive literally, such as an orange in the logo for an orange juice company (describes the product) or the peach in the Peachpit logo (depicts a word in the name).

  - Descriptive figuratively, implying the purpose or characteristics of the company or product. The logo for Before & After Magazine is a more figurative interpretation, using the black and white typography in the word "Before" as a contrast to the gaily colored typography in the word "After."

FIGURE 6.28 Logos

Peachpit Press
(www.peachpit.com, ©Pearson Education, Peachpit Press. All rights reserved.)

Ravenswood Winery
(www.ravenswoodwinery.com, ©2007 Ravenswood Winery, Sonoma, California.)

Before & After magazine
(www.bamagazine.com)

IBM® (IBM is a registered trademark of International Business Machines Corporation.)

It's an added bonus if a logo is clever, because visitors feel a sense of community or participation if they decipher hidden meanings, symbols, metaphors, or allusions. The Ravenswood logo is a good example of just such visitor involvement. Notice how the seemingly abstract circular design, vaguely Celtic in feeling, resolves into three ravens (from Ravenswood) upon closer inspection.

The first step in creating a logo is to look for visual symbolism, either literal (à la the peach in the Peachpit Press logo and the ravens in the Ravenswood logo) or figurative (the Before & After logo), associated with the company name or products. We might show objects that reflect the theme or people using the product, or employ a metaphor.

An alternative is to explore purely typographic manipulations, such as is used in the IBM logo. Play with the letters: What happens if they touch, or overlap, or change in size or style? The Before & After logo manages to combine both visual symbolism

("Before" in grayscale, "After" in brilliant color) as well as a typographic manipulation. Note how the colors changed, but the typeface did not, which keeps focus on the effect of the color change.

The next step is to create multiple visual representations of the generated ideas. One idea may be great, but 20 ideas are much better at this stage.

Just as a poem must be even more tightly and perfectly constructed than a 300-page book, so too must a logo be even more tightly and perfectly constructed than an entire web site, brochure, or advertisement. Many of the concepts presented in Chapter 4 apply to logos as well, only more so. As with designing a layout, we try to repeat lines, spacing, shapes, colors, and typographic treatments. Whenever possible, we align elements on an invisible grid and pay as much attention to the background and negative space as we do to foreground elements. And, most importantly, we do our best to simplify, to distill to just the essence of any idea we are exploring. For instance, the Peachpit logo in Figure 6.28 portrays only the most fundamental characteristics that make a peach recognizable: the silhouette, the crease that runs vertically around a peach, and the branch the peach hangs from. No attempt is made to show shading or leaves on the branch or any other element that doesn't directly contribute to distinguishing this as a peach. The point is that the very best logo is often the simplest imaginable design that manages to portray the organization's brand.

Image Design Inspiration

Design inspiration can come from many different sources, from printed materials to graphics in movie credits to wallpaper patterns. That said, **FIGURE 6.29** is a randomly-organized set of inspirational ideas.

FIGURE 6.29 Inspiration

Background Images

Background images, like all images, take time to download, while background colors alone do not. As a result, we should use background images cautiously, making sure the added impact is worth the resulting download hit. Another consideration is that busy background images are usually anathema to good design; rarely should a page background be the focus of attention. Still, a subtle background image can enhance the ambiance of a site.

Background Image Contrast

One way to make sure that a background image doesn't overwhelm the page or render the foreground text illegible is to use a low-contrast image, like the image in **FIGURE 6.30**. The colors in the image are very similar in tone and value, so the image can provide interest without overwhelming any foreground elements. As long as any foreground text is a dark color, it will show up effectively.

FIGURE 6.30 Low Contrast Background Image

What if we want to use an existing image, perhaps a photo, but its contrast is too high? **FIGURE 6.31A** shows just such a high contrast image that would distract from any content on the page and render text difficult to decipher. The remedy is to lower the image's contrast in an image-editing program. Simply tweak the "levels," brightness, contrast, or hue/color saturation controls, or overlay the entire image with a semi-transparent layer of white, black, or another color. **FIGURES 6.31B** and **C** show two methods that transform the original high-contrast image into one more suitable for a background.

A. High-contrast Image, Not Generally Suitable as a Background

B. High-Contrast Image, Overlaid with Semi-Transparent Red to Lower Contrast

FIGURE 6.31 Creating a Low-contrast Background Image

C. High-Contrast Image, With Levels Adjusted to Lower Contrast

Even if a high-contrast background is appropriate, we must then be careful that dark text isn't placed on dark areas of the background, and light text isn't placed over light areas, as illustrated in **FIGURE 6.32A**.

FIGURE 6.32 Text on a High
Contrast Background

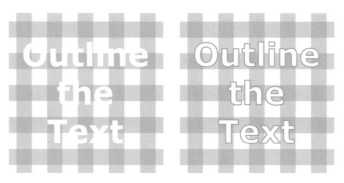

A. High Contrast Background,
Text Illegible

B. High Contrast Background,
Outline on Text

One remedy is to be very careful to lock light foreground elements in place on an area of dark background and vice versa, although that's much easier said than done on the web. Alternately, we could add a contrasting outline or glow to foreground elements, such that light foreground elements are outlined in a darker color, as in Figure 6.32B, and dark foreground elements are outlined in a light color. In this way, the text is legible regardless of whether it lands on a dark or a light area of the background. This still presents problems. First, although we can create images with outlined text for a limited number of page elements like headers, we can't do that for the HTML text that comprises most content. Additionally, not only does the background still look "busy," but now the text areas do, too. Busy-ness multiplied is rarely a good idea on a web page.

Let's look at each of the three general types of background images: tiled background images, full-screen background images, and partial-background images.

Tiled Background Images

If an image is too small to fill the entire background, the browser *tiles* (repeats) it horizontally and vertically until the background is filled. Because a tiled image is, by definition, smaller than a full-screen background image, it's inherently a smaller file.

Tiled backgrounds can take advantage of many different effects: textures, stripes, color gradients, random patterns, and checkerboards, to name a few. **FIGURE 6.33** illustrates several different background tiles and the effects they produce when tiled in a 200 x 200-pixel area.

What pixel dimensions are ideal for a background tile? Don't assume that the smaller the image, the better. There is a point when the image is so small that the download savings is more than offset by the time it takes for the browser to repeat the image over and over again. Ideally, an image should be in the range of 10,000 pixels (100 x 100 pixels, if the image is square). That number is just a guideline; the point is to try to avoid using tiles that are either too small or too large.

Additionally, if you're using a pattern or texture provided by an image-editing program, you must use a multiple of the pattern repeat (often around 100 pixels). For instance, the 100 x 100-pixel Oilslick tile in Figure 6.33 repeats seamlessly, while the seams show in the 50 x 50 Oilslick tile. Most patterns and textures built into Fireworks repeat seamlessly at around 100 x 100 pixels, give or take a few pixels, making it easy to create background tiles. In Photoshop, you can use Filter > Pattern Maker to create and test patterns.

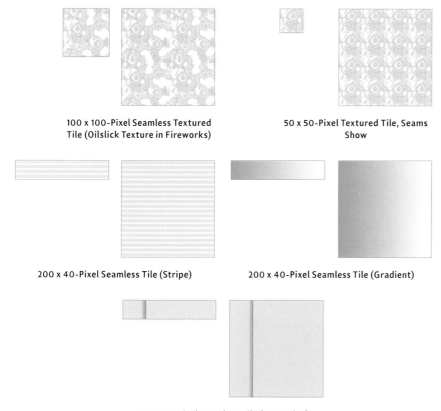

FIGURE 6.33 Background Tiles and Their Tiled Effects

100 x 100-Pixel Seamless Textured Tile (Oilslick Texture in Fireworks)

50 x 50-Pixel Textured Tile, Seams Show

200 x 40-Pixel Seamless Tile (Stripe)

200 x 40-Pixel Seamless Tile (Gradient)

200 x 40-Pixel Seamless Tile (3-D Ledge)

There is a technique to manually create your own seamless tile as well. **FIGURE 6.34** illustrates the process:

FIGURE 6.34 Creating a Custom Pattern Seamless Tile

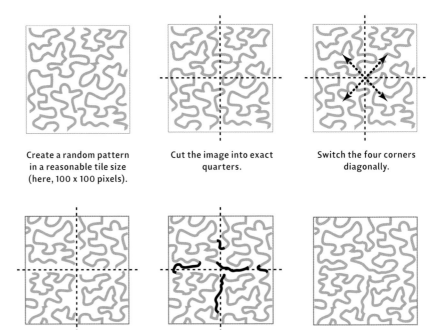

Create a random pattern in a reasonable tile size (here, 100 x 100 pixels).

Cut the image into exact quarters.

Switch the four corners diagonally.

The result of switching the four corners diagonally.

Fill in the center gaps so that the pattern carries on across the borders between the four quarters.

The completed tile.

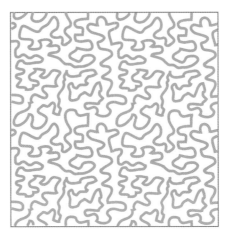

The tile as it would look when tiled into a 3 x 3 tile grid.

Full-screen Background Images

A full-screen background image is, of course, intended to fill the browser window from the upper left corner to the lower right corner. A full-screen JPG background photo has the potential to be a huge file, with a resulting huge download hit. Conversely, a full-screen GIF image with only a few shapes, two or three colors, mainly horizontal lines, and no gradients or patterns (as in Figure 6.30) could be a fairly small file. In any case, we should be certain that the image adds enough pizzazz to the page to make the download hit worthwhile.

The first consideration for a full-screen background image is its display size. If it's large enough to fill larger browser windows (say, 1600 x 1200 pixels), it can appear truncated and incomplete when displayed on smaller windows (like 800 x 600 pixels). Using a smaller image as a background for the entire page won't work, either, because, as we have seen, it often tiles unattractively to fill the entire page. **FIGURE 6.35** illustrates both problems. A photograph rarely works under these circumstances, although a well-planned abstract design might. In any case, you need to test a full-screen background at multiple window sizes.

FIGURE 6.35 Undesirable Background Tiling

Background Image Too Small for Window   **Background Image Too Large for Window**

Full-screen background images scroll by default, meaning that they move along with the content as the user scrolls down a page. We can use CSS to lock a background image in place so that it doesn't scroll:

```
body {background-image:url(someImage.gif); background-attachment:fixed;}
```

Now, the text scrolls over the top of the fixed background, just like movie credits often scroll over a fixed background image. In this case, it's especially critical that the background image is of low contrast internally but has high contrast with foreground elements, in order to avoid foreground elements becoming illegible as they scroll over areas of background that are too similar in value.

Non-tiling Partial Background Images

Sometimes, we want a background image that neither fills the screen nor tiles. There are two ways to show a partial background image:

- Specify a solid color background for the entire page, and a separate background image for the `<div>` or `<table>` that holds the main content, as in **FIGURE 6.36A**. You can also use CSS (see sidebar) to position the image precisely on the page, although it can be trickier to line up the content with the background image.

- Make the image the background for the entire page, and use a solid background color for the `<div>` or `<table>` that holds the main content (as in **FIGURE 6.36B**)—in short, the reverse of the previous method. The primary advantage to this technique is that you don't have to worry at all about whether or not the page background interferes with the legibility of the content.

FIGURE 6.36 Non-tiling Partial Background Image

A. Content over Background Image

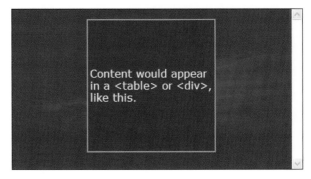

B. Content over a Solid Color Area

████ **USING CSS TO POSITION A SINGLE INSTANCE OF A BACKGROUND IMAGE**

Variations on the following <body> tag can be used to position a single copy of a background image:

```
<body style="background-color:#660000;
    background-image:url(backgroundImage.jpg);
    background-position: center 20px;
    background-repeat: no-repeat;">
```

In this case, the background image is centered horizontally in the window and drops down 20 pixels from the top of the window.

An Alternative to a Background Image

As we have seen, background images can add interest to a page. Even so, there is at least one way to get the look of a background image without actually using an image at all, by manipulating table cell background colors for graphic effects. **FIGURE 6.37** shows how such color blocking can give a very graphic, "Mondrian" effect to a page without using a single background image. Table cells or <div>s use appropriate background colors, while the dark lines are accomplished easily with wide spacing that allows the dark background to show through, or with wide borders.

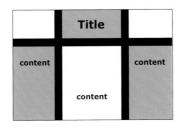

FIGURE 6.37 Using Table Cells to Create Graphic Effects

Hints on Working with Graphics

Here are miscellaneous working-with-graphics hints that don't fit neatly into the previous sections of this chapter.

Think in Pixels

Train yourself to think in pixels; don't even try to translate pixels to inches or centimeters in your head. Soon, you will start to not have to consciously figure out that a navigation column might be 100–150 pixels wide, a content column 500 pixels wide, a logo banner 100–200 pixels high, a thumbnail around 100 x 100 pixels. Although those pixels are not going to display at the same size on all systems, as we learned in Chapter 4, these guidelines give us a place to start. It doesn't take all that long, really, to become at ease with thinking in pixels.

Employ Visual Echoes

The visual consistency of a site is enhanced by repeating graphic elements throughout the site. Consider the following:

- Repeat an element from the logo elsewhere on a page. For instance, pick a simple shape from the logo and repeat it as an icon, a button, or a bullet.

- Choose a color from the logo or a photograph and repeat it elsewhere—in a background, on a bullet, or on text links. Use the eyedropper/color picker tools in Fireworks or Photoshop to identify the color code.

- Choose a consistent mood for graphics. For instance, organic shapes are rounded, flowing, and irregular. Manmade shapes are well-defined, with straight lines and right angles. In general, two distinctly different moods such as these don't play well together on a web page.

Keep a 1 x 1-Pixel GIF at Hand

A 1 x 1-pixel transparent GIF is a handy thing to have at your disposal. It can be used as a filler for empty table cells to avoid the tendency of older browsers to choke when exposed to an empty table cell. At the same time, it allows cells to be taken down to very small sizes, which filling with an   character won't allow.

A transparent GIF is also handy as a spacer. For instance, we might want extra space between two images. Although we could use multiple   characters for spacing, they don't deliver an exact number of empty pixels. A transparent GIF in an `<img />` tag, though, could specify an exact `height` and `width`. Normally we avoid stretching an image with `height` and `width`, but it's acceptable in this situation because we don't have to worry about the quality of the stretched image if it's invisible anyway.

A 1 x 1-pixel *colored* GIF can be useful as well. We can stretch it to make a square bullet of any size. It can also be repeated or stretched into horizontal or vertical rules (HTML doesn't provide vertical rules).

● ● ●

WHY NOT AN ?

The browser assumes that an   is the height and width of a space character in the current font specification. It then refuses to reduce the size of a table cell below that height or width.

Avoid Web Clichés

Avoid web clichés like spinning globes, spiders and webs, or animated envelopes for email. A spinning globe might be appropriate for NASA, but is not appropriate for, say, a site selling golf clubs, just because the site is on the "world-wide" web.

Consider Using Image Borders

In the "olden days" of the web, images generally sported the default HTML borders. Then, for a number of years, borders were viewed as passé and were turned off completely. These days, however, a graceful, one-pixel border seems to be coming back into style.

If the border is turned on but not otherwise styled, HTML renders the border for a normal image in the same color as normal text, and for link images in the same color as text links. You can, of course, use CSS to specify various border attributes, from style (dashed, double-dashed, dotted, etc.) to width to color. You can always embed a border in the graphic itself, too, before exporting it from within an image-editing program.

Use Dreamweaver to Create Remote Rollovers

We looked at graphic *rollovers* (also termed *mouseovers*) in depth in Chapter 3, since the most common use of rollovers is for navigational images. Here, though, we need to examine non-navigational *remote rollovers*, in which rollovers on text or image links change independent images elsewhere on the page. These rollovers are used for graphic effects, just to display alternating images, rather than as navigational affordances.

Like navigational rollovers, remote rollovers require JavaScript to implement, but we don't actually have to write the JavaScript ourselves. In fact, we can use Adobe Dreamweaver to create a standard rollover, and then manually convert it to a remote rollover:

1. In Dreamweaver, select Insert > Image Objects > Rollover Image.

2. In the resulting form:

   - Provide a unique image name, or use the generic name that Dreamweaver suggests.

   - Provide the URL for the original image as well as the URL for the rollover image.

   - Check "Preload rollover image."

   - Provide the alt text for the image.

   - Type "#" (used when the <a> tag isn't intended to load another page) in the "When clicked, Go to URL:" field.

3. Click "OK" so that Dreamweaver writes the HTML and JavaScript for the rollover.

4. Remove just the `<img />` tag from within the `<a>` tag that Dreamweaver gener-
    ated, and move it to the area on the page where the rollover image should
    actually render.

5. Replace the removed image in the `<a>` tag with the text or image that should
    instead serve as the rollover trigger.

Regardless of whether it's a local or a remote rollover, be sure that the two images
are identical in size, or else the rollover image might be squashed or stretched to fit
the footprint of the original image.

● ● ●

PRELOADING ROLLOVER IMAGES

The first time any type of rollover is invoked, the image swap effect might not show
up immediately, because the rollover image must be downloaded. In fact, the visitor
may have long since moved the mouse elsewhere before the rollover image is ready to
appear. The solution is to preload the image, which involves downloading the rollover
image at the time the rest of the page initially loads, even though the image won't be
needed until later. This way, the image is ready and waiting for its first appearance. In
Dreamweaver, you can check "preload image" when inserting the rollover, or you can
add "preload" to the image later, in the Behaviors panel.

Name Images by Function, Not Visual Attributes

When saving images, be sure to name them by function, not by some visual attribute, because visual attributes might change in the future. Let's say we have created a web site with red buttons for navigation and blue buttons for submitting
forms. If we name the buttons "buttonRed" and "buttonBlue" and then later the
color scheme of the web site changes, our button names become meaningless. On
the other hand, if we name the buttons "buttonSave" and "buttonSubmit," then the
sudden order from Management to change the color scheme of the site will not fill
us with dread and will in fact be relatively painless.

Animation

Including animation is, undoubtedly, tempting—perhaps even more tempting than
all the graphics- and photography-based elements we've discussed up until now.
But often it's more enjoyable for the designer to create than it is for the viewer to

watch. As "consumers," we have all experienced *splash pages* (introductory pages designed merely to entertain) that take forever to load, have no real purpose, are "glued on" to the site with no real relationship to the rest of the site, and are impossible to bypass. We have all endured an animation that continuously flashes at us from a corner of the screen, attracting (more like "distracting") our attention despite our best attempts to ignore it. And we have all tolerated (or not) even more irritating pages that have multiple animations going on at once, all vying for our notice. Finally, although as users we are not thinking about this as consciously, with animation we put up with increased file sizes and download times (since all animations contain multiple images, even when stored in an efficient format like Flash).

Although animation is not inherently evil, we should use it with restraint. If even a single animation on a page might be considered one animation too many, don't even think about multiple animations on a page. Furthermore, animation is counterproductive if it distracts from what you want to emphasize. Therefore, it should only be used to call attention to whatever is most important; if you want your viewer to click on the "Sale!" button, then it might make sense to animate the button. Finally, avoid animation that loops endlessly—it can be endlessly irritating. Instead, loop through a time or two and then stop, or at least provide the viewer with a way to halt it manually.

Animation Terminology

Before looking at the more common animation formats, we need to be clear about common terminology. A *frame* (called a *cell* in traditional animation) is a single drawing within an animation. A *keyframe* is the beginning or ending of a path of motion. An animated bouncing ball might have a keyframe at the top of its bounce and another one when it hits the ground. There might be ten frames between the keyframe at ground level and the keyframe at the top of the bounce arc, and another 10 frames on the downward half of the bounce.

Tweening is the process of creating the "in between" frames between two keyframes. Most animation-editing programs can tween automatically. That is, we specify the beginning and ending keyframes, and how many frames/tweens to insert in between. The program then creates the interim instances with interpolated attributes. Thus, we wouldn't have to create the ten frames between the bottom and top of the bounce of the ball, because the animation program tweens it for us.

We can use tweening to do more than just change the positioning of an object. Tweening can interpolate almost any object attribute, from shape to size to color. For instance, the shadow of the bouncing ball might be tweened to get bigger and lighter in color as the ball goes up, and smaller and darker as the ball comes down.

The more tweens there are between two keyframes, the smoother the animation appears. Traditionally, smoother animation has always been desirable. These days, the popularity of some modern TV cartoons like South Park, with very jerky animation, has freed web designers to experiment with animation smoothness, or lack thereof.

Looping is the process of replaying an animation repeatedly, either a preset number of times or endlessly.

Onion skinning refers to showing all the frames and objects at once, rather than just the current frame. The current frame is in full focus, while the lower frames that aren't currently being edited are somewhat "grayed out."

Most objects that are repeated in an animation should be entered to the program's *symbol library*—an efficient "place" for storing any number of elements for reuse, which might be familiar from vector-based graphics programs such as Illustrator. Editing objects within the library automatically updates every instance of that "symbol" that is used in your layout. A further benefit of using symbols is that the object is stored in the file only once, no matter how many times you use it, thereby resulting in a smaller file size.

Animation Formats

There are three common web animation formats: JavaScript, animated GIF, and Flash. JavaScript animation is well beyond the scope of this book, because it involves fairly heavy-duty programming skills. Luckily, however, you can find hundreds of free, pre-programmed animation scripts on the web, most of which require no programming skills at all to implement.

● ● ●

FREE JAVASCRIPT SCRIPTS

See www.javascriptsource.com for hundreds of free JavaScript scripts, including animations like the "falling snowflakes" background.

GIF Animation

Animated GIFs can be created in most image-editing programs that support standard GIFs. An animated GIF consists of multiple GIF images stacked on top of one another. The images are played in sequence to simulate movement. As you might expect, you can specify how many times the animation should loop and the time delay between frames. **FIGURE 6.38** shows two frames as they would display in the playback of a GIF animation, and one frame with the objects selected for editing.

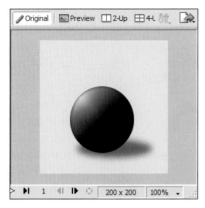

GIF Animation Frame

GIF Animation Frame

FIGURE 6.38 GIF Animation

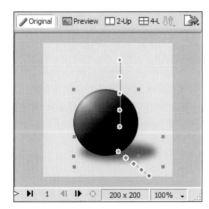

GIF Animation Frame during Editing,
showing the "handles" and lines of motion
for the animation.

Since GIF is a bitmapped format, every single pixel in every single GIF frame must be specified and rendered, which means the file size can get large quickly, depending upon how many GIF frames are used and how big each one is. An animated GIF doesn't require a plug-in; simply include the GIF in an `<img />` tag the way you would any other image.

Flash Animation

Flash is a vector-based graphics program, which, as discussed earlier, means that, in it, *shapes* are defined, rather than each individual pixel. Because vector graphics are usually more compact than bitmapped graphics, a Flash animation is generally a more compact file than its equivalent animated GIF. The fact that it's vector-based also means that Flash animations resize beautifully, without any loss of quality.

One option for Flash animations is specifying that the animation starts to play before the entire file is downloaded; the remainder of the file is downloaded in the background while the beginning sequences are playing. The visitor sees content more quickly, but at the same time the animation might need to pause midway through playback to allow the download to catch up.

The native format for an editable Flash file has the file extension .fla, but animations must be exported to a read-only SWF (Small Web Format, file extension .swf) file for replay in a browser. Although Flash requires a browser plug-in on the viewer's system, that plug-in is bundled with all modern browsers. Adobe states that as of July 2007, 98.7% of internet-enabled PCs included Flash Player (www.adobe.com/products/player_census/flashplayer/). Still, the remedy for those few remaining Flash-impaired visitors is to offer the option either to download Flash Player or to skip the Flash animation entirely.

Although Flash Player is free, programs to create Flash animations often are not. Adobe Flash is the most common program for creating Flash animations, of course.

Flash can be used to render an entire site, not just animation. Flash sites can be graphically stunning while at the same time generally smaller than the equivalent full-screen JPGs or GIFs. A Flash site uses just enough HTML to embed the SWF files, and Flash renders everything else, from images to text to navigation links to data pulled out of a server-side database. Flash as a tool to render an entire site is discussed a bit more fully in Chapter 4.

Graphics and Accessibility

Since graphics are, by their very nature, a visual medium, our primary focus is to make graphical information accessible to screen readers for the visually impaired. There are several ways we can facilitate this:

- Provide equivalent alternatives to visual content. At the very least, every non-text element (images, applets, Flash files, video files, and audio files) should include an `alt` attribute to describe the purpose of the element. Although the `alt` text should be complete enough that the purpose is clear, it should also be terse enough that visually impaired visitors aren't overly delayed by unnecessary description. Note that providing nothing more than the name of the file is not generally an acceptable use of the `alt` attribute.

- If a non-text element is a link, populate the `alt` attribute with a description of the link destination.

- If a longer description is necessary for any non-text element, use the `longdesc` attribute on the `<img />` tag to link to a separate page that contains the description.

- For complex non-text elements like graphs and charts, supplement them with detailed textual descriptions, either on the page itself or accessible by `longdesc`.

- For elements that are purely decorative, provide either a brief `alt` attribute (`alt="Company logo"`), or an empty alt attribute (`alt=""`). Under no circumstances should the `alt` attribute be omitted.

- Use the "Site" and then "Report" commands in Dreamweaver to check for accessibility lapses and missing `alt` tags.

- See www.w3.org/WAI/, www.usablenet.com, and www.adobe.com/accessibility/ for further information.

Summary

Graphics are critical in defining the ambiance, appeal, and professionalism of a site. While we try to deliver engaging graphics, we must also weigh the tradeoff of increasing the download times that heavy use of graphics can entail. Saving images in the proper format, minimizing image sizes, and using graphics appropriately can go a long way toward minimizing download times.

Design Checklist

The following checklist serves two functions: to summarize the major points and "rules" presented in this chapter, and to help ensure you've done all you should before finalizing any web site you are creating.

General—*Did you:*

- Avoid gratuitous graphics?
- Use an appropriate format: GIF, JPG, or PNG?
- Reuse graphics throughout the site, whenever possible?
- Crop or downsize images so that they display at the smallest reasonable size on the screen?
- Use `height` and `width` attributes appropriately?
- Use an `alt` attribute on each image?

JPG—*Did you:*

- Save photographs and other continuous tone images as JPGs, unless the images need transparency or animation?
- Export JPGs at the lowest compression that still looks reasonably good on a web page?

- Minimize JPG file size by adding a small amount of blur?
- Avoid saving over the original (master) JPG?

GIF—*Did you:*

- Save line-based images with areas of solid color (such as cartoons, line art, and graphic text) as GIFs?
- Select an appropriate GIF palette, either a web-snap or a non-safe adaptive palette?
- Explore transparent image backgrounds so that images no longer appear to be rectangles?
- Turn on dithering if there are more than 256 colors in an image?
- Specify interlacing, when appropriate?
- Keep in mind the file size implications of excessive colors, vertical stripes, anti-aliasing, gradients, dithering, and textures?
- Store a photograph as a GIF only if it needs transparency or animation, and then use a 256-color adaptive palette with dithering turned on?

PNG Images—*Did you:*

- Use PNG format if you have a flat color image that needs more than 256 colors?
- Remember that alpha transparency increases file sizes and may not be supported by all browsers?
- Specify interlacing, when appropriate?
- Store a photograph as a PNG only if it needs transparency or animation, and then use an appropriate palette with dithering turned on?
- Use only compressed PNG files (not native Fireworks PNG files) on the web?

Combination Images—*Did you:*

- Avoid combining GIF-appropriate and JPG-appropriate art in a single image?

Acquiring Images—*Did you:*

- Use stock photos and clip art when appropriate?
- Scrupulously obey copyright laws?
- Use screen capture software to acquire screen prints?

- Scan photos at the appropriate resolution?

- When possible, convert scanned images to vector format before resizing?

- Use a digital camera rather than a film-based camera, as appropriate?

Creating and Editing Images—*Did you:*

- Use anti-aliasing correctly, to avoid halos?

- Match colors across software packages?

- Use dingbat typefaces for ornaments, bullets, and icons, and for smoother small shapes?

Effects and Filters—*Did you:*

- Use effects and filters appropriately to embellish the page while avoiding effect overkill?

- Make sure that the light source for all 3-D elements on the page is at the same angle?

- Test your effects on a lower-end computer system?

- Contemplate using posterization, feathering, rounding, or putting an edge of some sort on a photo?

Logo Design—*Did you:*

- Create a logo that is:
  - Descriptive, literally or figuratively?
  - Compact and versatile?
  - Simple and distinctive?
  - Unique?
  - Universal?
  - Timeless?

- Create a clever logo, if appropriate?

- Use typographical manipulation?

- Create multiple versions from which to choose?

- Repeat and align elements?

Other hints—*Did you:*

- Use visual echoes by repeating shapes, colors, and mood?

- Use 1 x 1-pixel spacers appropriately?

- Avoid web clichés?

- Specify the `alt` tag on all images?

- Think about the alternatives for image borders?

- Include graphic rollovers?

- Name images by function, rather than by visual attributes?

Background Images—*Did you:*

- Create background images that are subtle and of low contrast, so that foreground elements are the focus and are legible?

- Plan foreground elements so that they show up well, even with a high-contrast background, either by locking them on appropriate areas of the background or by outlining them?

- Create a background tile of appropriate dimensions so that seams don't show?

- Use full-screen background images judiciously, and plan them to be relatively small files?

- Create a large background image so that it looks complete on small screens while, at the same time, avoids tiling on the larger ones?

- Specify the image as scrolling or fixed, depending upon which effect you want?

- Consider wrapping the "background" image in a table or `<div>` so that it is positioned where you want it on the page, without tiling?

- Consider using table cell background colors to mask the background image in content areas?

- Think about using table cell and `<div>` background colors to provide a color-blocked look without the use of background pattern at all?

Animation—*Did you:*

- Avoid animation unless to draw attention to the area you want to be the focus for your visitors?

- Choose an appropriate animation format?

Typography

DANIEL WILL-HARRIS, "CHOOSING & USING TYPE,"
WWW.WILL-HARRIS.COM/USE-TYPE.HTM:

"Type attracts attention, sets the style and tone of a document, colors how readers interpret the words, and defines the feeling of the page—usually without the reader recognizing a particular typeface."

Peruse a book, newspaper, or web site, and chances are the only time you notice the type is if it's annoying in some way—too small, too blurry, or too embellished to be legible. A choice of appropriate typography is usually transparent; that is, the reader doesn't even notice it. Thus, the primary function of type is to be utilitarian. Words must be set in a legible typeface, an appropriate size, and an appropriate color for the background upon which the words rest.

Even so, type has a subliminal effect. A typeface might be goofy, serious, breezy, exotic, saucy, corporate, feminine, or formal. A typeface should be visually consistent with the ambiance and sensibility of the site. A highly decorative, embellished typeface would be just as inappropriate on a banking site as a staid, sensible typeface would be on an online fantasy gaming site.

Type is much more powerful than we realize, so much so that a typeface can become associated with our site or company. For instance, the custom typefaces used in the Coca-Cola logo and the Harry Potter movies are instantly recognizable. That can happen with less obvious typefaces as well. For example, Daniel Will-Harris, a leading type authority, argues that we in the United States might well have a subliminal negative association with Helvetica because it's the typeface used on IRS tax forms. Whether or not this is actually the case, it's clear that choosing appropriate typefaces is critical to conveying our message.

Typography Basics

Basic typography concepts are pertinent whether the medium is the web, printed materials, or a billboard next to a superhighway. We will look at those universal concepts before examining how to apply them to the web.

Body Copy versus Display Type

Body copy or *body text* refers to the main content of a communication, that is, the paragraph content. *Display type*, also called *display text* or *headline text*, refers to text used for decoration and/or structure, such as logos, titles, headings, and sub-headings.

The primary focus for body copy is readability—no one wants to try to decipher an entire paragraph of a hard-to-read decorative typeface, especially at small sizes. Body copy should be set in a simple, legible, not-too-small typeface.

The primary focus of display type is to embellish or draw attention. Display type elements such as headings typically consist of only short phrases set in larger font sizes, in which case even very decorative typefaces can be legible. Accordingly, we have much more freedom to use somewhat less readable typefaces for display type.

Typefaces

Typeface (or simply *face* for short) refers to a particular design for characters, such as Courier, Times New Roman, Ariel, University, Curly, and so on. A *font* is a specific face in a specific size and a specific style (bold, italic, etc.). The Times New Roman typeface at 12 pixels in bold is one font, while Times New Roman at 14 pixels, bold, is technically a different font. Nevertheless, the computer world's insistence on calling a typeface by the term "font" means that most of us have come to use the terms interchangeably, even though they are in reality two somewhat different aspects of typography.

Most modern typefaces are *proportionally spaced.* That is, individual characters vary in the amount of horizontal space they use, so that an "i" consumes less space than an "M." In contrast, *monospaced* typefaces, such as Courier New, assign the same amount of space to each character. For instance, this "i" in the typeface `Courier New` is the same width as the letters "N" and "W" in the same typeface. Monospaced typefaces are useful when columns of characters must align vertically or when we need the feel of an old-fashioned, typewriter-based face.

A *font family*, in traditional typography terms, includes all the variations on a particular typeface, so that the Times New Roman font family includes a bold version, an italic version, and so on. As we will see later, "font family" means something very different in cascading style sheets (CSS).

Typefaces are loosely grouped as either serif or sans serif. *Serif* faces have small defined strokes or embellishments at both ends of the main letter strokes, as shown in **FIGURE 7.1**.

FIGURE 7.1 Text Typefaces. FYI, the three "headlines" in this list are set in Verdana—*the* san serif typeface for the web.

Sans serif faces, also shown in Figure 7.1, don't have embellishments at the termination of the main strokes, and are often viewed as providing a more modern effect. In fact, they seem to be the more common choice in today's corporate world.

There are also thousands of script and decorative faces with distinct personalities that defy categorization, also shown in Figure 7.1. Almost anything goes, from curlicues to "ice" hanging from letters to balloons floating above them. Although such faces are wonderful for display type, their very embellishment makes them illegible in smaller body copy.

Dingbat typefaces replace keyboard characters with symbols, shapes, and ornaments, as in **FIGURE 7.2**. See the book's web site for a chart of the keyboard equivalents for some of the more common and useful dingbat typefaces.

FIGURE 7.2 Dingbat Typefaces

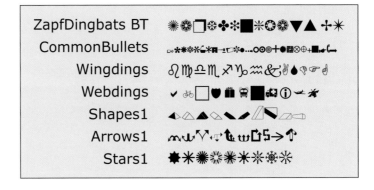

Some typefaces are tall and skinny, while others are short and fat. We can use the width-to-height ratio to our advantage, tailoring our typeface choices to accommodate "challenging" or limited spaces.

Use restraint in including multiple typefaces on a single document. Just because I've installed (at latest count) 1536 typefaces on my own computer doesn't mean I should subscribe to the "ransom note" school of typography by using all of them at once. Instead, as a general rule, it's best to use one simple typeface for body copy, and one or two decorative faces in the logo and/or headers. Those typefaces might contrast in structure; perhaps the body copy is a simple serif font while the logo uses a bigger and bolder version of the same font as well as another very decorative typeface. Often, it's best to choose two very different fonts that contrast sharply, rather than two or more very similar fonts.

Formatting and Contrast

Characteristics other than just the design of the typeface can create emphasis and typographical contrast:

- Size: big versus small.
- Weight: **bold** versus not bold.

- Color: you get the idea.

- Form: *italic*, ALL CAPS, or SMALL CAPS versus not italic (also called *roman*) and not caps (also called *lowercase*).

- Direction: whether the type is horizontal or at some other angle, such as running vertically, or on a curved path.

- Rhythm and spacing: characters that are s p a c e d differently, or even…   isolated. (We'll cover spacing in more depth, in the next section.)

- Embellishment: patterns, bevels, shadows, and glow, as shown in **FIGURE 7.3**.

- Texture: how a block of type arranges itself into a shape, either heavy (closely spaced text) or lighter (widely spaced text) in feel.

FIGURE 7.3 Text Embellishments

Once again, though, we must not be so dazzled by the infinite typographical possibilities that a page becomes visually chaotic. It's wise to use all of these attributes sparingly, with meaning attached. For instance, use bold, italics, or color contrast to draw attention to the structure or to give emphasis to the elements that should stand out in the visual hierarchy, not just for random decoration. One way to identify much too much typographical contrast is to stand back from the computer display and squint at the page. The most emphatic text elements will stand out from the blur. If there are too many areas of emphasis, some may need to be toned down.

● ● ●

TEXT BLOCKS FORM SHAPES

See Chapter 4 for more on how blocks of type can form shapes on a page.

Spacing

Leading refers to the empty space separating lines of horizontal text. **FIGURE 7.4** shows three different leading values: leading decreased by 20%, default single-spaced leading (in this case, equal to the text height), and leading increased by 20%. Print experts often recommend a *looser leading*, an extra 10–20% of space, because it makes it easier for the viewer's eyes to track from the end of one line to the beginning of the next. Looser leading is especially preferred for readability on longer lines of text. Tighter leading is preferred at larger font sizes, such as headings.

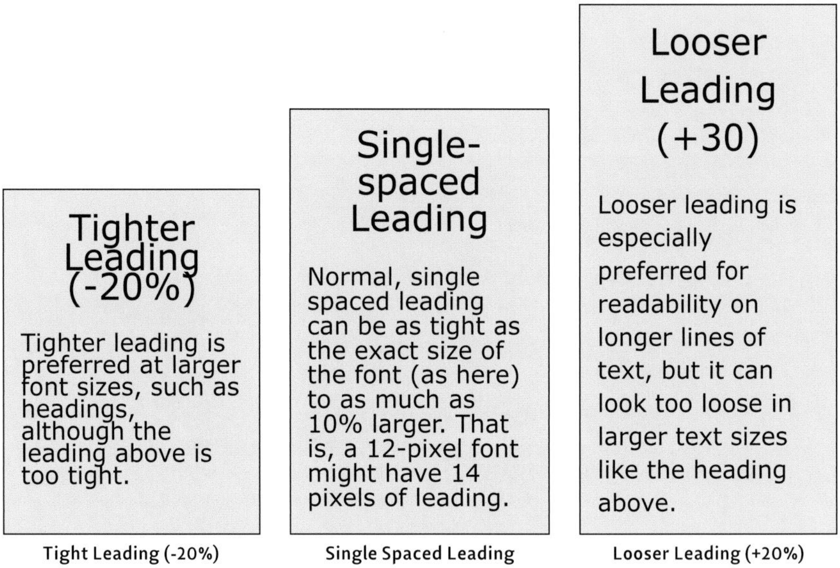

FIGURE 7.4 Leading Examples

Tighter Leading (-20%)

Tighter leading is preferred at larger font sizes, such as headings, although the leading above is too tight.

Tight Leading (-20%)

Single-spaced Leading

Normal, single spaced leading can be as tight as the exact size of the font (as here) to as much as 10% larger. That is, a 12-pixel font might have 14 pixels of leading.

Single Spaced Leading

Looser Leading (+30)

Looser leading is especially preferred for readability on longer lines of text, but it can look too loose in larger text sizes like the heading above.

Looser Leading (+20%)

Varying the leading can vary the "color" of a page. That is, it can make a page look darker and denser, or lighter and less dense, as the examples in Figure 7.4 illustrate.

While leading refers to the amount of space between lines of text, *letter spacing* (also called *letter tracking*) refers to the amount of space between individual characters within a paragraph or another selected chunk of text. Although wider spacing can be used for emphasis in headings and other decorative elements, if the spacing is too wide, readers can have difficulty grouping the letters into distinct words, as you can see here:

W i d e r   s p a c i n g   d o e s n ' t   n e c e s s a r i l y   l e a d   t o   g r e a t e r   l e g i b i l i t y .

Kerning is a specific type of letter spacing that adjusts the space between two neighboring characters, most typically used to nestle letters closer together to take advantage of adjacent parallel strokes, such as between an "A" and a "W." For example, the top row of text in **FIGURE 7.5** is not kerned. As a result, letters with parallel stokes in the word "AWAY" appear to be spaced more widely apart than the letters in the word "GO." Tighter kerning in the bottom row, however, remedies the perception of inconsistent spacing.

FIGURE 7.5 Kerning

Justification

FIGURE 7.6 illustrates several types of *text justification* (text alignment):

- **Left justified**—Body copy should *always* be justified left, *ragged right* (that is, the ends of the lines don't align) on the web.

- **Center justified** and **right justified**—Although appropriate for headers and other highlighted elements, neither one should be used for body copy. They are also inappropriate for bulleted or numbered lists, because the bullets or numbers don't line up.

- **Fully justified**—Full justification (when both the right and left margins are aligned on all but the last line of a paragraph) is good only if the medium allows for micro-spacing adjustments *and* the lines of text are long enough to spread those adjustments out. Otherwise, obviously uneven spacing can result, as in the last example of Figure 7.6.

FIGURE 7.6 Text Justification

Typography and Web Design

Besides the standard typography guidelines we've already examined, there are additional typographical and formatting issues to deal with on the web. For instance, we can manipulate some typographical characteristics with HTML and CSS (size, color, boldface, italic, and so on), but other effects like a bevel or drop shadow can be applied only within a graphic image. Let's look at both HTML text and graphic text in more depth.

HTML Text

HTML text is text that is embedded within HTML tags and that receives its formatting instructions from HTML and/or CSS.

HTML Typefaces

It's very important to know that a specified typeface displays in the viewer's browser only if that face is already installed on the viewer's computer system. If it isn't, the browser replaces the specified typeface with the resident typeface that it judges to be a reasonable replacement. Since browsers often make pretty poor decisions in this respect, we can take that responsibility away from the browser, as shown in the sidebar.

▬ HTML AND CSS REVIEW: SPECIFYING TYPEFACES

Here is how you can circumvent bad browser decisions and specify backup typefaces using CSS:

```
body {font-family: Georgia, Times, serif;}
```

As mentioned earlier, "font family" in traditional typography refers to variations on a particular typeface, including characteristics such as bold and italic. In CSS, though, "font-family" refers to the list of backup typefaces. When a font-family is specified, the browser works its way down the list, using the first typeface that it finds on the visitor's system. Thus, we can feel free to specify uncommon typefaces as long as we list commonly available backup typefaces as well.

Some newer browsers support downloading typefaces with the page. Alas, a standard decorative typeface might be 100K or more, which is an unreasonable download cost for routine body copy. As a result, this isn't a technique that we'll explore further. The alternative, of course, is to use a special typeface sparingly by putting it in graphic images, a technique we'll look at later in the chapter.

HTML's <font> tag is a deprecated method you're most likely to find on older sites, and you should not use it in new development. For new sites, stick with the CSS equivalent.

Most typefaces were originally designed for print media and are therefore not optimized for the low resolution of a computer display. To remedy this, Microsoft hired famed type designer Matthew Carter to create the faces Georgia (serif) and Verdana (sans serif) specifically for optimal screen display. The process took Carter two years but was well worth the effort. The characters of these fonts have better *hinting*; that is, larger and more uniform inter-character spacing, which does indeed improve legibility on the screen. We would be well advised to use one of these two typefaces on most body copy.

Typographers have long argued that printed body copy is more legible in a serif typeface, because the serifs provide quickly perceived cues to letter shape. In contrast, sans serif typefaces might be more legible on a monitor, because the resolution of monitors is so low that the serifs cannot be shown clearly—they tend to bleed together. But, of course, the key word here is *argued*—this debate is likely to go on indefinitely, and at least one study has shown that sans serif typefaces significantly improve onscreen readability *only* in sizes smaller than 12-point type.

• • •

THE DEBATE CONTINUES

For further (albeit non-definitive) argument on the subject of different typefaces on the web, see various articles at http://psychology.wichita.edu/surl.

HTML Font Sizes

HTML uses a scale of 1 to 7 for font sizes, with 1 being the smallest, 3 being the default size, and 7 being the largest. Despite what appear to be common size designators, different operating systems may well use a different number of pixels to build the fonts at each size. **TABLE 7.1** explains Windows versus Mac OS differences in this respect.

TABLE 7.1 DEFAULT FONT SIZE IN WINDOWS VERSUS MAC

	Assumed Text Resolution	Default Text Size (size="3")
Windows	96 pixels per inch	16 pixels high (1/6 of an inch)
Mac OS	72 pixels per inch	12 pixels high (1/6 of an inch)

Font size is specified in HTML with the `<font size="n">` tag. Since the `<font>` tag is deprecated, we will use only CSS font sizing in this discussion. With CSS, we can use either absolute or relative text sizing.

Absolute Text Sizing

We use *absolute text sizing* to stipulate a specific pixel height for text, completely disregarding any text sizing currently set in the visitor's browser. For example:

```
.largeText {font-size:18px;}
```

In older browsers, absolute sizing overrides font settings the visitor might have specified, which can cause problems for those with vision impairment. (Newer browsers allow visitors to override font settings on web sites.) Absolute sizing is most problematic when used to reduce (rather than enlarge) text size.

Relative Text Sizing

With relative text sizing, the font size currently in effect is increased or decreased by a certain proportion:

```
.largeText {font-size: 110%;}
.largeText {font-size: 1.1em;}
```

It's intuitively clear that the first example increases text size by 10%. The second example does the same thing, by referencing "em," the size of the letter M in the current font. See the sidebar for discussion of font size inheritance, which determines the base font to which the relative sizing applies.

RELATIVE FONT SIZE AND INHERITANCE

When using relative font size properties in CSS, such as `text-size:110%` or `text-size:1.1em`, the theory is that the relative size differential should be applied to whatever size characteristics the font has already inherited. For instance:

If the page's base font is size 3,

   And the font for tables is specified as 110%,

      And a header (contained in a table) is specified as 120%,

         Then, in theory, the header should be displayed at base font size x 110% x 120%.

Regrettably, not all browsers apply font size inheritance in the same way; some browsers have their own quirky way of interpreting inheritance. As always, be sure to test in all of your target browsers.

Absolute versus Relative Text Sizing

There are two major reasons for preferring relative text sizing:

- As we've already seen, absolute text sizing can override visitors' font size settings, thereby degrading accessibility for the visually impaired.

- As we saw in Table 7.1, text resolution changes when we cross the Windows PC versus Mac divide. If absolute sizing is used, specifying a text size of 24 pixels results in 1/3" (24/72) on a Mac but 1/4" (24/96) on a PC, a substantial difference. On the other hand, since their base font sizes are approximately the same, relative text sizing applied on top of those similar base fonts should result in text that's approximately the same size.

HTML Formatting

There are, of course, common formatting commands that we can use in HTML or CSS, as reviewed in **TABLE 7.2**. What we really need to examine right now, though, is when it is and is not appropriate to use such formatting.

TABLE 7.2 TEXT FORMATTING WITH HTML AND CSS

Format	HTML (deprecated in favor of CSS formatting)	CSS
Color	color="#nnnnnn"	{color:#nnnnnn;}
Bold	\<strong>, \<b>	{font-weight:bold;}
Italic	\<em>, \<i>	{font-style:italic;}
Reversed type	color="#ffffff" bgcolor="#000000"	{color:#nnnnnn;} for the font and {background-color:#mmmmmm;} for the area behind the text
ALL CAPS	Type all caps	{text-transform:uppercase;}
all lowercase	Type all lowercase	{text-transform:lowercase;}
Title Case	Type title case	{text-transform:capitalize;}
Underline	\<u>	{text-decoration:underline;}
Strikethrough	\<s>, \<strike>, \<del>	{text-decoration:line-through;}
FIRST LINE in uppercase	Type all caps	.allCaps:first-line {text-transform:uppercase;}
First letter larger	\<font size="..."> for first letter only	.largeCap:first-letter {font-size:200%;}

Color

Text color as it relates to background color is probably the most important formatting decision. Obviously, pale yellow text on a white background would be illegible because there is so little *value* (degree of lightness or darkness) contrast between foreground and background.

But while contrast is of paramount importance, it's not as limiting as it may sound. Although black text on a white background provides the most familiar and readable value contrast, a less extreme contrast can still be legible while providing a more serene mood to the site. For instance, a creamy yellow on top of a mid-value tan might be quite legible. Nonetheless, we must be even more careful to test such a site in grayscale mode to make sure it's accessible to color-blind visitors.

Light text on a dark background can sometimes be less legible than the more familiar dark-on-light scheme. We can often overcome this problem by making the text larger or bolder or by choosing a typeface with inherently thicker strokes.

Emphasis

For emphasizing words, our choices include all of the various formatting options in Table 7.2. Each style has its place. For instance, bold and italics are used in the print world to indicate vocabulary words (as in this book) or spoken emphasis. Many experts assert that bold renders more clearly on a display screen than italics, but it often depends on the typeface.

Setting text all in uppercase is a throwback to the days of typewriters, when uppercase was one of the few methods available to emphasize type. TODAY, WE GENERALLY AVOID USING ALL CAPS IN BODY TEXT BECAUSE IT MAKES THE CONTENT HARD TO READ, AS YOU CAN SEE. ADDITIONALLY, ALL CAPS HAVE THE NEGATIVE CONNOTATION OF SHOUTING IN EMAIL AND INSTANT MESSAGING. In general, the fewer capital letters, the easier text is to read, because the ascenders and descenders of the lowercase alphabet afford a more distinct word shape, thus increasing readability. All caps can be acceptable, though, in short headings.

Decoration

Using underlining for emphasis is another throwback to the ancient days of typewriters. Today, a visitor who encounters underlined text on the web is confused and annoyed if that text isn't clickable. Strikethrough is also seen as an outdated and potentially confusing formatting trick; don't use it unless you are attempting to display edited versions of documents such as legal contracts.

As shown in Table 7.2, now we've got CSS to help us add decorative effects. For instance, the first line in uppercase:

> FOUR SCORE AND SEVEN YEARS AGO OUR FATHERS BROUGHT FORTH on this continent, a new nation, conceived in Liberty, and dedicated to the proposition that all men are created equal.

…or the first letter of a paragraph larger:

> Four score and seven years ago our fathers brought forth on this continent, a new nation, conceived in Liberty, and dedicated to the proposition that all men are created equal.

Again, the HTML and CSS for these text formats is summarized in Table 7.2.

HTML Text Spacing

Altering the default line and character spacing can lighten the overall "grayness" of a bland page. In particular, increasing the leading from HTML's default single spacing can improve eye tracking from one line to the next, particularly on longer lines of text. Leading is controlled with CSS:

```
.largerLeading1 {line-height:1.1em}
.largerLeading2 {line-height:110%}
```

Extra spacing between letters or words can be used for emphasis, such as for headers. **FIGURE 7.7** shows how letter spacing/tracking and word spacing can be controlled by CSS (in the newer browsers), using absolute (pixels) or relative (ems and percents) text spacing.

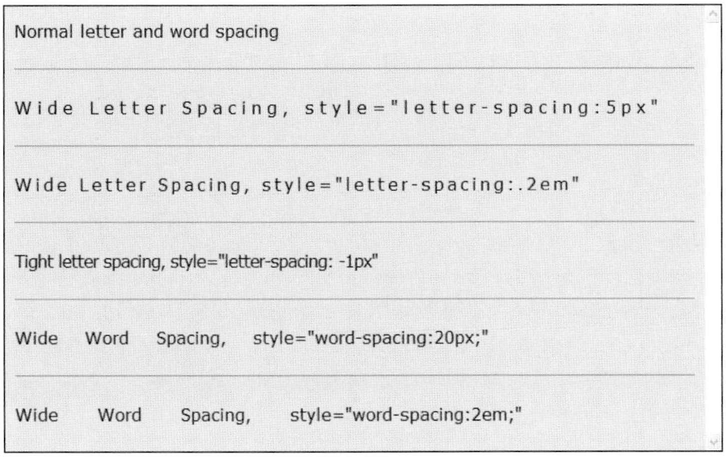

FIGURE 7.7 Letter and Word Spacing

The print industry has other spacing standards that we should follow on the web, too:

- Use only one space, not two, at the end of sentences. Fortunately, this is the default in HTML, since it doesn't recognize multiple adjacent spaces.

- Use either an indent at the beginning of a paragraph, or double spacing between paragraphs (this is the easier automatic option in HTML), but certainly not both.

- Ideally, allow the automatic blank line before a header tag, but use CSS margin styling to omit the automatic blank line after the tag. In that way, the header is closer and more visually connected to the content that it introduces:

```
h1 {margin-bottom:0em;}
```

Unfortunately, any <p> tag immediately following the header tag will add the extra spacing back in, as <p> tags are wont to do. Therefore, we must also remove the extra spacing from those <p> tags:

```
p.firstParagraph {margin-top:0em;}
```

HTML Text Justification

Left, right, and center justification are easy enough to do in HTML and CSS, using either HTML's deprecated align="..." attribute or the text-align property in CSS. However, full justification (text aligned on both the left and the right) is virtually impossible to pull off on a computer interface; the 72–100 ppi of a computer display cannot allow for subtle adjustments. At such low resolution, the result could well be letters or words spaced so far apart that they are difficult to read. For that reason, we should not use full justification at all.

HTML Text Layout

We examined general layout guidelines earlier in Chapter 4, but layout guidelines specific to HTML text should be considered, too.

Web readers skim content, rather than reading carefully. Therefore, it's important to *chunk* that content; that is, group content into small, identifiable sections using HTML tags such as <table>, <div>, <fieldset>, <ol>, and <ul>. For bulleted lists, we can use the default bullets supplied automatically by the browser (no CSS bullet styling), choose a specific browser-supplied bullet, or supply an image of our own:

```
.listItem1 {list-style-type: square}
.listItem2 {list-style-image: url(myBullet.gif)}
```

We can break up text in other ways as well. *Sidebars* (like those in this book) serve as footnotes of sorts, for displaying parenthetical content. Indenting an entire paragraph of text can serve the same function, using CSS's `text-indent` property.

Pull quotes (quotes pulled off to the side or inserted in the middle of body copy, as shown at right) can give visitors a particularly intriguing sample of the content, as a form of enticement. To further emphasize a pull quote, vary the typeface, its size, or its leading. It's more typographically correct if the initial quote marks of a pull quote can be set outside the framing lines of the text, as shown.

"A pull quote like this

can lure the viewer

into the content."

Line after uninterrupted line of text is visually boring, and lines of text that are particularly long are difficult to decipher, as we can see in **FIGURE 7.8**. As a result, we shouldn't completely fill a page with text, stretching from page border to page border. Instead, limit line length to perhaps 350–550 pixels by splitting wide pages into two or more columns, as discussed in Chapter 4.

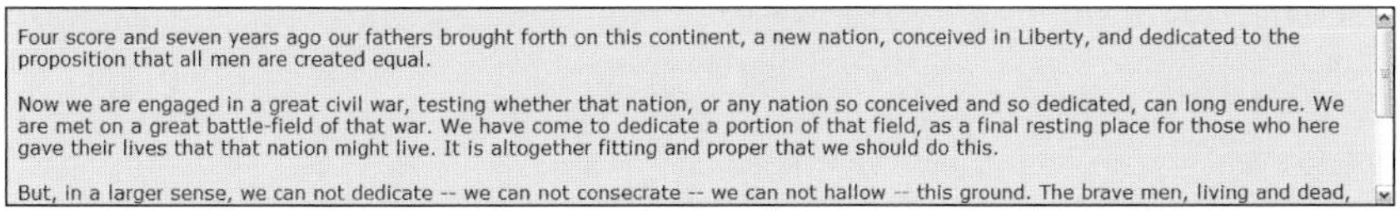
Four score and seven years ago our fathers brought forth on this continent, a new nation, conceived in Liberty, and dedicated to the proposition that all men are created equal.

Now we are engaged in a great civil war, testing whether that nation, or any nation so conceived and so dedicated, can long endure. We are met on a great battle-field of that war. We have come to dedicate a portion of that field, as a final resting place for those who here gave their lives that that nation might live. It is altogether fitting and proper that we should do this.

But, in a larger sense, we can not dedicate -- we can not consecrate -- we can not hallow -- this ground. The brave men, living and dead,

FIGURE 7.8 Excessively Long Lines of Text

HTML Special Characters and Punctuation Marks

Typography rules for print content have just as much bearing when that content appears on the web. A summary of the more valuable rules follows.

- Don't use excessive exclamation points in text! (Just look at how annoying this is!!!) Using numerous exclamation points dilutes their power to the point that they all become meaningless!
- Use *en dashes* (a hyphen the width of the letter N, like this –) to separate joined words, and true *em dashes* (longer, the width of the letter M, like this —) to separate sentence clauses. Often, we fake the em dash with two hyphens, but a true em dash looks more professional.

  en dash

  Example: "Limit line length to 30–70 characters."

  HTML code: `–` or `–`

  em dash

  Example: "Email—like snail mail—gets the job done."

  HTML code: `—` or `—`

DON'T FORGET SPELLING AND GRAMMAR

It's not HTML-specific, but it bears repeating: Always check spelling, grammar, and sentence structure. It's perfectly acceptable, even commendable, to have a friend or colleague read over the content to find mistakes that we might have missed. Everyone, even a web book author, needs an editor.

- Use proper "curly" quotes:

  Example: "curly quotes" versus "straight quotes"

  HTML codes:

    Curly left double quote: “ or “

    Curly right double quote: ” or ”

    Curly left single quote: ‘ or ‘

    Curly right single quote: ’ or ’

- Use the true ellipse (…), which is a single symbol, as opposed to three separate periods (...).

  Example: "em dash, en dash, curly quotes…"

  HTML code: &ellip; or …

- Use HTML codes for other special characters as appropriate. For example, you might want to embed an ampersand, "&" (&), a space ( ), or a copyright symbol "©" (©). See the book's web site for a listing of other codes.

UPPERCASE AND LOWERCASE NUMERALS, FOR THE TYPE-OBSESSED

Yes, believe it or not, some typefaces come with uppercase numerals (all the same size; also called *lining numbers*), while others come with lowercase numerals (with ascenders and descenders; also called *hanging numbers* or *oldstyle figures*):

- Verdana includes uppercase numerals: 123456789

- Georgia includes lowercase numerals: 123456789

Uppercase numerals appear too tall and blocky when mixed in with lowercase letters, while lowercase numerals hang inappropriately below a line of otherwise blocky uppercase letters. Examples:

- Unacceptable: different case letters and numbers

  - UPPERCASE LETTERS WITH LOWERCASE 123456789 NUMBERS

  - Lowercase letters accompanied by uppercase 123456789 numbers

- Acceptable: same case letters and numbers

  - UPPERCASE LETTERS WITH UPPERCASE 123456789 NUMBERS

  - Lower-case letters accompanied by lowercase 123456789 numbers

Since most typefaces include only uppercase or only lowercase numerals, we usually need to change typefaces to fix the mismatch.

Graphic Text

Graphic text is text created in an image-editing program like Photoshop or Fireworks, saved as an image and then embedded in HTML using <img /> tags. **FIGURE 7.9**, repeated from Chapter 6, shows just some of the effects and filters that can be applied to graphic text. (See Chapter 6 for more information on creating such images.)

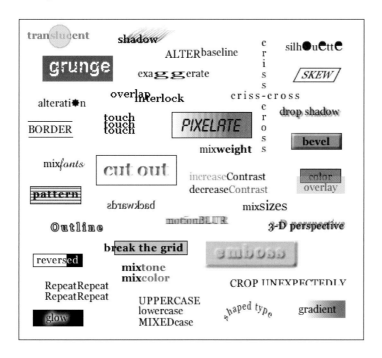

FIGURE 7.9 Effects for Graphic Text

Although text saved as an image is appropriate for decorative elements like logos, navigation buttons, and perhaps headers, text saved as a graphic should never be used for body copy. It's a sure mark of a new web designer, because experienced designers know that decorative body copy is never worth the download hit that embedding it in an image entails. Additionally, body copy embedded in an image is not searchable, not visible to search engines, not visible to screen readers for the visually impaired, and not easy to update if changes are needed later.

Many of the general typography concepts presented earlier for HTML text, including the differences in typefaces, sizes, and formatting, still hold true for text saved as an image. The major difference is that we have more freedom in graphic text to use effects, filters, and whatever typefaces we please, because we don't have to worry about whether or not the visitor has the typeface.

ANTI-ALIASING

See Chapter 6 for an extended explanation of anti-aliasing.

We can control graphic text anti-aliasing to make the type easier to read and less pixelated. Used inappropriately, however, anti-aliasing can make text almost illegible. Extremely small text becomes "mushy" when anti-aliased, with the letters running together and becoming indistinct. As type becomes larger, anti-aliasing can get stronger, although stronger anti-aliasing increases image file sizes.

The terminology for text anti-aliasing varies somewhat between image-editing programs. The terminology for anti-aliasing in Fireworks and Photoshop is listed in the sidebar below.

ANTI-ALIASING SETTINGS IN FIREWORKS AND PHOTOSHOP

Settings are listed in order from the least anti-aliasing to strongest.

Fireworks

- None
- Crisp
- Strong
- Smooth

Photoshop

- None
- Sharp
- Crisp
- Strong
- Smooth

Graphic text also allows us to turn kerning on and off for a given piece of text as well as apply kerning manually if we aren't happy with the automatic results. The larger the type, the more critical it is that the kerning is appropriate.

▨▨ EMPHASIZING TYPE IN IMAGES

When using a typeface with very thin strokes, making the text bold often doesn't provide enough emphasis for it to display well against the background. One remedy is to create an exact copy of the original anti-aliased text and position it directly on top of the original. By doubling the effect of the anti-aliasing, the type appears even stronger than bold alone. You might have to specify a wider letter spacing than normal, though, to prevent the characters from running together.

Another way to emphasize type, particularly when the type floats on top of a multicolored background, is to use not only a fill color but also an outline stroke. FIGURE 7.10, repeated from Chapter 6, shows a high-contrast example.

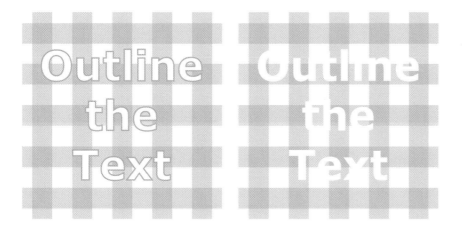

FIGURE 7.10 The Dramatic Difference Between Outlined Text And Unoutlined Text.

We can use smaller text in graphic images than we can in HTML text, because we can select a font designed for a specific, very tiny size without worrying if the visitor has the typeface on his or her computer. Three such fonts are Sevenet (precisely 7 pixels tall), Silkscreen (8 pixels tall), and Tenacity (10 pixels tall). These small fonts should be used *only* at the specified size, with anti-aliasing turned off.

By the same token, we can also employ characters from dingbat typefaces (see Figure 7.2), which, as we saw in Chapter 6, are often smoother and less pixelated than the same symbol drawn manually.

• • •

PHOTOSHOP ANTI-ALIASING HINT

If even small levels of anti-aliasing still look mushy, try deselecting the Fractional Width option in the Character palette menu.

Text and Accessibility

Accessibility has been addressed throughout the chapter, so only a recap should be needed here:

- Use relative text sizing on body copy (ems and percents), so as not to override the text-size settings that visitors have specified in their browsers. (Note that newer browsers permit the visitor to override any web site font-size settings, including absolute sizes.)

- Make sure that foreground text contrasts in value (the degree of lightness or darkness of a color) with the background so that the text is legible even to people who are color blind.

- Employ HTML's header tags (<h1>, <h2>, etc.) to provide the visually impaired with an outline of the hierarchical structure of a page.

- Include alt attributes on all images, including graphic text images. This is the single most important way to make image content accessible to the visually impaired. If the image is decorative only, with no meaning attached, use the empty alt tag (alt="") to avoid the delay of a screen reader speaking a meaningless description.

Summary

Nicely done typography is usually transparent—that is, if it is a legible typeface in an appropriate size and color for the background upon which it rests, the reader doesn't even notice it. Nonetheless, typography influences whether or not viewers read the content, as well as having a subtle effect on how they perceive your site. Choosing appropriate typefaces and controlling their presentation is critical to conveying your message.

The following checklist serves two functions: to summarize the major points and "rules" presented in the chapter, and to help you ensure you've done all you should before finalizing any web site you are creating.

HTML Text: Typefaces and Formatting—*Did you:*

- Use a non-decorative, screen-optimized typeface at a legible size for body copy?

- Use looser leading appropriately for longer lines of text, for emphasis, or to lighten the density of the page?

- Use wider letter and word spacing for emphasis?

- Set body copy as justified left, ragged right?

- Employ contrasting elements like different typefaces, size, weight, color, form, structure, bold, italic, reversing the type and background colors, all caps, texture, direction, rhythm, spacing, and embellishment to emphasize special areas of type?

- Use restraint on those elements just listed?

- Make use of CSS to set special capitalization rules (all uppercase, all lowercase, title case) automatically?

- Avoid using all caps in body text?

- Apply underlining only for links?

- Test the site in grayscale to make sure that foreground text contrasts sufficiently in value with background text?

- If using light text on a dark background, consider making the text bolder or choosing a typeface with inherently thicker strokes?

- Avoid strikethrough like this unless you are attempting to display edited versions of documents?

- Consider using CSS to style the first-letter or first-line of text for decorative effect?

HTML Text: Layout—*Did you:*

- Chunk content with headers, small paragraphs, bulleted lists, sidebars, indenting an entire a paragraph of text, or pull quotes?

- Limit line length to 350–550 pixels by splitting wide pages into two or more columns?

- Increase leading to improve readability on longer lines of text and to lighten the overall "color" of a page?

- Increase spacing between letters or words for emphasis?

- Use either an indent at the beginning of a paragraph, or double spacing between paragraphs, but not both?

- Avoid indenting the first paragraph following a header?

- Use double spacing before headings but single spacing between the heading and the content it introduces?

HTML Text: Content—*Did you:*

- Check spelling, grammar, and sentence structure?

- Limit the use of exclamation points?

- Specify proper typographic characters, including en dash, em dash, curly quotes, true ellipse, and upper and lowercase numerals?

Graphic Text—*Did you:*

- Make use of graphic text only when absolutely necessary, to avoid excessive download times?

- Choose appropriate embellishment, anti-aliasing, and kerning?

- For very small text, use typefaces designed for a specific size and turn off anti-aliasing?

- Consider employing symbol-based fonts for small graphics?

- For graphic text, follow the guidelines for graphics from Chapter 6?

Forms

JEF RASKIN, *THE HUMANE INTERFACE*:

"An interface is humane if it is responsive to human needs and considerate of human frailties."

ALAN COOPER, *ABOUT FACE 2.0:*
THE ESSENTIALS OF INTERACTION DESIGN:

"The poor writer is a visible writer, and a poor interaction designer looms with a clumsily visible presence in his software."

Input forms—the web-based equivalent of traditional data-entry forms—capture information from your visitors. In fact, any time a visitor enters data in a shopping cart, answers an online questionnaire, or fills out a "contact us" page, he or she is using a form. Forms are the foundation upon which interactive elements such as text fields, check boxes, radio buttons, and Submit buttons are built.

For a form to capture accurate information, it must be so obvious and unambiguous that the viewer has no doubt about what to enter in each field. Bad design in forms results in bad input. This chapter will examine the visual design characteristics and usability factors to keep in mind when designing input forms.

Principles of Form Design

Face it—visitors to web sites despise filling out forms. They want to accomplish a task in the minimum amount of time, with a minimum amount of hassle and effort. The longer the form, the more impatient they become; only the most motivated visitors will tolerate a form longer than one page. All of this relates to the principles of form design that follow.

Reduce physical effort

Most visitors don't much like typing and "keyboarding" any more than they have to. Consequently, we should take advantage of any chance we have to minimize a visitor's clicks, keystrokes, mouse movements, and scrolling. Specifically, don't request any piece of information more than once; whenever there's a chance of some input data being identical to previously entered data, take advantage of that fact. For instance, if a visitor has already entered a billing address, then provide her with the shortcut of checking a "same as billing address" box for the shipping address. Taking this a step further, we can remember data from a visitor's previous foray on our site, such as when Amazon asks permission to store a visitor's shipping and billing information so that she need not enter it the next time she stops in.

Reduce cognitive effort

In addition to minimizing the physical effort of typing, we also need to reduce cognitive effort. It almost goes without saying that a form should be simple and easy to understand. Sorting out a visually confusing page, with many seemingly unrelated and unorganized elements, requires more mental exertion than many users are willing to expend.

Avoid requiring any information perceived to be unnecessary

Visitors are most irritated by questions that they view as irrelevant to their own needs. They recognize that marketing questions (demographics, interests and hobbies, and so on) benefit not themselves but the web site's parent organization instead. It's a given that visitors will be exceedingly annoyed if such non-task-specific questions are mandatory.

We have to be careful about the way in which we ask for even required data. For instance, most users are turned off by a site that won't let them enter at all until they provide some personal information—how can they yet know if the site is worth the trouble? They aren't even sure if the site is trustworthy. As a result, many of them tap the Back button, and it's goodbye. In contrast, if visitors first see the contents of the site, they at least have the chance to become intrigued, and will likely be more willing to provide information. All this relates to the issue of *salience*, or importance, to visitors. The higher the salience, the more willing visitors are to jump through hoops.

If some of the information you're asking for is required, while other fields are optional, use some visual clue to signify which is which, so that visitors can choose to ignore the optional fields (which, of course, most of them will do). Placing an asterisk next to all of the required fields is a common technique that most visitors recognize, as in **FIGURE 8.1**.

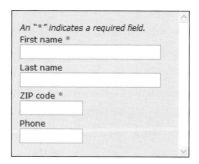

FIGURE 8.1 Indicating Required Fields

Collectively, the various form elements like text input areas and checkboxes are called *controls*, *form controls*, or *widgets*, the subject of the next section.

Input Controls

Input controls are wrapped in a `<form>` tag that specifies the name of the form as well as the method and action that should transpire when the form is submitted. Within a form, two general categories of controls capture visitor input:

- *Predefined choice controls* such as radio buttons, checkboxes, and list boxes.

- *Text controls* that allow the visitor to enter free-form text data.

Predefined choice controls minimize visitor keystrokes and ensure accuracy because there are a limited number of choices, all guaranteed to be valid. For example, typos and spelling errors are eliminated on state names if we provide a drop-down list of choices (all presumably spelled correctly). It's usually in our best interest to use predefined choice controls whenever there are a limited number of options from which the visitor must select.

● ● ●

TECHNICAL TERMS

Yes, "form control" really is the technical term for any field or button that you need to interact with as you move through the process of filling out a form. If it makes you feel any better to call it a "widget," that is a technologically correct alternative.

Sometimes, an early choice in the process may determine the options that are, or are not, available later in the process. These secondary options are called *dependent choices* (also called *filtered choices*). For instance, perhaps we offer cheaper shipping rates and one-day shipping only to those locations east of the Mississippi River. If a customer chooses "west of the Mississippi" instead, then one-day shipping isn't offered as an option in the selection that follows, as shown in **FIGURE 8.2**.

FIGURE 8.2 Dependent/Filtered Choices

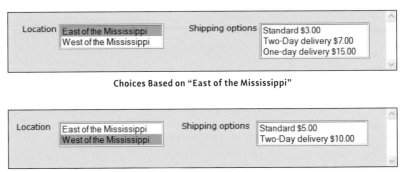

Essentially, if a visitor isn't allowed to choose an option, you should remove it; instead, filter out any options that become irrelevant because of earlier choices. Because filtering dependent choices on the same page as the initial choices can involve some rather tricky programming, it's often easier to put the dependent choices on subsequent pages, as we'll see in a bit when we look at wizards.

We'll look at each of the three predefined choice controls before moving on to the next general category of controls, text controls.

Radio Buttons

Radio buttons (or *option buttons* in Microsoft terminology) are used in single-choice situations; that is, only one choice is allowed from a grouping of related alternatives. (Think "Choose one of the following options.") **FIGURE 8.3** shows a radio button group for choosing a year in school. Radio buttons are circular, whereas HTML checkboxes (coming up soon) are square.

FIGURE 8.3 Radio Button Group

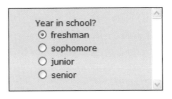

HTML FOR RADIO BUTTONS

Here is the HTML for the radio buttons in Figure 8.3.

```
<form name="inputForm">
   Year in school?<br />
   <input name="yearInSchool" type="radio" value="freshman" checked />
      freshman<br />
   <input name="yearinschool" type="radio" value="sophomore" />
      sophomore<br />
   <input name="yearInSchool" type="radio" value="junior" />
      junior<br />
   <input name="yearInSchool" type="radio" value="senior" />
      senior<br />
</form>
```

It's particularly important to chunk radio buttons visually somehow, so that it's clear which elements are grouped. As **FIGURE 8.4** shows, Dell accomplishes this by using a prominent header line between radio button groups. Another method would be to use the <fieldset> tag that we examined in Chapter 4. At the very least, provide extra white space around a radio group.

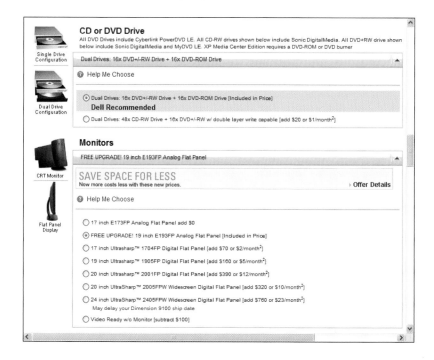

FIGURE 8.4 Text labels for a group of radio buttons can appear to either the right or the left of the buttons, as long as they're consistent and the buttons align vertically. (www.dell.com ©2007 Dell Inc. All Rights Reserved.)

Checkboxes

Checkboxes are similar to radio buttons, but they're used when the choices are *not* mutually exclusive. That is, the visitor can choose multiple items from within a checkbox group. (Think "Choose all that apply.")

FIGURE 8.5 shows a checkbox group after the user has made one choice. Notice that checkboxes are, as you might expect, a square box.

FIGURE 8.5 Checkbox Group

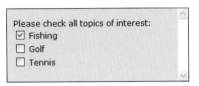

▊▊ HTML FOR CHECKBOXES

Here is the HTML for the checkboxes in Figure 8.5.

```
<form name="inputForm">
    Please check all topics of interest:<br />
    <input name="interests" type="checkbox" value="fishing" checked />
        Fishing<br />
    <input name="interests" type="checkbox" value="golf" />
        Golf<br />
    <input name="interests" type="checkbox" value="tennis" />
        Tennis<br />
</form>
```

The code in the sidebar shows grouped checkboxes, but checkboxes can also be used individually. The classic example of a single, binary "yes/no" checkbox is the one we've all encountered: the small type, automatically checked, "Yes, I want to receive special offers, otherwise known as spam" question posed by so many web sites. (Worded a bit less bluntly, of course.)

As with radio buttons, chunking checkboxes within a border and/or providing extra white space between the group and other page elements helps to show how the checkboxes are related. Any vertical list of checkboxes should align precisely, one above the other.

List Boxes

When options are so numerous that radio buttons or checkboxes would take up too much space on the screen, we can instead implement a list box. List boxes are commonly used for choices such as states, countries, or dates, as well as for jump menus. **FIGURE 8.6** shows a typical drop-down list box, first as it displays upon page load, and then as it might display when the visitor has clicked on the "down" arrow.

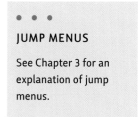

JUMP MENUS

See Chapter 3 for an explanation of jump menus.

FIGURE 8.6 Drop-down List Box

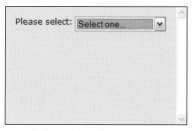

Before Clicking "Down" Arrow

After Clicking "Down" Arrow

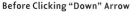 **HTML FOR A LIST BOX**

Here is the HTML for the list box in Figure 8.6.

```
<select name="hobbies" size="1">

   <option value="antiques">Select one...</option>

   <option value="antiques">Antiques</option>

   ...

</select>

</form>
```

Yes, list boxes do indeed irritate many users. Most of us would prefer entering a two-character state abbreviation in a text box rather than scrolling through a long list of states (especially if we live in Wyoming). Nevertheless, a list box absolutely guarantees that any submitted input is a valid choice. That alone makes list boxes worth their annoyance factor.

Think carefully about the order of the list items. Presenting the items in alphabetical or numerical order is the most obvious solution. However, in situations in which some elements on the list are chosen much more often than others, it can make sense to move those choices to the top of the list, and perhaps even specify the most common one as the selected default. For instance, a company based in the

United States might show USA as the default at the top of the list, as shown in **FIGURE 8.7**. Even so, usability experts are divided on the issue, with some suggesting that a standard order with a selected default choice is a better idea.

FIGURE 8.7 Displaying the
Most Common Choice at
the Top

A list box can be implemented as a drop-down list or as a scrollable list. Let's look at each.

Drop-down List Boxes

If you specify `size="1"`, which is actually the default on a `<select>` tag, only one option is initially displayed in the list box, and the remainder of the list drops down when the visitor clicks on the scroll arrow, as you saw in Figure 8.6. The first item is usually not a valid choice, but rather an explanation, as it is here with "Select one…". The HTML that renders this list as a drop-down is as follows:

```
<select name="hobbies" id="hobbies" size="1">
```

Scrollable List Boxes

A size greater than "1" provides a *scrollable* list box, with the `size` attribute determining how many choices show initially. The remaining choices are accessible by scrolling. **FIGURE 8.8** shows a list box with a `size="5"`:

```
<select name="hobbies" id="hobbies" size="5">
```

FIGURE 8.8 Scrolling List
Box (size="5 ")

Multiple-selection List Boxes

If the `multiple` attribute is included in a `<select>` tag, whether drop-down or scrollable, the visitor can choose multiple elements from the list, as shown in **FIGURE 8.9**. The only change from the HTML in the previous example is highlighted in this `<select>` tag:

```
<select name="hobbies" id="hobbies" size="5" multiple>
```

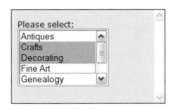

FIGURE 8.9 Multiple-selection List Box

▓▓▓ A COMMON "GOTCHA!": MULTIPLE AND SIZE="1"

The combination of `size="1"` and the `multiple` attribute, like this:

```
<select name="hobbies" id="hobbies" size="1" multiple>
```

changes the behavior of the `<select>` tag. Instead of displaying a drop-down list of all of the attributes, as it normally would if `size="1"`, the list is scrollable with only a single item showing at a time, as in FIGURE 8.10. Because seeing only a single item at a time is claustrophobic to visitors, it's usually better to specify a size of at least three or four items.

FIGURE 8.10 A Lonely Multiple-selection List Box, `size="1"`

Grouping List Box Options under a Header

Individual `<option>` items within a `<select>` can be grouped under a specially formatted, nonselectable header using the `<optgroup>` container. For instance, in
FIGURE 8.11, neither the "Hobbies" nor the "Sports" lines are selectable.

FIGURE 8.11 List Box with
optgroup Headers

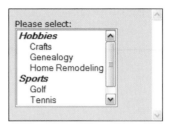

▮▮▮ DROP-DOWN LIST WITH OPTGROUP HEADERS

Here is the HTML for the drop-down list with optgroup headers in Figure 8.11.

```
<form name="inputForm" id="inputForm">
    Please select a topic of interest:<br />
    <select name="activities" size="7">
        <optgroup label="Hobbies">
            <option value="crafts">Crafts</option>
            <option value="genealogy">Genealogy</option>
            <option value="home remodeling">Home Remodeling</option>
        </optgroup>
        <optgroup label="Sports">
            <option value="golf">Golf</option>
            <option value="tennis">Tennis</option>
            <option value="fishing">Fishing</option>
        </optgroup>
    </select>
</form>
```

• • •

VISUAL SIZE OF FORM CONTROLS ACROSS BROWSERS

In the past, form controls displayed at widely differing sizes, depending upon the browser. These days, IE and Firefox, at least, display only minimal differences in the size of controls. Nonetheless, you should be sure to test your form in all target browsers. For further information on the exact sizes of the various controls in older browsers, see http://hotwired.lycos.com/webmonkey/99/41/index3a_page4.html?tw=design.

Single-line Text Input Areas

Single-line text input areas are specified with an `<input />` tag, like this:

```
<input type="text" name="city" id="city" value="Chicago" maxlength="30"
size="20" />
```

The optional `value` attribute provides a default value that not only displays in the input area upon page load but also is submitted for the field unless the visitor otherwise changes it. The optional `maxlength` attribute dictates the number of characters the visitor will be allowed to enter.

The optional `size` command specifies the horizontal space the input area takes up on the screen. Usually, the visual length of a field should reflect the actual length—that is, the `size` and `maxlength` attributes should roughly correspond. It would be silly to expect a visitor to enter a full last name (`maxlength="25"`) in an input area that appears to be only 6 characters long (`size="6"`), as in **FIGURE 8.12**. Although the field would scroll to allow entry of the full 25 characters, the user could see only a few characters at a time, which makes it hard to tell if he or she entered the text correctly. Conversely, it's equally inappropriate to provide the visitor with a 25-character `size` for a nine-digit postal code, as in the bottom input field in Figure 8.12.

FIGURE 8.12 Inappropriate Input Control Sizes…Don't Try This at Home.

What if a few visitors need substantially more characters than is typical for a particular input field? For instance, the vast majority of last names can be easily accommodated in 15 characters. Still, a rare visitor might need 25 characters. We might be reluctant to devote the extra screen space to accommodate those rare longer entries.

The compromise solution is to set the `size` to accommodate the majority of entries and the `maxlength` to accommodate the longer ones. For instance, we could set the `size` of the last-name field to 15 characters and the `maxlength` to 25 characters. Such specifications would permit most visitors to enter their names without scrolling, while the visitors with longer names would be accommodated by scrolling.

But even though we usually want the visual size of the input area to reflect the approximate number of characters allowed in the field, it can be visually chaotic to make every field a different length. In **FIGURE 8.13**, the form on the left lacks visual coherence because the right sides of the input fields don't line up with one another. The form on the right is much more visually pleasing, because fields are the same length whenever possible. It seems that we must find a compromise between indicating field lengths accurately and making the form aesthetically appealing, or at least not as chaotic.

FIGURE 8.13 Alignment of Form Fields

Form Fields of Differing Lengths   Form Fields of Similar Lengths

Punctuation and Formatting in Text Input Controls

If a field has punctuation embedded in it, such as dashes, slashes, or spaces, it's often a good idea to show that formatting, or at least give some indication to the user as to the formatting that we expect. For instance, **FIGURE 8.14** shows multiple ways of guiding visitors to enter a date correctly.

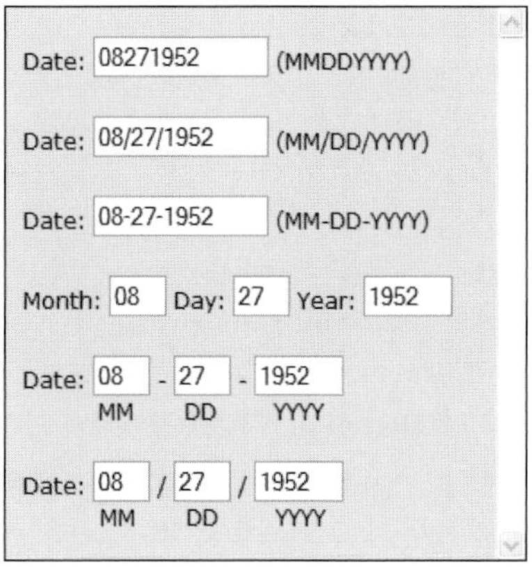

FIGURE 8.14 Input Controls Showing Formatting Options

The first line on Figure 8.14 is somewhat problematic. Although it conserves keystrokes because it omits punctuation, that omitted punctuation could aid in verifying the accuracy of data entry. For instance, it's much easier for a visitor to double-check a telephone number when it looks like 815-555-1212 rather than 8155551212. It may well be that in trying to "feed" the need of the busy web-visiting public to get everything done quickly, we're sacrificing accuracy for the sake of saving those few keystrokes.

Another alternative is to allow visitors to enter data in any way they please, while we use a scripting language like JavaScript to reformat and redisplay the data in our preferred format, including punctuation. For instance, a visitor might enter a telephone number in any of the following acceptable formats:

- 8155551212

- (815) 555-1212

- 815-555-1212

- 815.555.1212

We would then redisplay the field in its new, edited format so that the visitor can see that the field was entered properly. For instance, if the visitor typed 8155551212, the system might redisplay 815.555.1212.

Although many usability experts advocate such free-form entry, many visitors are understandably confused when they encounter an input field that doesn't provide any formatting clues at all. Such confusion tends to make a visitor pause, which defeats the very usability principles that recommend free-form entry in the first place.

Hiding Input Data on the Screen

Sometimes, one-line text areas should be protected so that someone looking over the visitor's shoulder can't read them. For instance, we don't normally display passwords on the screen where they can be read by any bystander. In such a case, you use `type="password"` on the `<input />` tag to display asterisks or dots instead of the characters actually being entered by the user. Note that `type="password"` doesn't protect or encrypt the data in any way whatsoever, just hides it on the screen.

Default Values for Text Input Controls

A default entry for the `value` attribute can save the user keystrokes in those cases where there's one possible value that's much more common than others. Let's say that 90% of our visitors are from Chicago. If we provide "Chicago" as the default `value` for city of residence, we save 90% of our users having to type that in. The tradeoff here is that our non-Chicagoans must go to the trouble of deleting "Chicago" from the field before entering a different value. Therefore, it's probably best to use a default only if it applies to 80% or more of our visitors.

It's possible make use of the `value` attribute to provide instructions to the visitor on what to enter in the field, as in **FIGURE 8.15**. However, this practice isn't much recommended, because it carries serious disadvantages:

- Deleting the instructions adds another layer of effort for all visitors—and all the more so for visitors with physical disabilities.

- The instructions disappear after the visitor starts typing a new value.

- If the visitor skips the field, the instructions will be submitted as the value unless you capture and handle that omission with a validation script.

FIGURE 8.15 Default Value Used for Instructions

Re-entering Critical Fields

For critical fields—those that cannot tolerate any type of a mistake at all, such as choosing a new password—we might require the visitor to type the field twice, as a way of catching most typos. One way to ensure that the visitor doesn't try to outsmart us by copying and pasting the first entry into the second one, thereby perpetuating any mistake entered in the first one, is to put the second entry on a second page. **FIGURE 8.16** shows how AMCORE Bank requires visitors to retype a billpayer account number on a second page.

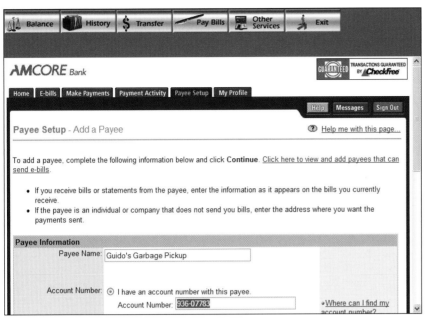

Enter Account Number on First Page

FIGURE 8.16 Entering Data Twice for Accuracy (www.amcore.com)

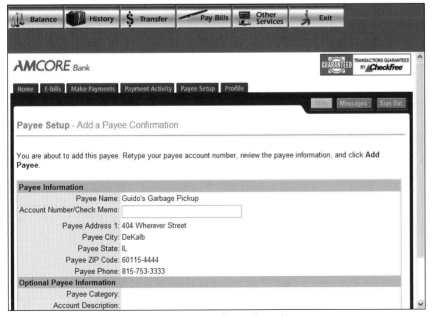

Re-enter Account Number on Second Page

Multi-line Text Input Areas

Often, text input can't be limited to just a single line; it needs to be the equivalent of a paragraph of text, as in **FIGURE 8.17**. Here's the HTML:

```
<textarea name="comments" id="comments" rows="4" cols="40" wrap="soft">
   No comment.
</textarea>
```

FIGURE 8.17 Multi-line textarea

The `cols` attribute specifies the approximate width of the field, while `rows` dictates the height of the box. If a visitor enters more characters than can be shown within the specified `rows` and `cols` attributes, a scrollbar appears automatically so that she can continue entering text. Keep in mind that the browser allocates space for the scrollbar within the `<textarea>` even it isn't needed.

The optional `wrap` attribute dictates whether text is wrapped within the allotted space and whether carriage returns are submitted along with the field. Since the `wrap` attribute is not included in the official HTML standard, some older browsers didn't support it. Modern browsers, however, seem to have settled on three possible values for this attribute:

- `soft` (the default): The text automatically wraps as the user types, but the automatically inserted carriage returns are not embedded in the field when it's submitted to the server.

- `hard`: Word wrap is turned on, just as it is with `soft`, but now the inserted carriage returns are submitted with the field.

- `off`: Word wrap is turned off, so the text area continues to scroll to the right as the visitor types. Only if the visitor presses the Return or Enter key does the cursor drop down to the next line.

The `<textarea>` tag has another use, beyond capturing visitor input; it can also be used to display informational text that needs to scroll. For instance, software license agreements are often shown using a `<textarea>` tag, whereby the visitor employs the scrollbar to read through the agreement (should he or she actually choose to read the software license, that is). **FIGURE 8.18** shows such an example. When used for display of text, rather than input, we can add the `readonly` attribute to the tag so that visitors can't change the displayed text.

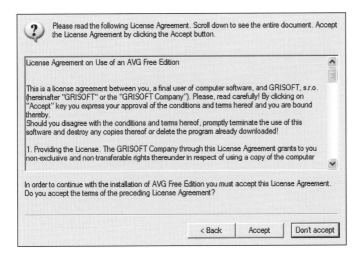

FIGURE 8.18 `<textarea>` for Display Only (www.grisoft.com)

Form Completion

We usually employ JavaScript to validate data locally on the client as much as possible, to make sure that we're not submitting obviously invalid data. Only after the data is validated do we ship it off to the web server. Let's look first at the specifics for validating data, and then at specifying Submit buttons.

Form Validation

Although this book doesn't cover the specifics of how to use JavaScript for validation, it is appropriate here to discuss the types of validation that should be done. Validation on the client is generally limited to completeness and format. For instance, we might validate a customer number to make sure it's not blank, that it's all numeric, that it contains the proper number of digits, and that it's within a certain allowable range. What we can't do from within the HTML document is make sure that a customer number matches an existing customer number in the database; such validation would require a server-side query to the customer database.

Ideally, we validate each field as soon as the focus moves away from it after it's been changed. That way, we can provide an error message and allow the visitor to re-enter the data immediately, before moving forward. After the entire form is submitted, all of the data should be validated again in order to catch any required fields that the visitor might have skipped over.

CLIENTS AND SERVERS

Refer to Chapter 1 for a quick review of how clients and web servers interact.

Web sites like http://javascript.internet.com provide free scripts for many common validating tasks. For instance, you might find scripts to validate email addresses, check for valid zip codes, or strip away excess spaces from a text entry.

The important thing to remember is that any efforts to trap formatting errors right away can save needless (and in some cases costly) queries against the server-side database. It's best to catch and correct as many errors as possible, as soon as possible, while the visitor is still on the page. We'll discuss contending with those errors in the Visitor Support section.

Submit Buttons

Submit buttons, of course, submit the form and all of its data using the `action` and `method` specified in the `<form>` tag. The button can be either a standard, browser-generated Submit button, or a custom button created in an image-editing program. **FIGURE 8.19** shows an example of each, and the sidebar reviews the HTML.

FIGURE 8.19 Submit Buttons

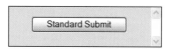

Browser-supplied

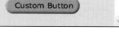

Custom Image

▓▓ BROWSER-SUPPLIED VERSUS CUSTOM SUBMIT BUTTONS

A standard Submit button is supplied by the browser, using code like this:

```
<input type="submit" value="Submit Form" />
```

A standard Submit button automatically submits the form to the server (unless you override with JavaScript). The `value` attribute specifies the text that appears on the button. If the `value` attribute is omitted, the browser supplies the wording, usually "Submit" or "Submit Query." The left image in Figure 8.19 shows how this Submit button appears in Internet Explorer.

A custom Submit button is nothing more than a button image created in the same way as any other navigational button. Here's the HTML for the right-hand button in Figure 8.19:

```
<a href="#" onClick="formName.submit();">
   <img src="submitButton2.gif" height="25" width="105" /></a>
```

Substitute whatever name you've chosen for the form for the name highlighted above.

Avoiding Multiple Submissions

Whether using a browser-supplied or a custom Submit button, we don't want the form to be accidentally submitted multiple times. We've all seen web pages that warn the visitor not to click a Submit button twice. Unfortunately, if the submission takes more than just a second or two, the visitor is left wondering if the click actually registered. At the same time, he's afraid to click a second time—after all, he's been warned of dire consequences if he clicks that second time. Just how long does the visitor wait in a case like this?

There are two user-friendly ways to avoid causing our visitors this kind of angst:

- Immediately reassure visitors with feedback that the form is in the process of being submitted, often done with some type of small animation. This is a great way, under any circumstances, of reassuring visitors that something is indeed happening.
- Use JavaScript to disable the Submit button after it's clicked, thereby preventing a double submission. See the sidebar for the code.

DISABLING A SUBMIT BUTTON

Add the following to the `<form>` tag:

```
onsubmit="this.submitButtonName.disabled=true"
```

Be aware that you might have to trace a hierarchy of path names to get to the button, if it's embedded within other elements like a table, and that the page would need to be reloaded completely to re-enable the Submit button. Getting this to work might be a bit trickier than it appears if you're unfamiliar with JavaScript and the Document Object Model (DOM).

Reset Buttons

Reset buttons clear a form's controls back to their initial values upon page load. Like Submit buttons, Reset buttons can be browser-supplied or custom. See the sidebar for the code.

BROWSER-SUPPLIED VERSUS CUSTOM RESET BUTTONS

A standard Reset button is supplied by the browser, using code like this:

```
<input type="reset" value="Clear Form" />
```

The optional `value` attribute specifies the text that appears on the button. Typical values include "Reset" (usually the default) and "Clear Form."

A custom reset button is simply a button image created in the same way as any other navigational button. Here's the HTML:

```
<a href="#" onClick="formName.reset();">
    <img src="resetButton.gif" height="25" width="105" /></a>
```

Substitute whatever name you've chosen for the form in place of the highlighted code above.

Many usability experts argue that we should never, ever, use a Reset button; it's far too easy for a visitor to hit it accidentally, thereby clearing several minutes of data entry. And just how often does a visitor deliberately want to clear an entire form, anyway? Rarely, it would seem. Most of the time, the visitor wants to retype a field or two but almost never needs to retype an entire form. Besides, hitting the browser's "refresh" button would serve the same function as a Reset button.

If you do feel the need to include a Reset button, use it with caution, and at least be sure to use JavaScript to capture the reset event in order to ask, "Are you sure…?", thus double-checking the visitor's intention before he or she does something irreversible.

Submit and Reset Button Hints

Submit and Reset buttons should be easy to see, and should be close to their related form controls. In any circumstance where the user has to choose between two or more action buttons, like Submit and Reset, be sure to position the safer or more positive action on the left, and the riskier or more negative action on the right. Also make sure default focus lands on the safer of the two actions, in case the visitor hits Enter without paying attention to the offered choices.

Any time there could be irreversible consequences for a visitor's action (so-called "ejector seat functions"), be sure to confirm that the action is what was actually intended. For example, never delete an account, submit an order, or change critical data in the database without first asking, "Are you sure you want to _____" (fill in the blank, of course, with a description of the critical action).

After a form has been submitted to the server, visitors are reassured if the server sends back a response page that redisplays the entered information. That way, they can double-check that the information they intended to provide was not only entered properly but also received correctly by the web site.

Transaction Structure

In the Site Architecture section of Chapter 2, we looked at creating a hierarchical or sequential organization to glue separate pages into an intuitive site architecture. One identified task was to categorize information and then use those categories to split content into individual pages. Now that we're working with input forms, however, we need to decide how to split the transaction structure across individual pages as well. For instance, if we have an interaction that requires a lot of information from the visitor, should the transaction be broken into multiple pages, one page per step, or should the entire interaction take place on a single page? The decision here is between using a wizard structure or a control-panel structure, both of which are legitimate choices, depending upon the circumstances.

Wizards

A *wizard* is a linear, step-by-step interaction that loads one page per step, in a defined order. For instance, a wizard for placing an order might present one page for reviewing the items currently in the shopping cart, another page for entering shipping information, and yet another page for entering payment information. See the first three pages of Amazon's checkout wizard in **FIGURE 8.20**.

Wizards have certain advantages:

- The entire process seems less overwhelming to visitors than a single-page version. After all, when presented with a single, long, complicated, scrolling form, visitors are bound to wonder if it's really worth the effort. If we conceal some of that complexity initially, visitors are more likely to continue.

- Wizards are ideal for processes in which some steps are dependent upon earlier choices. Take, for instance, the sign-in process (Step 2) in Figure 8.20. A returning visitor needs a somewhat different process than a new visitor, because the new visitor needs to register. With a wizard such as this, the subsequent page (register versus not needing to register, in this case) can depend upon the earlier choices.

- Wizards ensure that no steps are skipped or completed out of order, because visitors can't move forward until the current step is completed successfully.

- Errors are reported while the visitor is still focused on that particular step in the process.

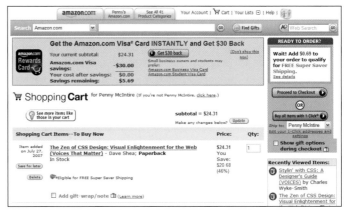

Step 1, Shopping Cart Contents

Step 2, Sign In

Step 3, Shipping Address and Methods

- Wizards are ideal for visitors who are not technically savvy or who perform the given task only occasionally.

But of course there are some disadvantages as well:

- Breaking the interaction across multiple pages entails multiple page loads, although that's at least somewhat offset by the fact that each smaller page downloads faster than one long page.

- Wizards seem tedious, cumbersome, and condescending to visitors who are already familiar with the process.

Control Panels

Instead of using a wizard structure, we could put the entire interaction on a single (possibly long) page, called a *control panel*. **FIGURE 8.21** presents a section of Dell's control panel for configuring a custom computer. The advantages and disadvantages are, for the most part, the reverse of those listed for wizards; control panels suit visitors who are familiar with the process and want to complete their tasks as quickly as possible. Note that Dell's custom configuration screen is probably going to be used primarily by computer-savvy customers anyway—other customers would be more inclined to buy a standard, non-customized system.

FIGURE 8.21 Dell's Build-Your-Own-Computer Control Panel (www.dell.com, ©2007 Dell Inc. All Rights Reserved.)

Dependent choices (discussed earlier under Input Controls) are more difficult to program for control panels than for wizards. For instance, there is only one HTML-only way to handle the returning visitor versus new visitor situation examined earlier. You'd have to present all of the information for both visitors on the same page, which could serve to confuse both audiences.

Input Form Page Layout

After deciding between a wizard and a control panel, we need to design layouts for the individual pages. Chapter 4 examined guidelines for page layout in general, including the characteristics of line, color, grids, and white space to create a visually coherent page. Nevertheless, we need to study some additional page-layout concerns specific to input forms.

Controlling Cursor Focus and Tab Order

A form control is said to have *focus* if the cursor is resting on it. Form controls naturally acquire focus following the sequence of their location in the HTML source code. For instance, the default values in the controls in **FIGURE 8.22A** show how the tab key would, by default, traverse the form controls left to right, then top to bottom. Most of the time, this order is the way we would want and expect the visitor to progress through the form, because that's how the majority of the Western world reads.

But sometimes—like here—that natural order doesn't make sense, and we might need to violate it. We would want the visitor to progress vertically down the left column before going to the top of the right, as in **FIGURE 8.22B**.

We can dictate this non-default tab order by assigning a `tabindex` value for each affected form element, like this:

```
<input type="text" tabindex="n" name="billAddress" id="billAddress" />
```

When the page loads, the cursor is initially positioned on the control with the lowest `tabindex` value greater than zero. The cursor then progresses through the remaining controls in order by ascending `tabindex`. Elements lacking a `tabindex` or with a `tabindex` of zero come last in the tabbing order, in order of their location in the document's HTML source code. (In Internet Explorer, a negative number removes the item from the tabbing order entirely.)

The sidebar shows the HTML for the "column first" tabbing order of Figure 8.22B, with the surrounding layout table, formatting, and irrelevant attributes removed for the sake of simplicity.

FIGURE 8.22 Tabbing Order

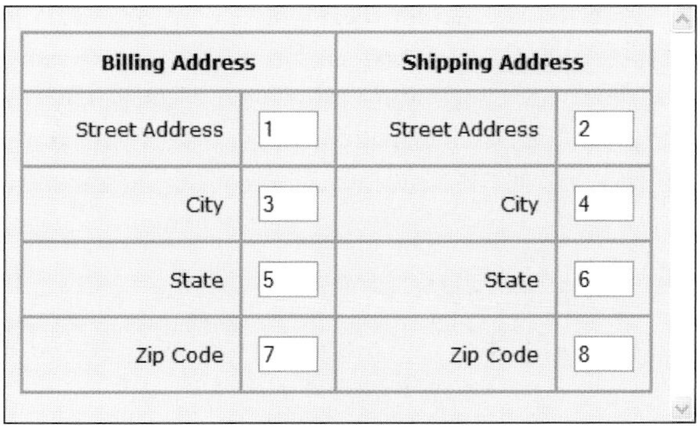

A. Default Tabbing Order

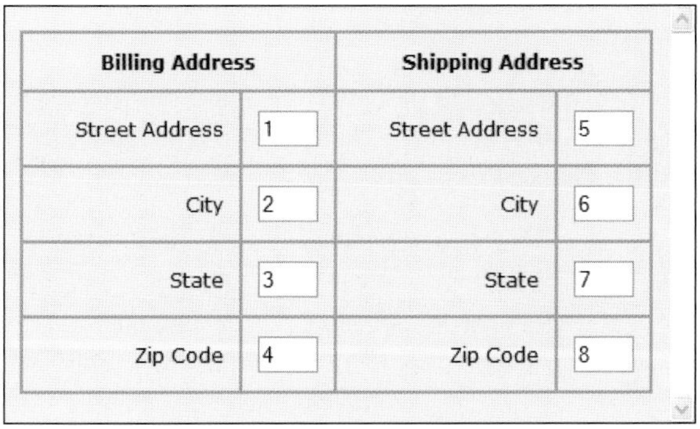

B. Non-standard Tabbing Order

NON-STANDARD TABBING ORDER FOR FIGURE 8.22B

```
<form>
<p>
  Street Address <input type="text" tabindex="1" value="1" />
  Street Address <input type="text" tabindex="5" value="5" /></p>
<p>
  City <input type="text" tabindex="2" value="2" />
  City <input type="text" tabindex="6" value="6" /></p>
<p>
  State <input type="text" tabindex="3" value="3" />
  State <input type="text" tabindex="7" value="7" /></p>
<p>
  Zip Code <input type="text" tabindex="4" value="4" />
  Zip Code <input type="text" tabindex="8" value="8" /></p>
</form>
```

Even if you don't need to specify a non-standard tabbing order, you can still set focus to a specific control where you want the visitor to start initial data entry. For instance, when a visitor opens www.google.com, the cursor is automatically positioned in the search input area, ready and waiting for the visitor to type in a search phrase. Automatically setting focus to the first form control illustrates how some thoughtful coding can save the visitor an unnecessary keystroke or mouse movement.

To set the focus upon initial page load, add the following onLoad attribute to the <body> tag, substituting your own form and field names for formName and fieldName:

```
<body onLoad="document.formName.fieldName.focus();">
```

Presenting Input Controls in the Expected Order

Regardless of where we set the focus, we should present input controls in the order that a visitor would expect to see them. For instance, we would all be confused if a form asked us for our address in the order shown in **FIGURE 8.23**, because we're accustomed to the standard street-city-state-zip format.

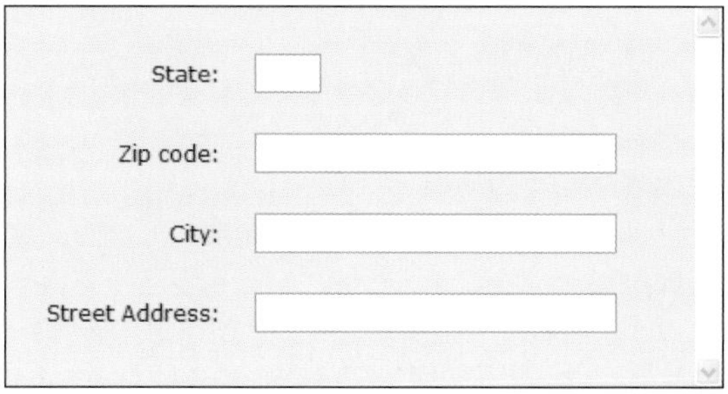

FIGURE 8.23 Inappropriate Entry Order

Another example of violating a user's order expectations would be to ask for a credit card number before displaying the items in the cart and calculating tax and shipping charges. After all, a visitor would want to verify that the order is correct before charging his credit card. The irregularity of the input order might even cause him to question if the site is really legitimate—maybe it's a site phishing for credit card numbers instead.

If visitors are consulting a paper source document as they enter data, the web page should present the fields in the same order as the source document. For instance, a site that's used to submit already-filled-out-on-paper income tax forms should follow the IRS's standard form layout. (One could certainly argue that changing the order of entry on IRS forms might be nothing but an improvement, but that's another issue.)

Chunking Input Controls by Category

We can clarify input form structure by chunking the controls by category. Such grouping is particularly welcome in a long control-panel layout. For instance, on the Dell control panel back in Figure 8.21, the category titles ("Hard Drive," "CD/DVD Drives," and so on) are featured with a pale gray background, which also serves to separate each category from its neighbors. Other options for visually chunking categories include using borders, the `<fieldset>` tag, and different font characteristics like size and color.

Visitor Support

Historically (meaning, essentially, pre-web), computer system designers went to great lengths to create extensive-but-separate instructions and Help documents to bail out users who were confused by or who encountered error conditions on their computers. These days, you very rarely see, let alone consult, separate Help pages on the web, and a visitor who loses patience simply abandons the site and moves on to an easier one. As a result, it's often wiser to expend your efforts on creating an intuitive and easy-to-use site rather than on instructions, help, and extensive error handling.

Principles of Visitor Support

Let's remind ourselves about the basic tenets of visitor support before we move on to specifics.

- **Practice defensive design**—Good design usually results in good input. Read that sentence again, slowly, and internalize its meaning: An intuitive form structure and helpful instructions can go a long way toward guiding visitors to use a form properly, thereby minimizing visitor confusion and its logical successor, visitor error (or the sad and just as logical outcome—site abandonment).

- **Cope gracefully**—Don't let problems and errors take you by surprise or somehow offend you by their existence. We must face up to the fact that issues, despite our best efforts, inevitably crop up. We'll talk more about that in the upcoming Error Handling section.

- **Less is more**—Too much information serves only to confuse visitors. If you have one piece of critical information buried in a long paragraph of unnecessary fluff, chances are most visitors won't read any of it, and the critical information will remain unnoticed. Therefore, try to be brief and salient, telling visitors only what they absolutely need to know to accomplish their tasks.

- **Provide obvious documentation for probabilities, not possibilities—**
When constructing both instructions and Help documents, we need to distinguish between probabilities and possibilities. A *probability* is something that is *likely* to happen. Providing obvious help and instruction for probabilities, those things that happen on a regular basis, can be worthwhile.

  Possibilities, on the other hand, are situations that arise infrequently; just because it's possible that it might happen doesn't mean there's much chance it will. For instance, it's possible that a visitor might accidentally enter only numbers into a first name field. But do we explicitly need a unique error message, just to handle numbers in the name field? Probably not. Instead, a generic error message such as "Please enter only alphabetic letters in the first name field" would suffice for all types of invalid entry.

  Although as web designers we are quite capable of wasting many a sleepless night thinking of every contingency, we should concentrate on making the probabilities visible, not the possibilities. Otherwise, we run the risk of bewildering visitors with too much information. Although we might still decide to include some of those possibilities, they should be placed out of the mainstream so that the normal visitor isn't forced to stumble over them.

We'll now look at the primary elements of visitor support: instructions, Help pages, feedback, and error handling.

Instructions

Instructions can be as simple as a clue about the format of an input field, such as showing "MM/DD/YYYY" adjacent to a date field, or as complicated as several sentences explaining a single input field. Here, we'll assume that instructions are on the same page as the fields to which they refer.

Instructions should:

- Accurately label each form control. (Since we've already discussed the subtleties of choosing good labels in the Site Architecture section of Chapter 2, we won't rehash the topic here.)

- Be in close proximity and visually connected to the fields they clarify. For example, explaining the format of a date control several lines below the control itself would not be constructive.

- Be unobtrusive, staying out of a visitor's way when not needed. For instance, we shouldn't automatically pop up a separate window with instructions that the visitor hasn't requested. Only the first-time visitor reads the message anyway, and veteran visitors will be annoyed by being forced to dismiss (translation: "close") the window.

- Use a consistent vocabulary. Don't describe a single process in multiple ways, such as "Enter the desired number" in one place, "Type your number" in another, and "Press your numeric choice" in yet another. If you aren't consistent, visitors might think that each of these different phrases refers to a different process.

- Be concise and to the point. As we discussed earlier, TMI (too much information) is either ignored or serves to overwhelm visitors. Edit all instructions down to a critical core.

- Include the `title` attribute on form elements to provide further instructions on rollover, if required.

Help Documents

If we provide adequate instructions on a page, our visitors should require separate Help pages only rarely. Still, some pages may have complicated tasks to perform. These, then, are the specific pages that cry out for meaningful Help documents, particularly for visitors who are brand new or who drop in only occasionally. Keep in mind that a visitor who consults Help is often already at a crisis point. Therefore, we need to be as "helpful" and concise as possible, to avoid further irritation.

The Help system could be as simple as integrated Help pages for just a few of the site's tasks, or as complicated as an extensively indexed, separate site-within-a-site consisting of dozens, even hundreds, of pages. Help can be *action-based*, such as a tutorial that leads visitors step-by-step through performing specific tasks, or it might be *reference-based*, in which case visitors are simply presented with an explanation of the requested topic.

In any case, Help can be accessed by links on the main menu system, as on Amazon's horizontal top menu (**FIGURE 8.24**), or by contextual links at the crisis point itself, as on the "View shipping rates and policies" link next to the shipping weight on Amazon's book page (**FIGURE 8.25**). Contextual help is usually more, well, helpful, because visitors don't have to worry about browsing or searching an entire help system to find what they need, nor do they have to worry about exactly which search phrase to use. Contextual help means you have to build your pages to be smart enough to discern which Help documents will be appropriate, depending upon what the visitor is attempting to do.

FIGURE 8.24 Amazon's Main Menu Help Link (www.amazon.com, © Amazon.com, Inc. or its affiliates. All Rights Reserved.)

FIGURE 8.25 Amazon's
Contextual Help
(www.amazon.com,
© Amazon.com, Inc. or
its affiliates. All Rights
Reserved.)

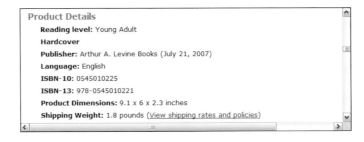

If the Help documentation consists of more than just a couple of pages, giving it a hot-linked table of contents or site map can be a lifesaver. For larger Help systems, a search feature is almost mandatory.

● ● ●

SITE MAPS AND SEARCH

See Chapter 3 for guidelines concerning site maps and search functions.

Periodically review your server logs to see which Help documents are accessed the most often, and what the user was attempting to do at the time help was consulted. If you discern that some tasks generate numerous Help requests, you should redesign those pages to make them easier to use.

Feedback

Visitors appreciate feedback that tells them they're on the right track or that they've encountered an error (although of course they appreciate the latter less!). For instance, if visitors enter shipping information on one page and credit card information on the next, the site should redisplay all of this information on a confirmation page before submitting the order. As a result, visitors are reassured that the system received the data as they intended to enter it. Furthermore, if an error arises, error feedback can notify visitors as soon as possible, while errors are still easily corrected.

Whether the message is positive or negative, there are two general types of feedback: modal and modeless. *Modal* feedback requires a response from the visitor before the flow of the activity can proceed, such as a dialog box that requires the visitor to click "OK" to dismiss the box before moving forward (as in **FIGURE 8.26**).

FIGURE 8.26 Modal
Feedback

In contrast, *modeless* feedback requires nothing of the visitor. Examples include using CSS's `a:link` to indicate that a click has been recognized, or providing a small animation that indicates progress as a file is downloading. The visitor need not dismiss the window when the activity is completed; transaction flow moves on to the next page automatically. Particularly when the activity requires a long wait, feedback such as this reassures the visitor that something is indeed happening. A similar type of feedback, but not requiring animation, might be to indicate how far a step-by-step process has progressed, such as "You've now completed Page Three out of five pages."

Since modal feedback interferes with the flow of an activity and requires the extra effort of a response from a visitor, avoid it whenever possible. For instance, you should normally avoid popping up a dialog box to report a normal condition, such as recognition of a valid password. Instead, simply proceed with the task. Use modal feedback when you need to interrupt the flow of an activity, either to double-check an action ("Are you sure you want to delete this file?") or to notify of a critical error condition ("Your credit card has expired. Please contact your credit card company.").

Error Handling

We should design our site to cope with errors gracefully when they do occur, a process called *contingency design*, or "when bad things happen to good people."

Error messages should:

- Be helpful—state what the error is, what its implications are, and precisely what the visitor should do to rectify the problem.

- Be clear and worded in non-technical language recognized by the visitors. Error codes by themselves are of little use to visitors, although they might be useful to your support staff. Even if we display error codes for internal use, we must explain the error in a way that can be understood by the general public. "Our UNIX server doesn't recognize URLs with embedded spaces" is not only confusing, but isn't at all helpful. "Please use only alphabetic letters, numbers, and underscores" frames the same error in terminology that anyone can understand and utilize. (Better yet, tell them that *before* they've entered the data.)

- Be concise. As we've already discussed, extraneous information merely obscures critical information.

- Be polite, tactful, non-accusatory, and apologetic. Error messages should never, ever, blame the user for the problem, even subtly. Instead, the site should shoulder the blame. After all, had our directions been clear enough, the error probably wouldn't have occurred at all.

- Avoid being funny, cute, or obnoxious. A visitor at a crisis point rarely appreciates humor.

• • •

MODAL AND MODELESS FEEDBACK

Modal and modeless are defined by Alan Cooper in *About Face 2.0: The Essentials of Interaction Design.*

• • •

TIP

Focus the cursor on the field that requires correction.

- Stand out on the page, with the fields or items in error highlighted somehow. Typical methods of highlighting include color-coding, colored asterisks, bold-face, or an error icon, like the exclamation point on a yellow triangle used by many Windows applications. **FIGURE 8.27** shows a form with an error indicated by a red asterisk.

FIGURE 8.27 Highlighting Error Messages and Fields

If, after submission to the server, the server-side application discovers that the data is somehow in error, there are two ways to address the situation:

- Present the entire form to the visitor again, retaining and redisplaying the valid fields while highlighting the invalid fields. The visitor re-enters just the invalid data and resubmits the form.

- Present a new, abbreviated form to the visitor, containing only those fields that were in error. Such an abbreviated form is particularly helpful to visitors when the original form was long or complicated. Thus, the visitor deals with only a field or two, instead of the entire form.

PROBLEM RESOLUTION

For more on how successful problem resolution solidifies customer relation-ships, see "Make No Mistake?" by Michael Schrage, in *Fortune* magazine, December 24, 2001.

Whichever method you choose, the important thing is to not require visitors to re-enter every field on the form just because a single field is in error. Unless they are highly motivated ("Free car if you fill out this form!"), most visitors would refuse, particularly on longer forms.

Avoid displaying the error message on a different page from the field that needs to be corrected, forcing the visitor to go back and forth between the error page and the input page as he or she sorts out what's actually wrong. The error message and the field requiring correction should be on the same page.

Regardless of the type of problem a visitor encounters on a site, the surprising news is that *successful resolution of a problem builds customer loyalty faster than delivering a product that performs flawlessly*. Seems hard to believe, but a cheerful and grace-ful problem resolution strategy can build loyalty to an organization faster than no problems at all. Let's say there's a problem with your car after the warranty expires.

If the company cheerfully offers to fix your car, free of charge, you've just had a positive experience that builds customer loyalty. Solving problems expeditiously and courteously can cement visitor good will.

Visual Design of Form Controls

A well-designed form is not only highly usable, it's also visually attractive and cohesive with the design of the site as a whole. All of the design guidelines we've looked at in previous chapters—layout, color, graphics, and typography—apply to forms just as they do to any other element on the site. But how do we actually apply those guidelines to forms and form controls?

There are many CSS properties that can be manipulated to coordinate a form with the rest of the site. **FIGURE 8.28** shows a form that displays both unstyled and styled examples of form controls. The HTML for this form is shown in the sidebar; examine it carefully so that you understand exactly how the formatting is applied.

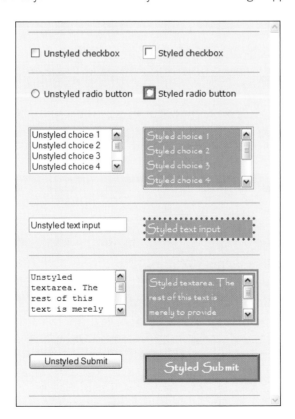

FIGURE 8.28 Using CSS to Style Form Controls

▓▓▓ STYLING FORM CONTROLS

Here is the HTML for the form shown in Figure 8.28. All non-styling attributes
(name, id, etc.) and tags have been removed for the sake of simplicity.

```
<form>
<!-- Checkboxes -->
    <input type="checkbox" /> Unstyled checkbox
    <input type="checkbox" style="border: #8bbbc1 solid 1px;
        background-color: #ffffff;" /> Styled checkbox
<!-- Radio Buttons -->
    <input type="radio" /> Unstyled radio button
    <input type="radio"
        style="background-color: #8bbbc1; border: 3px ridge #8bbbc1;" />
        Styled radio
<!-- List Box -->
    <select size="4">
        <option> Unstyled choice 1 </option>
        ...
    </select>
    <select size="4"
        style="background-color: #8bbbc1; font-size:14px;
        font-family: Papyrus, Arial, Helvetica, sans-serif;
        color: #ffffff;">
        <option> Styled choice 1 </option>
        ...
    </select>
<!-- Single Line Text Input -->
    <input type="text" value="Unstyled text input" size="21" />
    <input type="text" value="Styled text input" size="20"
        style="background-color: #8bbbc1; border: 4px #666666 dotted;
        font-family: Papyrus, Times New Roman, Times, serif;
        font-size: 1.3em; color:#ffffff;" />
<!-- Multi-line Text Input -->
    <textarea cols="16" rows="4">
        Unstyled textarea. The rest of this text is merely to provide
        enough text to generate a scrollbar.
    </textarea>
```

```
    <textarea name="textArea" cols="24" rows="3"
        style="background-color: #8bbbc1; border: 8px #999999 double;
        font-family: Papyrus, Arial, Helvetica, sans-serif;
        font-size: 14px; color: #ffffff;">
        Styled textarea, including scrollbar. The rest of this text is
        merely to provide enough text to generate a scrollbar.
    </textarea>
<!-- Submit Button-->
    <input type="submit" value="Unstyled Submit" />
    <input type="submit" value="Styled Submit"
        style="background-color: #8bbbc1; border: 5px #c2d7db ridge;
        font-family: Papyrus, Times New Roman, Times, serif;
        font-size: 1.3em; color: #ffffff; font-weight:600;" />
</form>
```

Note that this particular form is not intended to be pretty, but rather to show the wide possibilities for styling form elements. In fact, it serves as a graphic reminder that just because we *can* change every possible characteristic of form elements doesn't mean that we *should*. Additionally, we shouldn't change the default styling of a form control so much that it no longer resembles the control at all. For instance, the styled text input on Figure 8.28 now begins to resemble a button, and the styled radio button no longer looks like a radio button at all.

In any case, it should be clear from the previous chapters that any changes we make to color or borders or other attributes should coordinate with the overall look, feel, and mood of the site as a whole.

Visual characteristics of form elements and their associated text descriptions can help to guide our visitors through a form. For instance, we might use a contrasting color for the description next to all required fields in the form. Color, however, is not enough direction alone, because that color may not be visible to a visitor who is color blind. Therefore, some additional cue should be used, such as the ever-familiar asterisk next to the field description.

Another example of how styling can help gather accurate data is shown in **FIGURE 8.29**. Here, the different background colors are visual clues that heighten the value associations of the text descriptions.

FIGURE 8.29 Using Styling for Visual Cues

Input Forms and Accessibility

It's beyond the scope of this book to delve into the politics, policies, and nuts-and-bolts of making the forms fully accessible on your site, but our chapter on forms would not be complete without including information about accessibility.

Here, then, are the guidelines for making input forms accessible:

- Whenever possible, place labels to the left of input elements so that screen readers read the label first, and then the field requiring input.

- If a label must be placed somewhere other than to the left of a form element, or when other elements come between a label and its form element, link the label and the form element like this:

```
<input type="text" name="firstName" id="firstName" />
<label for="firstName">First name</label>
```

Screen readers for the visually impaired will then read the label along with the form element.

- To make visual category chunking explicit for screen readers, surround related form elements with `<fieldset>` tags, and include `<legend>` tags for labeling.

- Don't populate controls with instructional text as the default value, because that text makes it even tougher for access-impaired visitors to delete the instructions before continuing. Use proper labels and instructions on the form instead.

- Avoid using list boxes that use the `multiple` attribute; checkboxes are a more accessible option.

- Don't set the default value for a single yes/no checkbox to "yes."

- Use the `title` attribute to provide tooltips on rollover.

Summary

Forms can be painless or painful for visitors. Keep in mind that visitors want to get their tasks accomplished as quickly as possible, and with the least amount of effort. Proper planning and design can maximize task efficiency.

The following checklist serves two functions: to summarize the major points and "rules" presented in the chapter, and as a checklist before finalizing any web site you are creating.

Usability—*Did you:*

- Do everything possible to reduce visitor effort—visually, cognitively, and physically?
- Minimize visitor clicks, keystrokes, mouse movements, and scrolling?
- Avoid asking for any data until after visitors are aware of the benefits?
- Avoid asking for unnecessary or redundant data?
- Indicate which elements are required and which are optional?
- Present input controls in the expected order?
- Use wizards and control panels appropriately?
- If employing control panels, chunk the input elements by category?
- Specify an appropriate tab order and initial focus, when appropriate?

Selection Controls—*Did you:*

- Use `<input type="radio" />`, `<input type="checkbox" />`, or `<select>` for a limited number of choices?
- Filter out those options that become irrelevant because of earlier choices?
- Use `<input type="radio" />` for a short list of mutually exclusive choices?
- Use `<input type="checkbox" />` for a short list that allows multiple choices?
- Align checkboxes and radio buttons vertically?
- Visually chunk related radio buttons and checkboxes?
- Use `<select>` for a longer list that would cover too much screen real estate if all the choices were displayed at once?
- Decide whether or not to place the most common choices at the top of the list?
- Use `size="1"` for a drop-down list, and a `size` with a value greater than 1 for a scrollable list?
- Use `<optgroup>` to chunk related options within a select box?

Text Input Controls—*Did you:*

- Use `<input type="text" />` for one-line text input, or `<input type="password" />` for a one-line text input with the entered characters hidden by asterisks?
- Specify a `size` and `maxlength` that roughly correspond?
- Display relevant field formatting and punctuation, such as dashes within dates?

- Use the `value` attribute to specify a default value if 80% or more of the audience can use the default?
- Avoid using the `value` attribute to display instructions for the field?
- Use the `<textarea>` tag for multiple-line text input?
- Use `wrap="soft"`, `"hard"`, or `"off"` to determine whether carriage returns are used and whether they're saved with the `<textarea>` field?
- Use `<textarea>` to display informational text that needs to scroll?

Form Submission—*Did you:*

- Use the appropriate control to submit a form?
- Avoid telling visitors not to click a Submit button twice?
- Avoid using Reset buttons?
- If you do use a Reset button, verify that the user intended to click it?
- Position buttons in close proximity and visually connected to their form elements?
- Position the safer or more positive action button on the left, and the riskier or more negative action button on the right, making sure that default focus lands on the safer of the two actions?
- Confirm risky actions?
- After submission, reassure a visitor with a response page that redisplays the entered information?
- Verify completeness and format of all entries as much as possible before submitting the form to the server?

Visitor Support—*Did you:*

- Practice defensive design, so that the form is so intuitive and easy to use that little additional support is necessary?
- Try to be brief and salient, telling visitors only what they absolutely need to know to accomplish their tasks?
- Provide obvious documentation for probabilities, not possibilities?

Instructions—*Did you:*

- Provide adequate instructions so that separate help is rarely needed?
- Accurately label each form control, and place each in close proximity and visual connection to the fields it explains?

- Make documentation apparent but unobtrusive?

- Use a consistent vocabulary?

- Include the `title` attribute on form elements to provide concise instructions on rollover?

Help—*Did you:*

- Use contextual help whenever possible?

- Provide a hot-linked table of contents or site map, and a search function for larger Help systems?

Feedback—*Did you:*

- Provide feedback, particularly for long waits and errors?

- Use modeless, rather than modal, feedback whenever possible?

Error Handling—*Did you:*

- Provide error messages that are helpful, clear, non-technical, concise, polite, tactful, non-accusatory, apologetic, and visible?

- When a server-side error is encountered, either redisplay the entire form or just the subset of controls that are in error?

- Display an error message on the same page as the field that needs to be corrected?

- Remember that successful resolution of a problem builds stronger customer loyalty than delivering a product that performs flawlessly?

Accessibility—*Did you:*

- Whenever possible, place labels to the left of controls, or associate the label and its control with the `<label>` tag?

- Surround related form elements with `<fieldset>` tags and include the `<legend>` tag for labeling?

- Avoid populating controls with instructional text as the default value?

- Avoid using list boxes when multiple choices are possible (i.e., using the `multiple` attribute)?

- Avoid setting the default value for a single yes/no checkbox to "yes"?

- Use the `title` attribute to provide tooltips on rollover?

INDEX